One of the most positive effects you can have on the environment begins on your dinner plate. Chew Well!

COOL CUISINE

Laura Stec 11/08

COOL CUISINE
Taking the Bite out of Global Warming

Laura Stec with
Eugene Cordero, Ph.D.

GIBBS SMITH
TO ENRICH AND INSPIRE HUMANKIND
Salt Lake City | Charleston | Santa Fe | Santa Barbara

TO THOSE WORKING TOWARD CREATING A NEW VISION
AND SUSTAINABLE SOLUTIONS SO WE CAN ALL LIVE
IN HARMONY WITH THE EARTH.

First Edition

12 11 10 09 08   5 4 3 2 1

Text © 2008 Laura Stec
Photographs © 2008 Christine Krieg, unless otherwise noted
Other photo credits: © 2008 Istockphotos: xii (above right and center left), 1 (center left and below right), 21, 25, 96, 100 (below), 198; © 2008 Paul Baicich xii (below left), 23; © 2008 Terry Nathan: 1 (below left), 125; © 2008 Trevor Hunt design, 2; © 2008 Diane Choplin: 12, 13, 149; © 2008 Eugene Cordero: 17; © 2008 Laura Stec: 59, 67 (above left), 87 (below left), 98, 123, 143 (above right), 210; © 2008 David Stockdale (CUESA): 66 (above left); © 2008 Tyler Blank (CUESA): 66 (center right), 100 (above); © 2008 Samuel Gordon: 67 (above right); 87 (above right); © 2008 Coskata, Inc. archives: 116; © 2008 George Reekie: 119; © 2008 Kaiser Permanente archives, 121.

Published by
Gibbs Smith
P.O. Box 667
Layton, Utah 84041
Orders: 1.800.835.4993
www.gibbs-smith.com

Designed by Liddy Walseth
Printed and bound in China
Gibbs Smith books are printed on either recycled, 100% post consumer waste, or FSC certified papers.

Library of Congress Cataloging-in-Publication Data

Stec, Laura F.
  Cool cuisine : taking the bite out of global warming / Laura F. Stec and Eugene C. Cordero. —1st ed.
     p. cm.
  Includes index.
  ISBN-13: 978-1-4236-0392-4
  ISBN-10: 1-4236-0392-3
  1. Natural foods. 2. Environmental responsibility. 3. Sustainable living. 4. Global warming—Environmental aspects. I. Cordero, Eugene C. II. Title.
  TX369.S725 2008
  641.5'636—dc22
                        2008017369

Contents

Preface.. vi

Acknowledgments viii

Introduction xi

PART ONE BACKGROUND

1 The Global-Warming Diet 3

2 Why All the Oil in My Soil? 15

3 Global Warming and Tonight's Dinner 33

4 In Search of a Cool, Clean Drink..................... 51

PART TWO SOLUTIONS

5 The Summer of Grapes................................... 69

6 Holy Cow! 97

7 Seven Innovative Recipes for Success 117

PART THREE CULINARY HOW-TO

8 America's Changing Palate 145

9 Eat More Vegetables! 153

10 Great Grains... 177

11 A Cook's Look 199

Epilogue: The Secret 223

Appendix.. 224

Index 238

Preface

I HAVE BEEN ATTRACTED TO FOOD FOR GOOD AND BAD REASONS FOR MANY YEARS.

When I was in elementary school, I put on dinner parties for my family, cooking the foods and decorating the kitchen with souvenirs my parents brought back from their many trips overseas. I became a vegetarian in the early '80s and was inspired for seventeen years to follow that diet in search of better health for myself and for the environment. About that same time, I developed an eating disorder that negatively impacted my life for thirteen years: not anorexia or bulimia, but an obsessive-compulsive relationship with food where I handled stress with sugar, big time. In the late '80s, I discovered macrobiotics and started training at the East West Center in Eureka, California, under my first cooking teacher, Meredith McCarty. I also founded "EcoEaters," one the first food-and-environment education programs in the United States. For many years I went back and forth between the two worlds: totally inspired by and vocal about the positive effects that food has on our bodies and the planet, while silently struggling with an eating disorder that held me back personally and professionally.

The first cooking class I ever taught was to a group of eighth graders in Boulder, Colorado, in 1991. We made miso soup and a vegetarian burrito with whole-grain brown rice. I was so nervous teaching that I stumbled over the definition of miso, giving a most memorable explanation. What was supposed to come out as "miso is a food with tiny little organisms and friendly flora to help power our digestive system," came out as "tiny little orgasms" instead. The class, including the teacher, burst into laughter, and my face turned bright red. It was a fortuitous slip though—I bet those students never forgot the power of miso!

I continued to learn about food and health while training at the School of Natural Cookery in Boulder, the Vega Macrobiotic Study Center in Oroville, California, under Herman and Cornellia Aihara, and the Culinary Institute of America, at Greystone, St. Helena, California. In my early days of teaching, I primarily promoted the food and health connection: both the health of ourselves and health of the environment. However, along the way I realized most students weren't motivated by vitamins, minerals, or calorie counting (and now "carbon counting" must be added into that mix.) People listened to me speak about the connections and understood the concept, but it wasn't what inspired them to get going in the kitchen. And it wasn't what motivated me either. As important as health is (both our own health and that of the planet), what eaters are really motivated by is pleasure.

As the years passed, I healed myself from the eating disorder, added a little meat back into my diet, and taught students of many food philosophies how to get more satisfaction and enjoyment out of mealtime. In the process, I learned something very important: the pleasure derived from eating is not just about our stomach or filling our mouth with food. Cooking and eating are core to being human, and participating in that process is one of the ways we express ourselves. Recent authors who have written about the need for pigs to express their "pig-ness" and chickens to express their "chick-ness" got me thinking. How do we humans express our "human-ness?" One of the ways I have come to believe we do this is through our rituals around food and eating.

Today's industrial-chemical-agricultural-marketing system is stealing that ritual away, offering us a less healthy, less tasty food system where price and portability are king, and pollution, global warming, and a host of other planetary ills are the icing on the cake. By reconnecting to the sources of our food, however, and acknowledging the central role food plays in our lives, we can take that ritual back. And by valuing where our food comes from and the land, animals, and farmers who give it to us, food and eating can enrich our bodies as well as our minds and our spirits. This is how simple "eating becomes dining," as aptly described by French food philosopher Brillat-Savarin, and one important way we can finally be filled with the sense of true satisfaction that we hunger for.

The first two sections of this book are meant to appeal to the *reader* in you. They offer up-to-date information on a hot topic. The last section, however, is meant to appeal to the *eater* in you. Chew well on the early chapters about science, sociology, and innovation, but in the end, dear reader, remember the most important thing . . . to savor the flavor.

Acknowledgments

I would like to thank Dr. Eugene Cordero for his role as coauthor, researcher, and editor, and for "keeping me honest" throughout this entire process. Behind every good chef should be a scientist backing her or him up. Also to Clare Cordero for her overall help, much of which I probably did not see or know about. And a special thanks to everyone interviewed for the book, including Michael Ableman, Foxglove Farm; Paul Baicich, formerly of American Birding Association; Wes Bolsen, Coskata, Inc.; Dr. Sally Brown, University of Washington; Chris Choate, Norcal; Abe Collins, Carbon Farmers of America; Dave Culp, Kiteship; Aaron Dallek, EcoSynergy; John Dickman, formerly of Google; David Dunn, Central Vermont Public Service Corporation; Gail Feenstra, UC Davis; Dr. Gene Feldman, NASA; Dr. Anthony Fisher, UC Berkeley; Dr. Michael Hamm, Michigan State University; Will Harris, White Oak Pastures Inc.; Dr. William Horwath, UC Davis; Dr. Philip Howard, Michigan State University; Dr. Christine Jones, Amazing Carbon; Dr. Claire Kremen, UC Berkeley; Don Larson, Common Ground Organic Garden Supply and Education Center; Joe Lashlee, beekeeper; Brook Lucy, Bluebird Grain Farms; Dr. Preston Maring, Kaiser Permanente; Helene and Spencer Marshall, Marshall's Farm Natural Honey; Steven McCarthy, Prather Ranch Meat Co.; Robin Plutchok, Stopwaste.Org; Kathryn Renz, Seltzer Sisters; Robert Rice, Smithsonian Migratory Bird Center; Jo Robinson, Eatwild; Allan Savory, Holistic Management International; Paul Schmitt, master composter; David Stockdale, Center for Urban Education about Sustainable Agriculture (CUESA); Albert Straus, Straus Family Creamery; Lynn Giacomini Stray, Point Reyes Farmstead Cheese Co.; Louis Sukovaty, Crown S Ranch; Nathan Taylor, EcoSynergy; Aliza Wasserman, Community Alliance with Family Farmers (CAFF); John Wilcox, Duck Creek Farm; Dr. Douglas W. Williams, Williams Engineering Associates; Elise and Ron VanderYacht, Methow Valley Creamery, and Dr. Lewis Ziska, USDA.

Thanks to photographer Christine Krieg and others; designer Trevor Hunt; our editors Leslie Stitt and Jennifer Grillone and our publisher Gibbs Smith for supporting the book and the cause; our agent Ted Weinstein; editor Barbara Roth; and David Coale and Dr. Mike Sipe for technical support. I appreciated the help of my community editors Peter Neal, Sue Brown, Bart Westcott, Dorothy Bender, and Lynn Ahlberg; Brita Friedrich at Whole Foods; and my research assistants Elizabeth McMunn-Tetangco and Heather Nisen. Thanks also to environmental organization Acterra and my personal chef clients for their flexibility in my work schedule while writing this book. And lastly I express my appreciation to my parents, Edward and Helen Stec, and to God in all forms, for this amazing planet and home, filled with absolutely delicious food.

Laura Stec

I would like to thank my friends, family and colleagues for their continued encouragement and inspiration to write this book. I'm especially grateful to Dr. Steve Mauget, Dr. Andrew Watkins, and Professor David Karoly for their excellent science reviews and helpful suggestions. I benefited from many conversations about energy and carbon with Dr. Peter Seligman, and appreciate the research done by meteorology student Amanda Short on the food miles calculations. I would like to express my gratitude to Liz Whitaker for her careful reviews of my writing and to Professor Terry Nathan, both for his excellent photos and for the many years of collaboration and mentoring in the atmospheric sciences. Thanks also go to my parents for their moral support, and my wife Clare, who was a crucial part of our team. Clare's excellent research and editing skills improved the book immeasurably.

I would also like to acknowledge the Department of Meteorology at San José State University, which sponsored my yearlong sabbatical that allowed me to complete this project. I am also indebted to the National Science Foundation, who has supported my research and education interests through their Faculty Early Career Development Program (Grant ATM-0449996) over the last three years.

Finally, I'd like to thank Laura for her original idea of the Global-Warming Diet, for her energy and enthusiasm in getting this book off the ground, and for her easygoing and upbeat attitude throughout the project. This made working and learning together a real pleasure.

Eugene Cordero

Introduction

This book is organized into three sections: the first gives background to the global-warming problem, the second highlights solutions, and the third is a "culinary how-to," teaching simple techniques and tips. The research is based on interviews conducted in 2007 with more than thirty scientists, farmers, and industry experts, as well as our many years of classroom and industry experience.

The recipes at the end of each chapter offer a hands-on opportunity to learn about the chapter subjects by working directly with the food. Turn a dinner party or your book club into a pot-luck discussion, and use the "Book 'n' Cook Club" inserts as a way to deepen your knowledge. Serve the dishes made from these recipes when you meet, or better yet, get together and cook while you discuss the topic. We purposely did not include a lot of recipes in the book, just the most important ones—simple recipes you can build upon on a daily basis. I have plenty of cookbooks filled with recipes I never use. The trick is to get a basic understanding of techniques that work for you without following a recipe. Then you only need to refer to your cookbooks for new ideas and special occasions.

Dr. Eugene Cordero, professor of meteorology at San José State University, served as the science advisor for this book. He writes on the science of climate change and describes how energy used in our current food-system practices relates to global warming. This information is in the green-shaded sidebars throughout the book. I hope you find the mix of science and culinary art an enjoyable way to learn more about the daunting topic of global warming.

Changing your diet will not solve global warming all by itself, but it does represent an important piece of the solution and a fun way for you to get involved. Knowledge of where your food comes from and how to cook it easily will enhance your culinary life and set you up to be part of the solution.

PART ONE

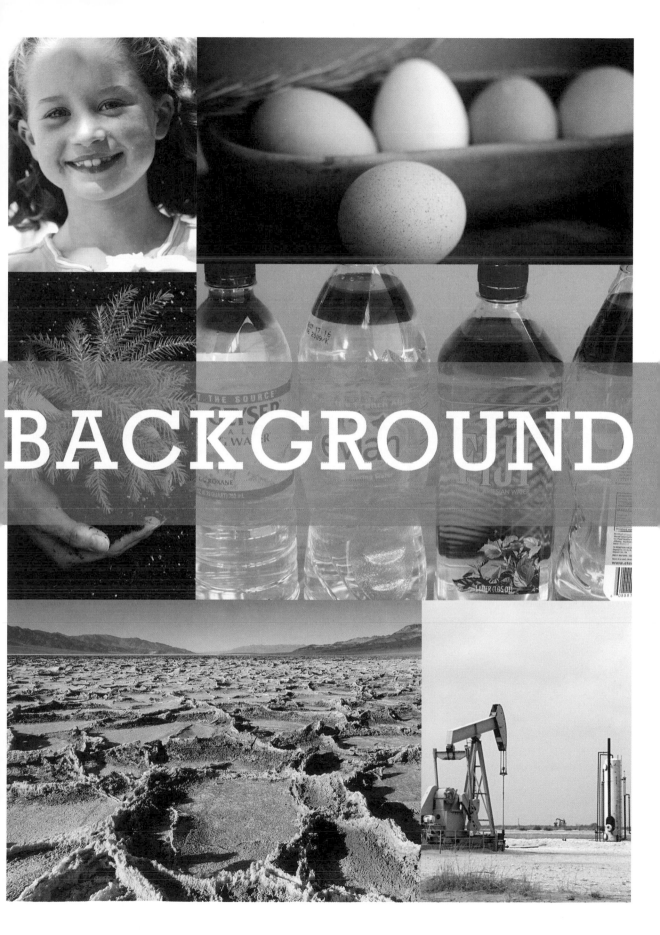

BACKGROUND

The Global-
Warming Diet

*Everyone talks about the weather, but nobody ever
does anything about it.* —Mark Twain

The most important thing I learned in culinary school had to do with energy. How to cut an onion, how to keep my knife sharp, and why water should be kept as far away as possible from vegetables are close seconds, but this is number one:

The energy of the cook goes into the food and the energy of the food goes into the cook.

If at first glance this statement appears to offer few clues on how to achieve culinary expertise, keep chewing on it. Food, like oil, is the sun's energy stored in a different form. It appears to be solid, but it is actually a mass of millions of atoms and electrons buzzing around one another. When we swallow that energy, it converts back to fuel, making us a world of solar-powered people. Like the gas we feed our cars, the better the food, the better the power. It behooves us to search out the best food we can find.

Using this energy to its full potential is what healthful cooking is really all about and what makes it exciting! Each carrot, grain of wheat, and piece of meat is a little package of bundled-up energy. Science explains that the power of food comes from the protein, carbohydrates, vitamins, minerals, and antioxidants found within. But the source of these compounds and the strength they exhibit are drawn from an elemental dance between sun, soil, water, and air,

Weather and Climate

An important distinction between the terms "weather" and "climate" is often misunderstood. Take a walk and notice the temperature, humidity, and wind direction. You are observing the weather. Weather happens at a specific location and time, and it changes from hour to hour and from day to day. Climate, however, is the accumulation of weather statistics taken over a long time period, and you need to gather a lot of weather data before you can determine the climate. Take summer in San Francisco as an example. San Francisco, on average, has a maximum daily temperature of 69 degrees F (20.5 degrees C) during July. This climate information, accumulated over the past thirty years of July weather, tells us what the average weather is like for that month. However, on any given day in July, the weather can be quite different, as tourists often discover when the cold fog rolls in under the Golden Gate Bridge. Climate is what you expect the weather to be, but, of course, on any given day the weather can be very different.

assisted by human energetic interaction. The end result is a gift, made just for you by the earth, wrapped in strawberry red, broccoli green, banana yellow, and all of the colors. Open up the package and bite in. Let those natural juices drip down your chin and the sun's energy release into you. Think about the elemental forces while you eat; it is they that nourish your body and soul.

Travel along today's culinary road, though, and what do you find? Potholes. Everywhere we turn, potholes line our path, blocking our way toward simple, real food. Highly processed, poor-quality foods stock the shelves of every store. Fast-food restaurants line every street and we supplement with delis and the frozen-foods section. High in fat, sodium, and ingredients we can't pronounce, this low-vibe food is prepared by "hands of indifference." Monster marts supply most of it—corporate conglomerates that seem to have forgotten that people are actually eating the stuff. Instead of growing fruits and vegetables with true flavor, our industrial food system buys bloated and bland produce grown in lifeless soil and hires "seasoning professionals" to dress it up and sell it to us as "value-added" product. By supporting this system, we have turned our Standard American Diet into its acronym: SAD—a diet low in natural goodness and high in saturated and trans fats, chemical additives, and refined sugar. And no matter what makes it onto your dinner plate tonight, guess what one of the other main ingredients will be? Oil. And I mean petroleum. From the wheat fields waving to the manufacturing and moving about of all our boxes and bags, our Standard American Diet has become a global-warming diet, too.

What Is the Global-Warming Diet?

D-I-E-T is a four-letter word. No one likes diets. Diet foods are boring, flavorless, and unsatisfying—words that describe the global-warming diet to a tee. It's a machine-cuisine we are eating today, and it takes about 500 gallons (1,890 l) of oil per person each year to produce it.[1] Talk about a greasy spoon—we emit similar amounts of carbon dioxide eating as we do by driving.[2] U.S. government research shows that our chemical fertilizer and herbicide-based food system contributes close to 20 percent of the nation's carbon dioxide emissions.

So how do food choices contribute to global warming? What's on the menu of the global-warming diet?

- Mountains of meat, especially beef. It takes more than ten times the fossil fuels to produce a calorie of beef protein than a calorie of grain protein.[3]

- Large amounts of imported food and drink.

- Foods grown with massive amounts of pesticides, herbicides, and fertilizers. We use 22 billion pounds (10 billion kg) of fertilizer just to grow the grain to feed our livestock.[4]

- A cornucopia of processed, frozen, and prepared foods. Processed food makes up three-quarters of global food sales by price (not by quantity) and typically requires more energy to make than what we get back when we eat it.[5]

- Piles of bottled water. More than half of all Americans drink bottled water; about a third of the public consumes it regularly. It takes approximately 17 million barrels of oil just to make the plastic for the 29-plus billion plastic water bottles used in the United States each year.[6]

Recipe for Making One Gallon of Gas

INGREDIENTS: 196,000 pounds of plants

DIRECTIONS: Find a field of about forty acres and harvest everything you can—plants, stalks, and roots (It should total about 196,000 pounds [89,000 kg].) Using a rather large utensil, such as a super-size potato masher, push your harvest down into the Earth's crust. In order to achieve the desired consistency, push plants into the crust about 6,500 feet (1,980 m), making sure to finish before they start to decay. Cover plants with very large porous rock. Set timer for 1 million years. Once cooked, remove from the ground.[7]

Climate Change and Global Warming

Climate change refers to the variations in the Earth's climate (e.g., temperature or rainfall) over time due to natural or human-related factors. Historically, the Earth's climate has warmed and cooled many times in response to natural changes such as volcanic eruptions or changes in the intensity of the sun. "Global warming," however, generally refers to contemporary climate change and the study of the natural and human-related processes responsible for the warming of the last hundred years and projected warming for the next hundred years. Many of today's scientists are working in the field of global warming; however, knowledge of past climate change is essential to improving our understanding of present and future climate.

- Gobs of high-fructose corn syrup. In 2000, Americans ate an average of thirty-one teaspoons of sugar a day, more than 15 percent of their caloric intake. Much of that was in drinks with added high-fructose corn syrup. The average American consumed almost 41.5 pounds (18.8 kg) of corn syrup in 2006, according to the U.S. Department of Agriculture. [8]

- Sizeable amounts of food waste. Nearly half of all the food harvested in the United States goes to waste each year.[9] Our food system generates 3,774 Calories per person every day, but we consume only approximately 2,100 Calories; the rest is wasted by overeating or by just throwing it away.[10]

- Plenty of packaging waste. We throw away 98 percent of the 380 billion plastic bags we use each year, along with the 12 million barrels of oil it takes to produce them.[11]

The truly sad thing about today's State of the Plate is that eaters don't benefit much from the greasy foods that are on it. Foods on the global-warming diet have less natural flavor, nutrition, and diversity and, in my opinion, are becoming less safe as more originate from factory farms than fields. U.S. food prices remain "the best deal in the world," and that's good. Or is it?

If it is true we only value what we pay for, it is understandable why we place so little value on food. Recently, I saw a woman pay for a hamburger just when her cell phone rang. She talked so long that the burger got cold, so she threw it away and bought a new one. Such inexpensive food has led our society into overeating and wasting sizable amounts of food—no matter what our income level is. In fact, income level is now an early indicator for obesity in the United States: lower income = higher chance of obesity.[12] That makes sense when some of the best deals at the grocery store, in terms of Calories per dollar, can be found in the junk food aisle. You can get 1,200 Calories of chips or 250 Calories of carrots for the same amount of money. This could be one reason why two-thirds of the U.S. population is overweight (one-third of those are obese).[13] We don't need food that is this cheap, certainly not junk food.

The Cost of Food

One of the reasons why junk food in the United States costs less than healthy food is because we prepay for a lot of it in the form of the U.S. Farm Bill. Every year, each American contributes about $250 in tax dollars ($289 billion total in 2008) to this massive piece of legislation that is supposed to help farmers but is really a subsidy for the country's largest agricultural producers. Rewarding the overproduction of crops such as corn, soybeans, and wheat creates a cheap supply of animal feed for factory farms, as well as an abundant source of raw material to make the high-fructose corn syrup, white flour, and soy oils in today's junk foods. The subsidies help create enormous profits for the large producers while pushing the family farmer out of business. Our annual $250 contribution promotes the growth of fields of corn, destined to become junk food for humans and cows. Fruits, vegetables, and nuts, on the other hand, are considered "specialty crops" in the bill, making them ineligible for funds.

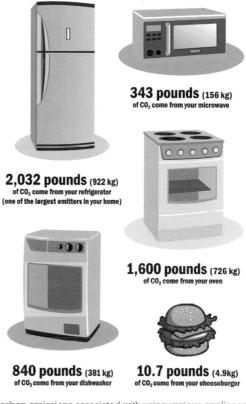

ANNUAL HOUSEHOLD EMISSIONS

343 pounds (156 kg) of CO$_2$ come from your microwave

2,032 pounds (922 kg) of CO$_2$ come from your refrigerator (one of the largest emitters in your home)

1,600 pounds (726 kg) of CO$_2$ come from your oven

840 pounds (381 kg) of CO$_2$ come from your dishwasher

10.7 pounds (4.9kg) of CO$_2$ come from your cheeseburger

Carbon emissions associated with using various appliances over a year [14] compared to the carbon emissions associated with a single cheeseburger (i.e., energy to grow food and cattle related methane emissions).[15] If a family of four were to eat one cheeseburger each week for a year, the emissions (2,225 pounds [1,007 kg]) would be greater than the energy required to operate the refrigerator for a year.

HIDDEN COSTS OF FOOD	
Farm Bill 2008 (for five years)	**$289 billion ($58 billion per year)**
Environmental cleanup externalities	**$11 billion average**
Increased medical costs due to weight gain and obesity	**$117 billion**
TOTAL	**$186 billion per year**

How might this be better spent? Compare these amounts to the annual research funding the United States gives to alternative energy (3 billion) and health care (30 billion).

Another thing that affects the cost of food is that we don't pay the true cost, or we pay for it in other ways. Collateral damage from our machine-cuisine creates problems for both our environmental and personal health. Environmental cleanup costs associated with industrial agricultural have been estimated at $6 to $17 billion a year.[16] And where we used to spend 18 percent of our income on food and 5 percent on health care in the 1960s, we now spend less than 9.5 percent on food and 16 percent on health care. Increased medical costs due to weight gain and obesity alone run $117 billion per year.[17]

Food costs are going up, but that's due more to increased fuel costs than increased quality. In general, Americans don't value food enough to pay a little more for better quality. Instead we seem to prefer an abundance of cheap food that is not very good. When price is the primary concern, produce and animals are produced like machine parts, not real food. In essence, our food has no more value than the plastic widgets coming off assembly lines (powered by a lot of cheap oil). We seem to have lost a connection to the deeper role that food and eating play in our fast-paced human lives. There's no comparison between machine-cuisine and real food, or between the satisfaction we get from vine-ripened produce compared to what we get from artificially ripened produce, picked to travel. We're not investing as a nation in the quality or health of our food system, and we have forgotten why this is so vitally important.

Cool Cuisine: The Ultimate Low-Carb(on) Solution

So what would a cool cuisine look like? In determining the carbon footprint of your next meal, consider these questions:

- How far do I travel to buy food and how do I get there?
- How much food am I buying—will I eat it all?
- What kind of food am I buying—is it plant based or animal based?
- Geographically, where is my food coming from?
- Is my food organic?
- How processed is my food?
- What kind of packaging is used for my food?
- Do I buy too many processed foods that need to be frozen or refrigerated?
- How am I disposing of the food and packaging waste?

A cool cuisine would reduce your overall carbon footprint by using fewer animal products, fewer processed foods, less bottled water, and less food and packaging waste and using more fresh, organic, seasonal, and locally grown whole foods such as vegetables, fruits, and whole grains. The benefits of eating this way are nothing new, but now we realize that our planet, as well as our body, is paying the price for an industrialized food system. It is time for a new perspective on a very old problem.

I propose that solutions to global warming may be the best thing that has happened to the culinary world in a long time, and that is what this book is about. Forget the gloom-and-doom statistics surrounding the fate of the planet; this book offers inspirational ideas on what people are doing to make it better, how you can participate, and what you get out of it by doing so.

Evidence of Twentieth-Century Warming

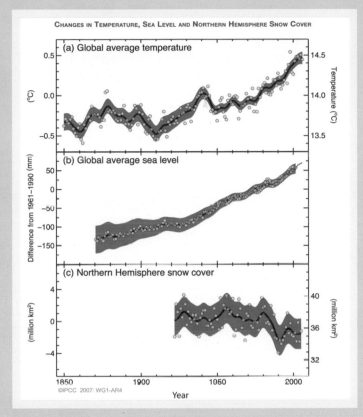

(a) Global average temperature

(b) Global average sea level

(c) Northern Hemisphere snow cover

©IPCC 2007: WG1-AR4

Figure 1. Observed changes in (a) global average surface temperature, (b) global average sea level where tide-gauge data is in blue and satellite data is in red, and (c) Northern Hemisphere snow cover for March-April. All changes are relative to corresponding averages for the period 1961–1990. Smoothed curves represent decadal average values while circles show yearly values. The shaded areas represent the uncertainty.[18] (Source: IPCC 2007).

Daily observations of temperature have been gathered from meteorological stations around the globe for many decades. Figure 1 shows global temperatures from 1850 to the present. The most obvious feature is the gradual warming of the planet, although you can also notice decades when the global temperature remained constant or even cooled. These variations reflect the competition between warming and cooling factors, with both natural and human origin. However, the most prominent signal of change has been the steady warming of the Earth since 1970: the warmest years on record (1998 and 2005), the warmest decade on record (the 1990s), and by 2007, eleven out of twelve of the warmest years have been in the past twelve years.[19] Clearly, over the last century, our planet has been warming.

Other signals of a warming planet or "fingerprints" of climate change have also been identified.[20] Fingerprints include the melting of glaciers, the rise in sea level, and the changes in distribution of plant and animal species. Today most glaciers in the world are in retreat, some of them very rapidly.[21] Sea-level rise has also been observed around the world.[22] Plants and animals are also sensitive to temperature, and migrations in numerous insect and marine animal populations toward higher altitudes or higher latitudes (where it's cooler) have been observed.[23] Taken together, these collections of fingerprints present further evidence that the planet is warming.

Human Connections: Greenhouse Gases

Since the Industrial Revolution, the global increases in carbon dioxide (CO_2) concentrations are primarily due to burning fossil fuels (such as coal, petroleum, and natural gas) and deforestation, while increases in methane (CH_4), and nitrous oxide (N_2O), are primarily due to agriculture.[24] Fossil fuels come from the fossilized remains of organic matter from plants and animals that, over millions of years, have been compressed, heated, and chemically altered by the Earth. Records of greenhouse-gas concentrations over the last thousand years using ice-core data and recent atmospheric measurements show that levels were nearly constant between the years 1000 and 1800, and then began to increase from 1850 (see Figure 2). The most important of these gases is carbon dioxide. Since 1850, CO_2 concentrations have risen from about 280 parts per million (ppm) to around 380 ppm today.[25] However, the rise has been most rapid in the last few decades. Considering the increase of 100 ppm of extra carbon dioxide in the atmosphere, it took 125 years for CO_2 levels to increase the first 50 ppm (between 1850–1975), whereas it only took thirty years for CO_2 levels to increase the last 50 ppm (between 1975 and 2005). Today's levels of carbon dioxide are likely higher than anytime in the last 650,000 years,[26] and if steps to reduce emissions are not taken, levels of carbon dioxide are forecast to double (compared to preindustrial levels) by 2050.[27]

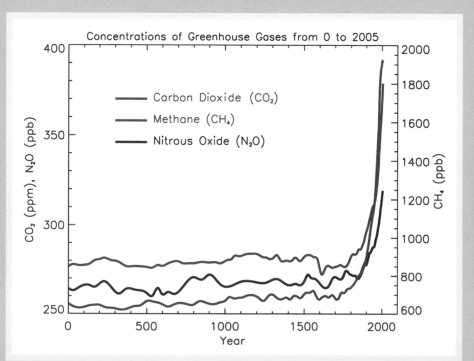

Figure 2. Atmospheric concentrations of important long-lived greenhouse gases over the last 2,000 years. Concentration units are parts per million (ppm) or parts per billion (ppb), indicating the number of molecules of the greenhouse gas per million or billion air molecules, respectively, in an atmospheric sample.[28] (Source: IPCC 2007.)

Use it as a tool to excite and inspire you to spend a little more time in your kitchen.

When you are considering changes in dietary habits, however, remember the age-old saying, "Everything in moderation, including moderation." Any food can be "good" or "bad" depending on a variety of different factors. Balance is the key. And though many things do motivate us, our ultimate motivation is pleasure. So have fun with this. Don't guilt yourself or anyone else *out* of doing things; instead, inspire them *in* to new ways of cooking and eating. Most importantly, "Don't let the perfect be the enemy of the good," wise words from French philosopher Voltaire. Changes in your diet, no matter what ideals guide you, can only be sustained by celebrating the small steps while you learn how to make food that you actually enjoy eating.

Cooking and eating are two of our most primal human pleasures. Learning more about where food comes from, valuing a local food system that brings it to us, and improving our cooking skills can bring years of increased motivation, satisfaction, connection, health, and culinary joy. It just so happens that, along the way, we can also have a significant impact on the health of our planet. And by doing so, our pleasure can become even greater.

Largest Global-Warming Diet Contributors

- Livestock
- Synthetic nitrogen fertilizers
- Greenhouses
- Air freight
- Food waste
- Consumer travel to and from store

—University of California, Davis, 2007

Cool Cuisine—Stage One

Here's a partial list of things you can do. Start with small changes and add on new steps as you go—the higher the stages, the greater the change. Have fun with it!

• Reduce meat consumption, specifically beef, by 20 percent. Replace with three meatless meals per week (or replace a beef meal with chicken).

• Start buying seasonal produce. Use our "What's in Season When?" chart in chapter 5 as a guide.

• Buy produce grown within your own country. Reduce consumption of tropical fruits.

• Reduce consumption of bottled water. Drink water bottled in your own country.

• Reduce food waste—eat what you buy.

• Bring your own bags to the grocery store.

Cool Cuisine—Stage Two

• Reduce meat consumption, specifically beef, by 30 percent. Replace with four or five meatless meals a week.

• Replace two factory-farmed meat meals with meat from grass-fed, pasture-raised animals.

• Eat one or two meals a week using no animal products at all (no meat, cheese, or egg).

• Start shopping at a farmers market, or purchase a community-supported agriculture (CSA) box of produce. Bike to the market when you can.

- Learn how to flavor foods with herbs, spices, and seasonings rather than animal fat.

- Eat three meals a week using organic foods.

- Refill plastic water bottles once from the tap before tossing the bottle (see chapter 4).

- Cook one to three meals a week using unprocessed, unpackaged foods. Buy in bulk if possible.

Cool Cuisine—Stage Three

- Eat three or more meals a week using no animal products (no meat, cheese, or egg).

- Eat five or more meals a week using organic foods.

- Stop drinking bottled water altogether. Buy a water filter and reusable bottles and refill them from your home tap.

- Bring your own cup to the coffee shop. Bike to get there.

- Buy fair-trade, organic, bird-friendly coffee and chocolate.

- Start your own home food-scrap compost pile or convince your city to start one.

2

Why All the Oil in My Soil?

I learned a lot about soil the first time I went snorkeling. It was off the coast of Malaysia, just after getting fired for not marrying my boss. I met my "short-term employer" at the Vega Macrobiotic Study Center in Oroville, California, near completion of a yearlong kitchen apprenticeship in 1996. Vega was a world-renowned school run by Herman and Cornellia Aihara, two of the leaders credited with bringing macrobiotics (a study of health through food and a holistic lifestyle) into the United States. My boss was a student at Vega, visiting from Singapore. Before returning home, he offered me a job as a macrobiotics teacher and personal chef. I flew to Singapore following graduation and, after only five days of work, he asked me to marry him! (I guess he really liked my cooking.) He didn't, however, like my answer: "Absolutely not." Saying "no" doesn't go over well in an Asian culture because it offers the receiver no chance to "save face." I've been told that a better answer—and one that could have bought me a few more days on the job—might have been, "I'm not quite ready," or even, "Please get back to me after the Jalapeño Rum Beans are cooked." (For those of you who have never cooked dried beans from scratch, they do take a while, but they are worth the wait. The recipe is at the end of this chapter.)

I took advantage of my newly unemployed status by traveling around Malaysia. This brought great adventure and a trip to Pilau Tioman, the island in the movie *South Pacific* referred to as "Bali Ha'i." It was there that I snorkeled for the first time and marveled at the unexpected mini circus performing just below the surface. Shiny, spotted sea creatures, vibrant coral, and fluorescent fish filled the space beyond my goggles. I was awestruck and deeply moved by this secret world that would have forever remained elusive had I not stopped to look.

Snorkeling helps me think more deeply about soil—this moist yet friable, mysterious, alive substance to which we literally owe our very survival. If ground goggles were available for soil snorkeling, we would be able to see a crepuscular world much more diverse than the seas of Malaysia. Soil is alive, a hotbed of movement and vivacity. David Montgomery, author of *Dirt: The Erosion of Civilizations,* writes:

> Look closely and you find a whole world of life eating life, a biological orgy recycling the dead back into new life. Healthy soil has an enticing and whole-some aroma—the smell of life itself. [1]

I am not a gardener, but I have come to see that making good soil has similarities to making wine or an artisanal soy sauce. We gain a new appreciation for our food by learning about the soil. Approximately 9 billion microorganisms can be found in only one tablespoon of soil. An acre of healthy soil is reported to contain approximately 900 pounds (408 kg) of earthworms, 2,400 pounds (1,089 kg) of fungi, 1,500 pounds (680 kg) of bacteria, 133 pounds (60 kg) of protozoa, and 890 pounds (404 kg) of arthropods and algae! [2] Healthy soil is vital for healthy plants and better-tasting food. And while we used to believe that nutrition, or "chemistry" (the amount of nitrogen, phosphorus, and potassium), was the most important contributor to soil health, we now acknowledge that microorganisms (the soil bugs), or the "biology" of soil, is the key.

In relationship to global warming, soil serves as an important "carbon sink" (a reservoir that absorbs carbon), enhanced by the amount of organic matter found within it. The Earth's soil contains about three times the amount of carbon found in the atmosphere, and about four times more than in all of the Earth's vegetation. [3] Think of the grasslands as one big natural solar panel, sucking up the sun and storing the carbon for later use in the form of plant matter and soil humus. More carbon in the soil means more plants, more earthworms, more life in general. Healthier soil produces more nutrient-rich fruits and vegetables, what I call "high-vibe" food.

> Healthier soil produces more nutrient-rich fruits and vegetables, what I call "high-vibe" food.

Agriculture, whether conventional or organic, can have a deleterious effect on the Earth's soil. Some agricultural practices are particularly hard on the environment and contribute to our global-warming diet. What are they?

The Greenhouse Effect

To understand the science of global warming, we can start by looking at a greenhouse. Essentially a small house made of glass, a greenhouse allows the sun's energy to pass through easily while inhibiting the heat from leaving. The Earth's atmosphere works in a similar way. A majority of the sun's radiation passes through the cloudless atmosphere and acts to warm the Earth's surfaces and the oceans. In turn, the land and ocean give off energy that is headed out to space. Most of this energy does not escape to space, rather it is absorbed by naturally occurring greenhouse gases such as water vapor (H_2O), carbon dioxide (CO_2), methane (CH_4), and nitrous oxide (N_2O). After they absorb the Earth's energy, they, in turn, re-emit some of that energy back toward the Earth's surface and provide additional warming of the Earth. This is what we call the greenhouse effect because, although the sun's energy is able to pass through the greenhouse gases, these same greenhouse gases trap the Earth's outgoing energy.

It turns out that greenhouse gases play a very important role in our climate system. Remove all the greenhouse gases in the atmosphere and the Earth's average temperature would be a very chilly 0 degrees F (-18 degrees C), and most of the planet would be frozen. However, in a manner similar to putting blankets on to trap your body heat when you go to bed, the layer of greenhouse gases acts as a blanket to keep the Earth a comfortable temperature of 59 degrees F (15 degrees C). And just as you can expect to sleep warmer if you add extra blankets to your bed, you can expect the Earth to get warmer if you add extra greenhouse gases to the atmosphere.

So where are these greenhouse gases and how many of them are around? Well, take a deep breath. You have just inhaled an assortment of molecules that primarily include nitrogen and oxygen, and also small amounts of greenhouse gases such as water vapor and carbon dioxide. It's actually these molecules in relatively small concentrations, which exist everywhere in the atmosphere, that turn out to be important for shaping our climate. *(You can now exhale!)*

To Till or Not to Till—
That Is the Question

Tilling has long been a part of farming practices, with archaeological records of the plow dating back to 6,300 BC.[4] Farmers till the soil to loosen and aerate it, to assist with weed control, and to add compost and other soil amendments. The process is under intense observation lately as farmers and scientists consider the issues of carbon emissions and carbon sequestration (the long-term storage of carbon in the biosphere, underground, or the ocean) in relation to soil. As tilling opens up the soil, it exposes the organic matter to oxygen, and carbon dioxide is emitted. Heavy tilling machinery passing back and forth over fields compacts the subsoil while guzzling up fossil fuels along the way. Compacted subsoil causes problems with water drainage and root growth, making the soil less healthy and less able to store carbon. Tilling also wreaks havoc with the bacteria and fungi networks that assist nitrogen fixation of the soil, which, in turn, increases the need for more oil-based fertilizers.

Conventional farms don't till much because they add little or no compost (read—good energy) back into the soil. Instead, machines that "slit" the ground to plant the seeds have begun to replace tilling, and herbicides are used to reduce any leftover plant matter that remains on top of the soil. Industry cites this practice as environmentally friendly because it creates less soil disturbance and helps keep carbon in the soil.

The next time you go to the farmers market, ask the farmers what they think about tilling and how they do it. Every farmer I interviewed for this book had a different perspective on what some termed the "necessary evil." There are, however, a few new plows that are more in tune with organic growing. One from the Rodale Institute in Pennsylvania uses a front roller to crush the cover crop and a back roller to slit through the cover crop and ground and plant the seeds. This one-step process reduces soil compaction, tillage, and fossil-fuel use, allowing for better carbon retention.

Fertilizers, Pesticides, and
Candy-Coated Brie

Back in the 1800s, European farmers harvested seabird guano for use as one of the first commercial fertilizers. Guano was found on islands off the coast of Peru, piled as deep as two hundred feet on some of the islands, preserved by the relatively rain-free environment. Guano export became big business because it provided an excellent source of nitrogen—essential for growing plants.

In 1901, as the islands were being stripped of their guano, two German chemists, Fritz Haber and Carl Bosch, made modern-day fertilizer by combining atmospheric nitrogen with hydrogen from fossil fuels to get liquid ammonia. Known as the Haber-Bosch process, this process "fixes nitrogen" for use on fields, enabling farmers to bypass the work of legumes and soil microbes. Observing a farm's first contact with oil-based fertilizers has been aptly described by farmers as "watching the soil become a drug addict." With the overabundance of accessible nitrogen appearing to produce more food than organic agriculture, this addiction has been encouraged. However, today's organic farms are beginning to successfully challenge this assumption.[5]

Approximately 22 billion pounds (10 billion kg) of chemical-based fertilizers are used each year just to grow the grains for America's livestock.[6] That's like 18.3 million average-size cows piled on top of one another. Strangely enough, massive amounts of fertilizer sprayed over the surface of the soil reminds me of one of my favorite "Martha" recipes for candy-coated Brie (Brie is made in many other countries besides France, including in the United States). To make it, caramelize sugar in a small pot until it is a beautiful, glistening gold liquid and then pour it over a round of Brie to harden. (See detailed recipe at the end of the chapter.) Guests love slicing through the crackling coating into the creamy Brie inside. Put a piece to your lips, and your tongue will smile. Savor it for a moment, suspending cheese and sugar between tongue and mouth, then crunch down slowly and swallow. It's a perfect combination of rich, tangy cheese and a crispy sweet topping—definitely what I want from my cheese, but not what I want for my soil. Overfertilized, hardened, crackly dead soil does nothing for the taste or quality of my food; it's an unsavory outcome of a global-warming diet.

Overdependence on oil-based fertilizers and industrial agriculture produces nitrous oxide as a by-product, a greenhouse gas with a global-warming potential per molecule that is more than three hundred times stronger than that of carbon dioxide. Nitrous oxide is produced when soil is low in oxygen, which occurs for a number of reasons, including compaction from heavy machinery and failure to compost

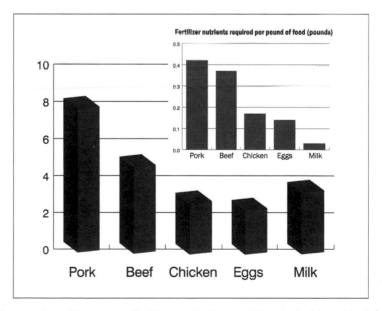

Fertilizer nutrients used per year (billion pounds)

Fertilizer nutrients required per pound of food (pounds)

A comparison of the amount of fertilizer required to grow different animal-based foods.[7]

or add organic matter back into the soil. A healthy soil has a balance of anaerobic and aerobic bugs that use each other's gases for food. Soil low in oxygen is bad for aerobic bugs but ideal for anaerobic bugs. If the system becomes out of balance, underutilized gases from anaerobic bugs are released into the atmosphere as nitrogen gas or nitrous oxide. Agriculture accounts for approximately 37 percent of the nitrous oxide released in the United States.[8]

Different foods require different amounts of fertilizer. Raising livestock on grain requires much more fertilizer than growing fruits and vegetables. One pound of fertilizer is needed to produce two and a half pounds of feedlot pork (pigs eat mostly grain). Feedlot cows come in second after pigs as inefficient converters of grain to meat, requiring one pound of fertilizer for every three pounds of beef produced. Factory-farmed chickens and eggs generally require only half the amount of fertilizer as beef and pork.[9]

By growing our food this way, we have become addicted to cheap sources of oil not only to move us about but to feed us as well. Drugs (in the form of fertilizers and pesticides) have replaced natural growing processes and degraded our soil. David Montgomery writes:

> The USDA estimates that about half the fertilizer used each year in the United States simply replaces soil nutrients lost by topsoil erosion. This puts the United States in the odd position of consuming fossil fuels—geologically one of the rarest and most useful resources ever discovered—to provide a substitute for dirt—the cheapest and most widely available agricultural input imaginable.[10]

Monocropping Is Bad for Dinner Parties

Monocropping is an agricultural practice of growing large fields of the same crop on the exact same piece of land, year after year. Fueled by chemical fertilizers, monocropping creates an unnatural, unsustainable ecosystem. Look around you. Nature is balanced with variations in foliage for a number of reasons; pest control is one of them. Bugs like some plants and can't stand others; they stay with their favorites. Diversity keeps everybody under control. Fill a field with only one plant and it becomes an exclusive country club with no need for bouncers. Bugs can lay out their lawn chairs and feast on an endless smorgasbord of corn, wheat, or whatever their preferred *amuse-bouche* may be. These bugs are like houseguests from hell. They eat everything, replace nothing, and trash the place. Once they get going, only an oil-based entrée (read "pesticide") can dampen the party. In a healthy ecosystem, the carbon cycle (composting plant and animal matter) replaces nutrients taken up by growing plants. In a monocropped field, fertilizers do all the work. No need for compost there.

What is the Carbon Cycle?

Carbon exists in all living things and has been called the building block of life. Carbon also exists in nonliving things, such as carbon dioxide (an invisible gas) and rocks such as limestone. Our understanding of how carbon moves between the atmosphere, ocean, and land is central to quantifying how increases in greenhouse gases and changes in land surface (i.e., deforestation and soil erosion) will affect climate in the future.

The carbon cycle is a complex series of processes that describes how carbon is exchanged between the atmosphere, ocean, and land (i.e., plants, soil, and the Earth's crust). One component of the carbon cycle is the exchange of carbon between the atmosphere and plants (i.e., carbon dioxide absorbed by plants via photosynthesis), while volcanic eruptions that inject carbon dioxide into the atmosphere represent an exchange of carbon between the Earth's crust and the atmosphere. Although carbon is constantly moving between different parts of the Earth, the total amount of carbon on the planet is constant. In this way, if the amount of carbon in the ocean were to go down, then the amount of carbon in the atmosphere or land would have to go up. This property of carbon conservation allows us in theory to keep track of all carbon movements throughout the Earth.

Today, the burning of coal and petroleum for energy is just an acceleration of one component of the carbon cycle. For example, the carbon in coal would normally remain in the ground for thousands of years until erosion or plate tectonics eventually released this carbon back into the atmosphere. So when humans burn fossil fuels they are really just moving carbon from the land into the atmosphere.[11]

Well-defined estimates exist for how much carbon goes into the atmosphere each year due to the burning of fossil fuels and changes in the land surface. There are also various organizations that are working to take carbon out of the atmosphere and put it back into the land. For example, the planting of a tree over a period of time will store atmospheric carbon in the trunk, branches, and roots of the tree. However, true to the carbon cycle, if that tree were to burn in a fire, the carbon would be liberated back into the atmosphere. So careful monitoring of the carbon cycle is necessary to understand how human factors affect atmospheric carbon levels and climate.

Creating a healthy agricultural ecosystem is a lot like planning a successful dinner party. You don't serve five dishes of the exact same food to a group of uninvited guests who overstay their welcome. And after the meal is done and your guests have gone home, please don't leave the table bare. The party energy can continue if you cover the table with something nice, such as seasonal placemats or a tablecloth. The same holds true for the fields. Planting diverse crops, interspersing hedgerows, and putting down a cover crop between harvests keeps the invited bugs eating, drinking, and making good soil. It is one of the most effective ways to increase soil carbon and create healthier soil, as we will see in chapters 5 and 6.

Now that automobiles have begun to quaff the nectar out of America's monocropped cornfields, we have all been witness to what happens as stomachs start competing with cars. Plans call for one-third of the U.S. corn harvest moving from food to fuel, but recent international food shortages and riots make it clear this strategy is fuelish; food is too precious of a commodity to use as fuel. Besides, corn-based ethanol seems an inefficient way to harvest the sun's energy, possibly using a similar amount of energy to produce as it generates as a fuel.[12] Developing biofuels that use cellulose-rich plants such as sugarcane may be a better solution, but not if it requires the continued destruction of forests. Forget monocropping altogether—let's focus on harvesting the sun's energy directly. The daily amount of sunlight that falls on this planet is 5,000 times more than the amount of fossil fuel we burn each day. Economic incentives are needed to encourage planting rows of solar panels between strawberries and green beans, instead of planting rows of corn for fuel. Or better yet, let's invent paper-thin solar panels to tie onto field poles. They could sparkle and flutter in the wind (like the Mylar tape does now), capturing the sunlight and scaring away the birds, all at the same time.

Deforestation and Shady Coffee and Chocolate

http://nationalzoo.si.edu/Conservation
AndScience/MigratoryBirds/Coffee

Ongoing rainforest deforestation is another result of current agricultural trends, accommodating an ever-growing monocropped diet of foods such as oranges and beef. According to the Climate, Community, and Biodiversity Alliance (CCBA), tropical deforestation is the second leading cause of climate change after the power sector, accounting for 20 to 25 percent of all greenhouse gas emissions. Six million acres (25,000 square km) of Amazon rainforest are cleared each year for grazing cattle and growing the soybeans that feed them.[13] Standing trees help moderate levels of atmospheric carbon dioxide by taking in carbon dioxide and giving off oxygen. Once the trees are

Shade-grown coffee plant.

gone, the carbon dioxide is ultimately released back into the atmosphere, and the land becomes subject to overgrazing and erosion, decreasing the soil's health and its ability to hold carbon.

Forests are also clear cut to plant monocropped fields of coffee and cocoa. When grown this way, both foods have a "large ecological footprint," due to forest destruction as well as the amount of fertilizers and pesticides required to grow the plants in unnatural habitats. However, a recent movement to support sustainably grown coffee and cocoa is gaining steam. Chocoholics can relax.

Coffee is the second most traded commodity in the international economy after petroleum. Between 20 to 25 million farmers grow coffee around the world, the majority based in Brazil, Colombia, and Vietnam. Vietnam got into the business after Agent Orange cleared the forests during the Vietnam War, leaving large open spaces in their place.[14] Worldwide, cocoa is farmed on more than 17 million acres (69,000 square km) by 15 million farmers. Most of these are small farms and, by searching out their product, we not only support their livelihood, we can sequester carbon and preserve rainforest as well.

Robert A. Rice, a geographer with the Smithsonian Migratory Bird Center (SMBC), tells us that coffee plants prefer naturally shaded, biologically diverse habitats. Coffee is a very "sociable plant" that grows well around other crops and under the canopy of trees. Though it is increasingly common to grow coffee and cocoa in full sun to increase production, the process ruins the natural habitat and pushes out the small family farmer.

Shade-grown, Bird-Friendly® (SMBC's shade certification) coffee has been around since 1998; it is an idea that's slowly growing. It's more than just organic; it also promotes biodiversity protection. The Migratory Bird Center is specifically concerned with shade trees being part of the agro-forest system. If it looks like a rainforest, the migratory song birds will use it because birds are attracted to areas with plenty of food. Large farms are often "coffee factories in the field," but well-managed small farms (grown on the outskirts of the rainforest) offer so much more than coffee. They grow mango, citrus, leguminous nitrogen-fixing trees—often more than twenty different species of plants. They can't replace natural rainforests, but they do support an agricultural system that supplies food and income while providing bird habitat. The greater the diversity of the environment, the greater the diversity of birds. Birds are an indicator of forest health.

Cocoa trees also grow in naturally shaded areas, and some chocolate manufacturers are beginning to highlight the unique flavors of small-farmed cocoa beans, creating artisan products that use beans from certain growing regions—similar to wine and olive oil. Chocolate is made by roasting and grinding up the center of the cocoa bean (called the nib) and processing it into a cocoa liquor. The nibs are high in the antioxidants or flavonols, which are associated with cardiovascular health. Without the addition of milk solids (which may reduce the benefit of flavonols), sugar or cocoa butter, nibs are slightly bitter, somewhat crumbly, and taste strongly of chocolate. Eating one ounce of rainforest-certified dark chocolate (at least 70 percent cocoa) or chocolate nibs daily can support your own health and that of small farms and forests. Find recipes using nibs and dark chocolate at the end of this chapter.

Although "shade grown" is an increasingly common claim on coffee bags and chocolate bars, watch out—it is still an unregulated term. A plant grown in the shade of one tree can be called shade grown. If you can't find Bird-Friendly® coffee or Rainforest Alliance–certified chocolate, look for organic and fair-trade products from Latin America. When all these are on the label, chances are good that the product will be shade grown and bird and forest friendly.

Erosion Versus Earthworms (the True Iron Chefs)

Natural erosion by wind and water is Earth's way of refreshing the soil, but modern-day agriculture may be using up the soil faster than natural processes can replenish it. Erosion becomes a problem when unhealthy soil lacks enough plant matter and other carbon substances to keep it together, a direct result of the global-warming diet.

Far from a new concern, soil exhaustion was addressed by Greek philosophers Plato and Aristotle, along with the Mayans and early Europeans. In 1935, the United States Congress declared soil erosion a "national menace."[15] The USDA estimated that an alarming 2 billion tons of topsoil eroded from U.S. croplands in 2001,[16] with our agricultural system responsible for 60 percent of it.[17]

Erosion decreases when soil is healthy, filled with minerals, decaying organic matter, and soil microbes such as protozoa, arthropods, and earthworms. Earthworms are key to the process of soil formation, as noted by naturalist Charles Darwin, who wrote, "It may be doubted if there are any other animals which have played such an important part in history of the world as these lowly creatures." Masters of their craft, earthworms are the true Iron Chefs. Their favorite recipe? Carbon-rich soil. Their secret ingredient? Rocks (made up of iron, no less). Talk about tough; an earthworm grabs a leaf and rock dinner with its pharynx (throat), pushes the delicacy into its gizzard (stomachlike organ) and grinds it up with teethlike stomach muscles, turning the recipe into soil. While estimates suggest that without a rich abundance of soil animals it can take hundreds of years to build up an inch of topsoil, Darwin found that under favorable conditions earthworms can do it in five to ten years.[18] Industrial farming creates hostile environments for earthworms and keeps the national menace of soil erosion unchecked. We'll look more closely at ways a cool cuisine can change directions for the better in the following chapters.

Carbon Dioxide: Year by Year

An interesting illustration of human impact on the Earth's atmosphere comes from Hawaii. Since 1958, daily measurements of carbon dioxide have been taken from the Hawaiian mountain of Mauna Loa, at 13,680 feet (4,170 m) above sea level. In Figure 3, the solid black line is the five-year average measurement mean; the red line represents the actual monthly measurements. The average CO_2 concentration has steadily increased over

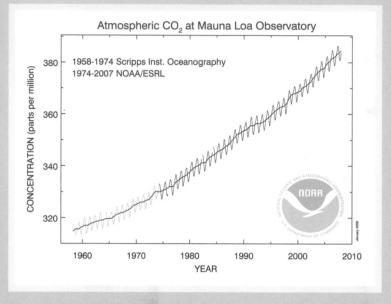

Figure 3. Monthly values of atmospheric carbon dioxide concentrations at Mauna Loa Observatory, Hawaii, measured in parts per million (ppm) indicating the number of molecules of carbon dioxide per million air molecules. The black curve represents the smoothed data.[19] (Source: NOAA.)

the last fifty years. Because carbon dioxide is relatively well mixed in the atmosphere, the measurements at Mauna Loa are a good estimate of the global average. Using ice-core measurements from Antarctica, scientists believe that today's concentration of carbon dioxide is higher than at any time over the last 650,000 years.[20]

In addition to the steady rise in carbon dioxide, the annual rise and fall of carbon dioxide in the atmosphere is also striking. Every year CO_2 concentrations go through a cycle in which they slightly decrease between April and July and slightly increase in September and October. This regular pattern reveals the connection between the atmosphere and all living plant matter on Earth. Here is how it works.

In spring and early summer, new growth on trees, plants, and grasses returns with the warming weather. Because plants take in carbon dioxide as they grow, CO_2 levels start to decrease, and by the summertime—the peak growing season—CO_2 levels have noticeably dropped. In the cooler weather of fall, plants start to lose their leaves which break down and return carbon to the atmosphere, and CO_2 levels then start to increase. Some people have suggested that the annual cycle in carbon dioxide is an example of the Earth breathing. During the spring and summer, the Earth's plant life is growing and thus taking in carbon dioxide, whereas in fall and winter, plants have died back and carbon dioxide is returned to the atmosphere.

Book 'n' Cook Club Ideas

Recipes

Ruth Leserman's
  Caramel Brie

Nitrogen-Fixing
  Pot o' Beans

Jalapeño Rum Beans

Dark Chocolate Chili

Popping Chocolate
  Gomashio

Video Documentaries

King Corn (2007)

Our Daily Bread (2005)

Birdsong and Coffee, A Wakeup Call
  (2006)

Books

Dirt: The Erosion of Civilizations, by
  David Montgomery

Field Trips

1. Check out a local chocolate factory for public tours (and free samples!).
2. Tour a municipal organic composting facility.
3. Go outside and probe the soil or look under fallen leaves for earthworms. Say thank you.

Small Things Matter

• Buy/make orange juice from oranges grown in or near your own country.

• Leave behind the monocropped lifestyle by reducing consumption of processed foods or trying new grains such as emmer, millet, and quinoa (see chapter 10).

• Replace one or more meat meals with beans.

• Start a compost pile and make your own live soil (see chapter 7).

• Purchase organic and fair-trade coffee. Look for "Bird-Friendly®" and Rainforest Alliance-certified seals.

• Buy coffee online from farmers in Latin America. Search for direct sales from small-farm cooperatives. Farmers make more profit this way, and their farms support natural habitat.

Recipes

Ruth Leserman's Caramel Brie

This is a great combination of creamy cheese with crunchy sugar. Choose Brie made in your country, and look for organic sugar. Reprinted with permission from *Martha Stewart's Hors D'Oeuvres Handbook.*

SERVES 36

1 wheel of ripe Brie (60 percent butterfat), 2.4 to 2.8 pounds
2 cups sugar
1/2 cup water
12 to 16 walnut or pecan halves (optional)

Place the Brie on a rack over a large sheet of parchment paper or aluminum foil. Combine the sugar and water in a small heavy saucepan and melt the sugar, swirling the pan from time to time, over high heat. Do not stir. When the mixture begins to boil, cover the pan to allow condensation to drip back down and melt the crystallized sugar on the side of the pan. Uncover the pan after 3 to 5 minutes and continue cooking over high heat until the sugar becomes a deep amber color.

Immediately pour the caramel over the cheese to cover the top evenly, allowing the excess to drip down the sides. You may have to tilt the cheese a little to spread the caramel evenly. Being very careful not to touch the hot caramel, press nuts around the perimeter, if desired. The caramel will harden quickly. Once cool enough to handle, transfer the wheel of Brie to a serving platter. Serve within 1 hour.

Nitrogen-Fixing Pot o' Beans

Do your part to help kick the planet's oil-based fertilizer addiction: replace a few meat meals with beans and legumes. They work with soil microbes to nitrogen-fix the soil, thus eliminating the need for additional fertilizers. Legumes such as alfalfa and clover are most often grown to do this, but even green beans, lentils, black beans, pinto beans, and split peas have a beneficial effect, even if the crops are harvested rather than just tilled back into the ground.

MAKES 3 CUPS

1 cup beans (black, pinto, small red, garbanzo, or a local brand)
4 cups water
1 (3-inch) piece kombu sea vegetable (adds flavor, helps with digestion)
Salt, to taste

Place dry beans on a plate and sort through for stones or dirt. Wash the beans, place in a medium-size saucepan, and cover with water. Use one of the following two methods to soak your beans, depending on how much time you have.

QUICK SOAK: Cover the saucepan. Bring the beans and water to a boil. Remove from heat and let sit, covered, for 1 hour.
LONG SOAK: Cover the saucepan. Let the beans soak overnight (6 to 8 hours).

Once beans have soaked, drain and rinse. Return to the saucepan and add 4 cups of water and the kombu. Cover the pot and bring to a boil, and then reduce the heat and simmer for 1 hour, or until the beans are tender. In the last 15 minutes, add salt to taste. Remove the kombu, chop it up, and put it back in the pot. Drain the beans and eat, or don't drain and use the whole pot as a base for soup.

Jalapeño Rum Beans

Season your beans with this easy recipe. It works well with freshly cooked or canned beans.
SERVES 3

1 1/2 cups beans, freshly cooked or canned
1 cup vegetable or chicken broth
1 tablespoon dark rum (optional)
1 tablespoon red wine vinegar
1 clove garlic, sliced thin
1 teaspoon minced jalapeño pepper
Freshly ground pepper and good salt, to taste

Place all the ingredients in a small saucepan. Bring to a light boil, then reduce the heat and let it simmer for 15 to 20 minutes. Drain the beans, save the cooking liquid for a soup stock or other purpose. Serve the beans as is or incorporate them into another dish.

For more flavor and to save energy, turn off the heat and let the beans marinate in the sauce for an hour on the stovetop.

Dark Chocolate Chili

Put that forest-friendly chocolate to work! A vegetarian chili benefits from a complexity of flavors and ingredients that make up for the missing complex compounds found in meat. Dried peppers are really worth the extra effort because they "fill in" the chili, giving it more body. This recipe has many ingredients, but they are easily assembled into a slow cooker. Using a slow cooker helps the flavors meld together. Use low heat for best results.

SERVES 6

3 tablespoons olive oil, divided

1 red onion, diced

4 medium tomatoes, peeled and seeded

2 yams, diced

1 red pepper, diced

1 (14.5-ounce) can diced tomatoes (organic fire-roasted preferred)

1 (16-ounce) can baked beans (not rinsed)

2 zucchinis, diced

3 stalks celery, diced

1 cup vegetable stock

1/4 cup dry red wine

3/4 cup beer

1/4 cup bulgur

10 whole cloves garlic, peeled

5 dried apricots, diced small

2 teaspoons coriander

2 teaspoons cumin

3 tablespoons chili powder

2 tablespoons Worcestershire sauce

1 tablespoon dark soy sauce

1 teaspoon molasses

1/2–1 teaspoon salt

3 dried negro chiles

3 dried ancho chiles

2 tablespoons fresh lime juice

1/2 (of a 3.5-ounce) dark chocolate bar, broken into small pieces (70 percent cocoa content or more)

1/4 cup chopped cilantro

Heat 1 tablespoon olive oil in a medium sauté pan; add the onion and cook until it is softened (about 4 minutes). Remove the pan from the heat. Chop peeled tomatoes coarsely and purée in a food processor or blender. Mix together the onions, tomato purée, the next 19 ingredients (yams through salt), and the second tablespoon of olive oil in a 5- or 6-quart slow cooker. Place the six dried chiles on top of everything and push down slightly into the mixture. Cover and cook on low heat for 6–7 hours or on high heat for 4–5 hours.

Halfway through cooking, remove the now-moistened dry chiles to a separate bowl. When chiles are cool enough to handle, remove the stems, slit down the center, and remove any big chunks of seeds. Place the chiles in a small food processor or blender with the third tablespoon of olive oil and the lime juice. Process into a paste. Remove from blender and push the paste through a medium-size sieve, with holes large enough for the paste to get through, but not the seeds or pepper skins. Scrape the paste off the bottom of the sieve and stir all of it into the chili. Compost the seeds and skins.

One-half hour before serving, turn off the slow cooker. Add the chocolate and cilantro; stir. Adjust seasoning to taste.

Popping Chocolate Gomashio

Eating carbon dioxide pop rocks won't solve global warming, but they are a great conversation starter about the issues and a fun addition to any dinner party. Gomashio (goma = seed, shio = salt) is a Japanese condiment, most often used on whole grains. (See more gomashio recipes in later chapters.) Sprinkle this sweet gomashio over your local organic ice cream, yogurt, pudding, fruit, or anything else in need of a crunchy, popping garnish. Sesame seeds are a great source of calcium, and freshly popped seeds are best.

MAKES 1/2 CUP

3 tablespoons brown sesame seeds

1/4 cup chocolate nibs (look for fair trade and organic)

1 teaspoons organic brown sugar (see Note)

2 tablespoons sliced almonds

2 tablespoons pastry pop rocks (optional—sold at pastry stores and online)

Heat a stainless steel frying pan (with a lid) on high. When hot, pour in 1/2 of the sesame seeds (you want a single layer of seeds.) Cover; the seeds should start popping immediately. Toast while shaking the pan as if you were popping popcorn, 30–60 seconds. Watch and listen closely because the seeds burn quickly. The seeds should be lightly toasted, not dark brown or black. Pour popped seeds from the skillet into a medium-size bowl while they are still popping. Repeat with remaining seeds. Add the chocolate nibs, almonds, and sugar; combine. Right before serving, mix in the pop rocks.

NOTE: Look for organic, fair trade sugars and unique varieties, such as dark brown molasses sugar.

3

Global Warming
and Tonight's Dinner

Believe it or not, the United States began studying potential effects of climate change on agriculture in the 1960s. In 1990, Congress passed, and President George Bush Sr. signed, the Global Change Reserve Act, aimed at understanding how humans were contributing to global warming. In 1993 the Global Change Research Information Office was established, and it is still in operation today. In 1995 it issued the report *Potential Impacts of Climate Change on Agriculture and Food Supply.*[1] We tracked some of its findings for an updated look at how today's scientists think global warming might affect tonight's dinner.

Global Warming and Tonight's Japanese Hot Pot with Carrots and Kudzu

Everyone talks about temperature in relation to climate change, but how might increased carbon dioxide levels affect the growth of crops and weeds? Plants that evolved before the ice ages, when atmospheric carbon levels were up to four times greater than they are today, are called C4 plants. After CO_2 levels dropped in the last 25 to 30 million years, another group of plants emerged that were able to survive with less carbon dioxide. These are called C3 plants. During photosynthesis, C3 plants form one less carbon molecule than C4 plants do, making them deficient in the amount of carbon dioxide they need (but adaptable to current levels). If CO_2 levels rise farther, the C3 plants will likely respond much more vigorously than C4 plants do, due to the increased availability of carbon, an essential resource. Most of today's crops—such as wheat, rice, and soybeans—as well as many invasive weeds, are C3 plants; in fact, 95 percent of all plant species are C3s. C4 plants include corn, sorghum, sugarcane, and millet. Because the majority of crops are C3, shouldn't climate change and the rise of carbon dioxide in the atmosphere be a good thing? Shouldn't it *benefit* agriculture?

In 2003, the USDA's Agricultural Research Station compared how the invasive weeds velvet-leaf (C3) and redwood pigweed (C4) and the grain sorghum (C4) reacted in a controlled CO_2 experiment. Researchers found that when CO_2 levels were increased, the yield of weeds (whether C3 or C4) increased, while the sorghum yields decreased. [2]

"Carbon dioxide is a principal global-warming gas, but it is also the carbon supply for all food and all plants," says Dr. Lewis Ziska, the USDA study's lead scientist. I read about Dr. Ziska's work while updating research from the 1995 governmental report on climate change and agriculture. What struck me (besides the fact that the government was even studying the issue) was his breadth of knowledge on the subject coupled with a straightforwardness about the limitations of this science. Dr. Ziska was the first scientist I contacted while researching for this book. When I asked for an interview, his response—"Sure, I am happy to share with people what I do not know"—surprised me. Little did I know that many of the scientists I would interview would offer similar disclaimers. Even though I had been reading about global warming in newspapers and hearing reports on the TV, it wasn't until after speaking directly to the scientists that the idea finally hit home. Though there is little doubt in the scientific community about the reality of climate change and the connection with humans, no one can predict exactly what the outcomes will be—on the environment, on our food sources, or on ourselves. He continued:

> Rising levels of atmospheric carbon dioxide [will] have a dramatic effect on 95 percent of the plants, and science has only a small understanding of what will actually occur. We need to start talking about this.
>
> When you change carbon dioxide levels you qualitatively and quantitatively change the food that is grown. We expect weeds will respond more than crops to changes in carbon dioxide and temperature. Weeds always respond better to uncertain and varying conditions. This has us worried that crop losses will increase as carbon dioxide increases, especially for the rice, wheat, and corn that supply food for half the world's population.

Dr. Ziska mentioned how increasing carbon dioxide could easily make poison oak much more toxic and make natural habitats even more overrun by nonnative plants. On the edible side, invasive weeds such as kudzu (also known as kuzu) might become a lot more invasive, too, which means kudzu stands to win the fight that many of us are tackling in our own backyards. Thank goodness kudzu is actually a desirable food in the kitchen, so let's learn how to use it. Sold in natural foods stores as a white powder or in small rock-size pieces, kudzu is an effective thickener, more gel-like than cornstarch. Praised for its medicinal properties, kudzu has been known to help with intestinal disorders, headaches, colds, and hangovers. It is calming to the nerves and soothing to the stomach. Our Japanese Hot Pot with Carrots and Kudzu is an easy way to put those increasing carbon dioxide levels to work. You will appreciate how kudzu thickens a sauce and how good you feel after you eat it. (Find the recipe at the end of the chapter.)

Dr. Ziska finished by explaining how rising carbon dioxide levels, of and by themselves, affect the makeup of our food.

> The plant world has four major "food groups" from which plants derive the substances they need to grow and produce: water, light, nutrients (such as phosphorus and nitrogen), and carbon. If humans made a 20 percent change in one of our food groups—for instance, if we started consuming 20 percent less meat or 20 percent more vegetables—we would expect it to affect us in some way, yes? Plants are no different. Since the 1960s, plants have seen a 20 percent increase in the amount of atmospheric carbon dioxide available for

Past Climate Change: Does a Few Degrees Matter?

The Earth's climate over the last 4 billion years has changed many times. The swings between warmer and cooler climates are well documented from records such as ice cores or the thickness of tree rings, and indicate that periods of warm and cold climates can last for hundreds or thousands of years.[3] These records also indicate that seemingly small changes in global temperature are the difference between an ice age and warmer periods like today. For example, 20,000 years ago, Earth's average temperature was about 8 degrees F (4.4 degrees C) colder than it is today. That was during our last ice age, when North America was largely covered with ice.[4] Step back a further 100,000 years, and the temperature of the Earth was warmer by about 3 degrees F (1.6 degrees C). Most of the Earth's ice had retreated toward the poles, and sea level was at least twenty feet (6 m) higher than today.[5] So based on historical records, a few degrees difference in the Earth's global temperature can have a big impact on the planet.

them to "eat." From this we anticipate nutritional changes, some positive, some negative, but overall, we anticipate food, particularly cereals, to have more starch and less protein.

Global Warming and Tonight's Seasonal Fruit Salad with Candied Ginger

How will increased temperatures affect crops? Increasing temperatures are a mixed bag for agriculture, another part of the "grand experiment" we are involved in. With global temperatures on the rise, agricultural areas are expected to shift northward (or southward in the Southern Hemisphere), benefiting countries such as Russia and Canada. This is good because it gives these countries a longer and hotter growing season, but it's problematic if plants can't adapt to lower soil-fertility levels and increased hours of sunlight. Higher temperatures may accelerate the respiration of plants (the rate at which they release carbon dioxide), which is good if they can self-regulate the carbon increases or bad if plant growth is slowed. Although there is nothing like hotter temperatures to generate a delicious-tasting tomato, if it gets too hot, the pollen of the tomato can be damaged and the plant won't grow at all.

Higher temperatures can also affect "chill hours," the number of hours below a certain temperature required for some fruits to reproduce effectively. Without enough chill hours, some crops become less productive, and flavors can be affected, specifically stone fruits such as cherries, peaches, and plums.

In a 2006 interview with the Union of Concerned Scientists, Steve Pomeroy, a cherry farmer from Contra Costa County, California, reported a dramatic change over the last ten years in the average number of California chill hours. For his cherries, 1300 to 1400 chill hours per year is optimum and used to be quite common, with 900 hours per year on the low side. These days, Steve says he's getting only 400 to 600 hours, a change that is affecting both yield and quality.[6]

Higher temperatures are also beneficial for pests. A longer growing season gives bugs more time to reproduce and the opportunity to get really, really big. This means I should have included a recipe for extra-large beetles dipped in fair-trade, organic Latin American chocolate. Larvae may even start surviving the warmer winters, which means there could be even more varieties to candy coat. We'll save those recipes for the next book.

Though we can't manipulate the chill hours in favor of our fruit salads, we can affect the flavor of the salad by choosing good fruits. The best-tasting fruit salads are made with fruit that is

Evidence for Human Contribution: The Climate Model

Probably the most important tools in use today for understanding climate change and predicting the future are global-climate models. These highly sophisticated models are mathematical descriptions of the atmosphere and ocean. Similar to weather-forecast models that predict the weather within the next few days, global-climate models can develop projections for how the climate will change over the next few decades. And just as we know that weather-prediction models sometimes yield the wrong answer, climate models also have their limitations. So, how do we know that today's climate models are good enough to make accurate predictions of the future?

The test for climate models is to see if they can reproduce the climate of the twentieth century, for which there are lots of observations for comparison. We start the model in the year 1900 and simulate the climate for one hundred years. We can also run experiments where we pose different questions, such as, "What would the climate of the twentieth century be like if humans were not around?"

The results of such a series of experiments are shown in Figure 4, where the thick black line indicates the observed global temperature, and the colors indicate the results of various climate-model predictions during the twentieth century. The blue shading indicates the global temperature in simulations that include only natural changes to our climate system, such as changes in solar radiation and the major volcanic eruptions of the twentieth century. The red shading indicates simulations that include both natural changes and human influences (that is, emissions of greenhouse gases and aerosols). The model simulations that include both natural and human processes actually match the observations fairly well, whereas the models that neglect human-produced gases do not show the warming trend observed since 1970. These experiments therefore demonstrate two important points. First, it is very likely that human-produced greenhouse gases are responsible for a large fraction of recent warming, especially over the last fifty years.[8] And second, they provide us with confidence that model predictions of the next one hundred years will have some legitimacy.

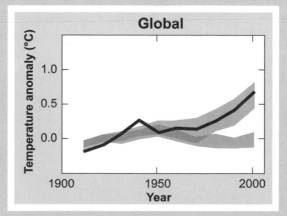

Figure 4. Comparison of global surface temperature with results simulated by climate models using natural and human forcings.[7] (Source: IPCC 2007.)

in season. This means none of those off-colored cantaloupe and watermelon chunks on the Christmas morning fruit plate. Our Seasonal Fruit Salad with Candied Ginger gives you ideas on which fruits to include in which seasons. In chapter 5 we'll learn more about how eating seasonally helps solve the global-warming diet.

Global Warming and Tonight's Water (No Ice) with Dinner

The Worldwatch Institute and the United Nations estimate that every country in the world will face shortages of water by 2020.[9] This is problematic for agriculture because three-quarters of the world's freshwater is already committed to growing food (in the United States, the figure is 85 percent).[10] Much of the water used to grow half of all fruits and vegetables consumed in the United States is stored in the California Sierra snowpack.[11] Precipitation in the Sierra is expected to remain relatively constant in spite of climate change, but the "water-to-snow ratio" is what concerns Anthony Fisher from the University of California, Berkeley. A professor of agricultural and resource economics, Dr. Fisher says, "Warmer winters with less snow and more rain will reduce the Sierra's natural winter storage capacity, resulting in quicker runoff, and possible serious flooding, followed by potentially devastating summer droughts."

Research by the International Food Policy Research Institute (IFPRI) suggests that by 2025, water scarcity may result in annual losses of 350 million tons of food—almost equivalent to losing the entire world rice harvest or U.S. grain crop.[12] Putting this into perspective, science communicator Julian Cribb notes that the "agricultural challenge of the coming generation will be to more than double food production [using] approximately 50–60 percent of [what is] currently available—in other words [we will need] to achieve a 300–400 percent gain in water use efficiency worldwide."[13] Professor Fisher elaborates:

> This is all a lot of guesswork on the part of scientists. We aren't sure how quickly farmers will be able to adapt to things like changes in water supply. Climate change will have significant impacts, but they can be largely avoided if policy choices are made relatively soon. It's important to act quickly, but this is hard to do politically because the impacts are pushed far off into the future. In order to solve the issues, costs will have to be felt upfront, but the beneficiaries will be largely the people living twenty to fifty years from now who have no political influence. By and large, the beneficiaries and those hurt are not the same.

Now let's look more closely at how these changes will affect a favorite Friday summer dinner—a nice piece of grilled fish with Peach-Ginger-Mint Relish, homemade Rice Miso Bread, and a glass of California wine . . .

Projections of Future Climate

What will the climate be like in twenty, fifty, or one hundred years? It turns out there is no definite answer to this question, in large part because the decisions we make today, such as a continued reliance upon fossil fuels, will impact the climate of tomorrow. What we can say, using climate models, is how the climate will change if we follow a particular scenario. The Intergovernmental Panel on Climate Change (IPCC)[14] has developed various scenarios that characterize possible future worlds based on the amount of greenhouse gases and aerosols emitted over the next hundred years. These scenarios are called "storylines," and each storyline describes how the population grows, the type of global economies present, and the types of energy in use.[15] Economists and social scientists work to develop realistic scenarios that encompass a range of possible future worlds. At one end are the high-emission scenarios, which describe a world that promotes and values very rapid economic growth in a material-based economy that relies heavily on fossil fuels. At the other end are the low-emission scenarios, where the world has moved toward more service and information economies and the adoption of clean and efficient-energy

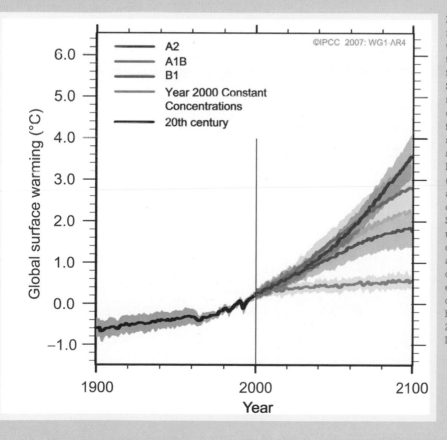

Figure 5. Climate model projections for temperature in the twenty-first century for different scenarios. Solid lines are climate-model global averages of surface warming for the high-emission scenario (A2), middle scenario (A1B), and low-emission scenario (B1), shown as continuations of the twentieth-century simulations. Shading denotes the uncertainty range of individual model annual averages. The orange line is for the experiment where concentrations were held constant at year 2000 values.[16] (Source: IPCC 2007.)

technologies. From both of these examples, the amount of greenhouse gases in the atmosphere can be calculated and then fed into a climate model to predict how the climate will change under these conditions. In this manner, we can estimate the range of possible climates expected under these scenarios.

Predictions from more than twenty climate-model simulations using both low- and high-emission scenarios from the most recent IPCC report[17] are shown in Figure 5. In the low-emission scenario, temperatures will rise by about 3 degrees F (1.8 degrees C) by the end of the twenty-first century, whereas in the high-emission scenario, temperatures may be up to 6.5 degrees F (3.6 degrees C) warmer than they are today. Although models also vary in their predictions based on different model formulations and assumptions, all models and scenarios predict steady warming throughout the twenty-first century.

A couple of points should be highlighted. First, remember that the Earth is quite sensitive to seemingly small temperature changes. If the climate shift from the ice age of 20,000 years ago to current conditions was marked by an 8 degree F (4.4 degree C) increase in surface air temperature, then a further 8 degree F (4.4 degree C) increase in one hundred years, as seen in the high-emission scenarios, might also cause some very noticeable changes. The other point is that the low-emission scenario is essentially the goal of the Kyoto Protocol, an international agreement aiming to stabilize greenhouse-gas concentrations at a level that prevents dangerous climate change. So even in this case where significant emission reductions are made, the Earth will continue to warm over the next century. It should be noted that even if greenhouse-gas concentrations were to stay constant at year 2000 levels, the accumulated heat in the oceans would still cause increases in temperature of about 1 degree F (0.5 C) over the next hundred years.[18]

Although predictions of the future are typically complicated, the message here is that our climate will continue to warm, and, if left unchecked, the warming will push the Earth's temperature to a level that will more than likely be dangerous to natural systems on the planet.[19] The scenarios are like paths, and presently we have the choice of which path to take. As you can see, the paths all start relatively close together, but by around 2030 they start to diverge. If society wants to avoid the largest increases in temperature associated with the high-emission scenarios, the challenge will be to move onto one of the lower-emission paths within the next decade.

Global Warming and Tonight's Glass of Wine— Red, White, or Green?

At the current rate of climate change, "Wine Drinkers for Global Warming" could become a popular bumper sticker, as higher temperatures and less water can improve the flavor of grapes. On the other hand, costly changes would be needed for vineyards to adjust. An upward shift in temperature of 1 to 2 degrees F (.5 to 1.1 degrees C) would deepen the flavor of heat-loving Zinfandel, Syrah, and Merlot grapes. It could mean grapes with higher sugar content and wines higher in alcohol but lower in acids, and you can certainly sign me up for that wine club. If, however, temperatures get too hot—such as a shift of 6 to 8 degrees F (3.3 to 4.4 degrees C), which is in line with projections if carbon emissions are not reduced—the harvests could be severely damaged and the party will be over. In general, grape-growing regions around the world are expected to shift northward (or southward in the Southern Hemisphere) toward cooler environments, coastal zones, or higher elevations. Cool-loving grapes such as Chardonnay, Pinot Noir, Viognier, and Riesling would branch out into new areas, and warm-loving grapes such as Syrah and Zinfandel would move into the regions where cool grapes used to grow.

Reductions in water availability may also affect wine flavor, with some vines more adaptable than others. Grapes, like tomatoes and other produce, can benefit when grown with less water. Using only natural rainfall for irrigation (a process called dry farming) can result in more concentrated flavors. Dry-farming grapes requires vines with drought-resistant roots that penetrate deep into the soil. It is a common practice in Europe and used to be common in California until the 1980s when vines were replaced with water loving vines because of pest infestation. Water is also a factor in production when eight gallons (30 liters) of water are needed to make one gallon (3.8 liters) of wine. During harvest, this makes vineyards one of the largest users of electricity among agricultural and food-processors.

Motivated by these and other factors, "red, white, or green" will probably be the wine choices of the future. Vintners have started to power facilities with rooftop solar and geothermal energy systems to save energy. Others are incorporating agricultural practices common one hundred years ago, convinced that green growing practices, using less water and fewer herbicides, pesticides, and fossil fuel, will improve the taste of their product.

A good example of this is California-based Benziger Family Winery, known for bringing nature back into the vineyard. Many of their acres are farmed "biodynamically," a holistic approach to agriculture that considers a farm to be an individual living organism. With the goal of creating a

"Red, white, or green" will probably be the wine choices of the future.

functioning ecosystem rather than a monocultured environment, diverse habitats of plants and animals balance each other and even do some of the work. For instance, Benziger has planted an "insect garden" to attract beneficial insects that do the work of pesticides. Cover crops control erosion as well as supply habitat for insects. Man-made ponds are used to naturally filter wastewater. Scottish Highlander cows produce manure used for fertilizer, and horses pull some of the equipment through the more "prized" vineyards. Benziger believes that the end product is a better bottle of wine.

Global Warming and Tonight's Best Choice Seafood Dinner with Peach-Ginger-Mint Relish

NASA Oceanographer Gene Carl Feldman has learned that if you want to find out what's really happening in the ocean, you might just need to go up in space. For twenty years he's been keeping tabs on the sea with satellite imagery.

> People think it is strange to be studying the ocean from space, but it's one of the best ways to do it. The oceans cover the largest portion of the Earth, and conditions can change that are unable to be measured from the deck of a slow-moving ship. For instance, a million square kilometer satellite image showing the abundance of phytoplankton (microscopic floating plants and a primary food source) or sea temperature (an indicator of the physical state of the ocean) can take years for a ship to measure but only minutes for the satellite. . . . Studying the ocean is like doing a giant jigsaw puzzle blindfolded. We don't know if we have all the pieces and we don't even know what the final picture looks like, but we are getting better at it.

Feldman says that most scientists agree that increased levels of atmospheric carbon dioxide will cause significant changes in the ocean. When carbon dioxide dissolves in the ocean, it changes the pH, or the degree of acidity of the water, which can endanger coral reefs. Coral is an animal that takes carbon dioxide out of the water and secretes it in the form of calcium carbonate to make an external limestone "skeleton" (which is their home). If the pH changes just slightly, it's more difficult for the coral to deposit the limestone. If too much carbon dioxide is in the water, the reefs and many other shell-forming creatures may start to dissolve. The coral reefs create stable habitats in the ocean and are some of the most biodiverse ecosystems on the planet. Feldman says this is important because "it takes a very stable ecosystem to support a highly diverse and specialized food web, and very subtle changes in any part of that system could have profound and, at this time, unforeseen consequences."

The carbonic acid that results from increasing levels of carbon dioxide in the ocean is also a corrosive agent. It can dissolve the shells of oysters and clams, and, most importantly, the shells of tiny oceanic snails called pterapods that are critical food sources for many creatures. Feldman says:

> Much life in the sea relies on these little guys, and they will probably be one of the first creatures to be affected with increasing levels of carbon dioxide. Even the slightest change in the lowest levels of the food web will produce dramatic changes higher up because of the way food and, consequently, energy is transferred from one level in the food chain to the next. With each level in the food chain that we go up, there is about a factor of-ten loss of energy. For instance, for every ten pounds of plankton produced, we may get, at the most, one pound of zooplankton, one-tenth pound of larval fish, and one-hundredth pound of grownup fish (like salmon or tuna).

Dr. Feldman made it clear that any serious disruptions of the lower levels of the marine food web will mean our fish dinners may look very different in the future. Recent changes in ocean surface temperatures, although relatively small, have been shown to significantly alter the ability of phytoplankton to grow, which means changes in the entire food web. So, if you want to be food energy efficient, eat low! Shellfish such as mussels and clams eat plankton (microscopic plants) directly. Anchovies, sardines, and herring eat plankton or zooplankton (microscopic animals). Tilapia is a good choice because it is an herbivore, unlike tuna, which is a carnivore. Our recipe for Umami Broccoli combines anchovies and broccoli for a hearty vegetable dish, low on the food chain. Feldman concludes:

> There is no longer any question that the Earth is changing. We've been able to measure the physical systems that drive the planet's environment such as temperature, wind, and rain for quite a while but until very recently haven't been able to understand the response to these changes. Now we are entering a very exciting period in earth sciences. For the first time in history, we can actually monitor the biological consequences of this change—to see how the things we do, and how natural variability, affects the Earth's ability to support life as we know it. Just like a doctor measures our vital signs to see how healthy we are, scientists are learning how the different systems interact and how those interactions set the stage upon which life flourishes.

If you want to be energy efficient, eat low!

Global Warming and Tonight's Rice Miso Bread

Wheat is the world's largest cereal crop, supplying 20 to 35 percent of the international food supply. Wheat, as well as corn and rice, is very sensitive to changes in temperature, precipitation, and CO_2 levels, and global warming could pose serious threats to harvests. Worldwide, there has been a steady decrease in grain availability. Production levels have fallen behind the level of consumption, a factor behind recent food shortages and riots. Surpluses are kept for times of international emergency or crop failure, but current reserves are at about fifty-seven days, the lowest level in thirty-four years. If a broad-scale crop failure were to occur, the world could run out of food before the next harvest would come in.

Photosynthesis of some grains could stop altogether if the temperature gets too hot. Grain-growing countries such as Sudan and northern India are particularly vulnerable as grain already grows at the top end of its temperature tolerance. "The impact of climate change will fall disproportionately on the world's poorest countries, many of them in Africa," said former secretary-general of the United Nations, Kofi Annan. "Tropical regions may experience the greatest increase in temperature, and this could put up to 200 million people at risk of hunger."[20]

Not satisfied with just the stats and numbers showing future wheat having "more starch and less protein," Dr. Ziska and his team from the USDA put on chefs' coats and took the matter into their own hands. There was something they still "kneaded" to know. In 2004, the USDA grew, milled, and baked into bread four different lines of hard-red spring wheat cultivated over the last ninety-three years.[21] The USDA received seeds from a South Dakota State University seed bank dating from 1903, 1921, 1965, and 1996—and grew them in varying CO_2-controlled environments. As CO_2 levels increased, plant growth increased, as expected. The seeds were then milled and turned into bread, and the result was completely different from a usual loaf of homemade bread. The flour grown in increased carbon dioxide did indeed have less protein and more starch. It also had more moisture, needed less mixing, and didn't rise as well. (Uh-oh—time to go back to culinary school.) Ziska noted:

> In general, the nutritional quality of food will certainly change due to differing CO_2 levels. It's fascinating from a scientific point of view because there are so many different questions to be answered. We are affecting a process that alters all life on the planet and doing it in a way where we do not know what the consequences will be. Understanding those consequences is tremendously important in terms of their impacts as well as our adaptations.

Book 'n' Cook Club Ideas

Recipes

Japanese Hot Pot with Carrots and Kudzu

Seasonal Fruit Salad with Candied Ginger

Best Choice Seafood Dinner with Peach-Ginger-Mint Relish

Umami Broccoli

Rice Miso Bread

Video Documentaries

Planet Earth: Visions of the Earth from Space: Oceania (2001)

John Cleese's Wine for the Confused (2004)

Books

Controversies in Science and Technology Volume 2: From Climate to Chromosomes, by Lewis H. Ziska

Field Trip: To the Forest

Learn to cook with edible weeds such as burdock, watercress, dandelion greens, nettles, purslane, and sea vegetables. Find them at farmers markets and natural foods stores too.

Small Things Matter

• Refer to the Monterey Bay Aquarium Sustainable Seafood Guide when buying fish—it's a free wallet-size card listing the best seafood choices for your region, www.mbayaq.org/cr/SeafoodWatch.asp.

• Buy bread made with organic wheat or other whole grains.

• Search out dry-farmed tomatoes at your farmers market.

• Support "green" wine makers and learn their stories. Having a connection to the vineyard adds so much to the experience of drinking the wine.

• Save water. Don't let the water run while you are cleaning vegetables; run the dishwasher only when it is full (using the shortest cycle); and use the garbage disposal less—compost instead!

Recipes

Japanese Hot Pot with Carrots and Kudzu

Put that kudzu to work! This is a quick, soothing dish, easy enough for any day.

SERVES 5

2 cups cooked grain of choice (see chapter 10)

1 tablespoon olive oil

1 onion, thinly sliced

$1/4$ teaspoon salt

4 teaspoons kudzu (powdered or chunk style, arrowroot or cornstarch may be substituted)

4 teaspoons water

3 carrots, cut into 1-inch rounds

1 head cauliflower, broken into large florets

1 cup stock, plus extra for deglazing pan

4 ounces smoked packaged tofu, cut into $1/2$-inch chunks (optional—or you can substitute
  in chicken)

1 to 2 tablespoons soy sauce

2 teaspoons grated fresh ginger

Salt to taste

Green onions or nori, sliced thin, for garnish

Prepare 2 cups of cooked grain using the "Grain Cooking Chart" on page 181 in chapter 10.

While grain is cooking, heat a medium-size, heavy-bottomed pot over medium heat. Add oil
and sauté onion with salt until translucent, about 5 minutes. While onions cook, dissolve kudzu
in a small bowl with 4 teaspoons water. Set aside. After 5 minutes, move onions to one side of
the pot; add half of the carrots. Spread onions on top of the carrots, and then add the remaining half of the carrots on top of the onions. Add a little stock as needed. Cover and cook over
medium heat about 7 minutes. Add cauliflower florets on top of the carrots. Add a little stock as
needed. Cover and cook an additional 7 minutes or so, until vegetables are tender. Add tofu
and stir. By now the kudzu/water mixture will have hardened. Stir it well and combine with 1
cup stock, soy sauce, and ginger. Add to the pot and bring to a boil, stirring until sauce thickens. Check consistency; add more kudzu (diluted in water) or stock if needed. Garnish with
green onions, sliced nori, and Condiment Plate (see page 183).

Seasonal Fruit Salad with Candied Ginger

Fruit is tastiest and most affordable when grown locally and eaten in season. Adding a garnish of dried or candied fruit is a nice easy touch that guests love, especially in the winter and spring when fruit choices are more limited.

SERVES 4

4 cups seasonal fruit
$1/4$ cup candied ginger or other dried fruit

Slice fruit and transfer to serving bowl. Sprinkle with candied ginger or other toppings.

WINTER
Fruit: apples, grapefruit, kiwi, pears, oranges, tangerines
Garnish: candied lemon or grapefruit rinds, dried persimmons

SPRING
Fruit: cherries, kiwi, strawberries
Garnish: candied ginger, candied walnuts

SUMMER
Fruit: apricots, blackberries, blueberries, cherries, melons, nectarines, dates, peaches, plums, raspberries
Garnish: dried dates

FALL
Fruit: apples, figs, grapes, kiwi, pears, persimmons, pomegranate
Garnish: dried strawberries, blueberries, cranberries

CHEF'S NOTE:

Eggs Full Monty

Egg shells, like ocean coral, are primarily made up of calcium carbonate. What happens when an egg sits in vinegar for forty-eight hours, and what can it teach us about the acidification of the oceans due to global warming? Find out with this science experiment.

Get three raw eggs and a cheap bottle of vinegar. Put eggs in a flat container and cover with vinegar (do not let the eggs touch). Cover and refrigerate. After twenty-four hours, pour out the vinegar and replace with fresh vinegar. After another twenty-four hours, remove the eggs. The vinegar will have dissolved the shells, leaving only the membrane to hold the eggs together.

Best Choice Seafood with Peach-Ginger-Mint Relish

Make this relish in the summer when peaches are at their best. It works well with a variety of fish, so follow your Monterey Bay Aquarium pocket guide for the best choices for your region.

SERVES 2 OR 3

Rub

1 tablespoon cinnamon

1 tablespoon nutmeg

1 tablespoon sesame seeds

Salt and pepper to taste

1 pound sustainable fish fillet

Relish

1 peach, pitted and cut into $1/2$-inch pieces

$1/2$ teaspoon grated fresh ginger

Splash brown rice vinegar

$1/2$ teaspoon walnut oil

$1/2$ teaspoon chopped fresh mint

$1/4$ teaspoon finely chopped jalapeño pepper

Salt and pepper, to taste

Heat the grill, making sure grill grates are clean. For the rub, combine the cinnamon, nutmeg, sesame seeds, and a sprinkle of salt and pepper in a small bowl. Rub the entire surface of the fish with the mix. Place fish on a hot grill and cook 10–12 minutes, flipping only once. Meanwhile, combine the relish ingredients and season with salt and pepper. Serve fish with the relish.

Umami Broccoli

You can still have a meaty flavor in your dishes even if you reduce the amount of meat in your cooking. The trick is to season with umami in mind. Umami is the Japanese word for "savory," and it is the fifth basic taste along with sweet, sour, bitter, and salty. Anchovies offer umami to this dish without being overpowering and support eating seafood that is "lower on the food chain."

SERVES 4

1 (1-ounce) jar oil-packed anchovies, drained and chopped

$1/4$ cup olive oil

3 cloves garlic, chopped

2 tablespoons chopped green onion

3 cups broccoli chopped into long, thin, diagonal pieces

2 tablespoons dry white wine

In a mini food processor or blender, make Umami Paste by puréeing the first four ingredients. Heat a sauté pan on medium high. Add 2 tablespoons of paste and the broccoli; stir and cover immediately. Cook for 4 minutes and then add the wine. Cover immediately and force-steam the broccoli while shaking the pan. Cook 1 more minute, or until tender.

NOTE: The pan should be hot and dry enough to slightly brown or caramelize the broccoli (another way to bring on umami).

Rice Miso Bread

This is a hearty yet moist bread—the "bread of the future" if carbon dioxide levels get high enough to affect the way wheat rises. It is a perfect use for leftover grains and an easy way to incorporate more grain into your diet. This bread doesn't use store-bought yeast—just the natural yeasts from the leftover grains.

MAKES 1 LOAF

3 cups cooked brown rice

2 tablespoons miso (barley, brown rice, chickpea)

1 1/2 cups water

2 cups whole wheat flour

1 cup barley flour

Let the cooked rice stand at room temperature for 24 hours.

Combine the miso with the water; mix well. Add the flours to the rice and mix well. Combine the miso/water mixture with the flour mixture and transfer to a lightly floured board. Knead the dough 50 to 100 times. If it appears too wet, add a little more flour. The end result will be sticky, so keep your board lightly floured. Place dough in an oiled bread pan. Cover and let it rise in a warm place for 6–8 hours.

Preheat oven to 375 degrees F. Place bread in the oven and bake for 1/2 hour. Reduce heat to 325 degrees F and bake for an additional 1 1/4 to 1 1/2 hours.

In Search of a
Cool, Clean Drink

What began as a search for a drink of water turned out to be so much more. It started after a visit to my local recycling center, in the early days of writing this book.

I love going to the recycling center. I am really good at getting rid of things (the only things I still can't seem to get rid of are old boyfriends). My inner-anal organizer takes over at the recycling center and loves seeing all the neat little piles of the same little things, stacked up and ready to move on to a brand new life. One day while jogging near the center, I made a beeline through it in search of a water fountain and an opportunity to run my hands through the Styrofoam peanuts. Cruising around the corner, I was greeted by a huge plastic wall of multicolored bottles squished together in a solid chunk that stopped me dead in my tracks. It looked like something that had just fallen from outer space. Thirsting, I stared up at the wall. Who drank all this water, where did all these bottles come from, and where on earth were they going?

What's the Story Behind
All Those Bottles?

Americans drink a lot of bottled water, and bottled water containers drink a lot of oil. It takes approximately 17 million barrels of oil just to make the plastic for the 29-plus billion plastic water

Impacts of a Warmer World: Past and Future

As the Earth warms, we can expect to see a variety of changes. Direct changes that have been documented during the twentieth century include higher maximum and minimum temperatures; changes in the amount, location, and intensity of precipitation; and a steady increase in sea level. Other manifestations of a warmer world include increases in the severity of drought and in flooding associated with extreme precipitation events.[1] For example, Australia is currently in the midst of its worst drought in at least a century, with scientists predicting that parts of inhabited Australia will essentially remain drier during the coming century.[2] While many cities have been forced to enact severe water restrictions (e.g., Brisbane imposed level-five restrictions in 2007[3]), a number of cities have declared that some level of water restrictions will become permanent.

The increased occurrence of drought and floods are in part related to shifts in storm tracks and thus shifts in rainfall patterns. Since modern civilizations have developed around access to freshwater, if there are changes to the locations of freshwater due to lack of rain, inadequate snow/ice melting, or coastal intrusions of saltwater into freshwater lakes, then the viability of some societies could be significantly compromised.

Other signals of a warmer world include the increase in intensity of tropical cyclones. Although the connection between hurricane intensity and human-induced warming is still an area of active research,[4] rising sea levels and, more importantly, increases in coastal populations will make the types of damage seen in New Orleans in 2005 more likely in the future. Less controversial but just as devastating are the increased occurrences of extreme heat events and heat waves.[5] The most prominent recent example is the European heat wave of 2003, in which more than 30,000 people died as temperatures soared for weeks.[6] Although no single weather event can be attributed to climate change, some research suggests that human-influenced global warming has doubled the risk of heat waves of this magnitude.[7] It is also clear that if the warming continues, events such as these are expected to occur more frequently.

The impacts of a warmer world affect other biological life on Earth as well. The earlier arrival of spring and the overall warmer minimum temperatures have a particularly important influence on bird and insect migration. For example, disease-carrying mosquitoes are expected to spread to higher altitudes and other areas previously too cold for their survival. Many examples of more northerly migrations are already occurring, ranging from the Pacific starfish slowly migrating north along the Californian coast[8] to the recent arrival of the famously colored puffin birds in northern Alaska.[9] These migrations change the natural balance between food and predators and may subject some species to further danger.

bottles Americans use each year.[10] If connected end to end, supposedly they would circle the Earth 150 times. Don't plan on the bottles biodegrading anytime soon, because plastic doesn't seem to disappear. No one knows how long it takes plastic to biodegrade because it hasn't yet. The first plastics invented 144 years ago are supposedly still around. While paper and most other natural products take anywhere from months to years to break down into simple chemical elements (carbon dioxide and water), plastics take hundreds of years or more to completely break down.[12]

Increased recycling would help, but we don't offer

ABC News reports that it takes two ounces (57 g) of oil to make and transport 33.8 ounces (1 liter) of water from France to Chicago,[11] a distance of 4,138 miles (6,660 km). Using this number as a baseline, we extended the calculation to three other types of bottled water (see chart below). In the photo above, the oil required for each bottle was added to the water.

PLACE TO PLACE	MILES (KM)	AMOUNT OF OIL
San Francisco to Chicago	1,846 miles (2971 km)	1 ounces
France (Paris) to Chicago	4,138 miles (6,660 km)	2 ounces
Fiji (Suva) to Chicago	7,250 miles (11,667 km)	3 ounces
New Zealand (Auckland) to Chicago	8,203 miles (13,200 km)	4 ounces

economic incentives or even collect enough raw materials (used plastic bottles) to keep businesses running in the United States. Currently, less than 20 percent of our plastic water bottles are recycled. Much of what we do recycle is shipped overseas to countries with environmental standards lower than those in the United States. Shipping our plastics to other countries is no solution; it may create more environmental damage than just throwing the bottles in a landfill.

How About Reusing?

Here's one solution to reduce global warming: What if everyone refilled their plastic water bottles once, from the tap, and we cut the amount of oil used and bottles thrown away by half? I compiled a list of reasons why people might *not* be inclined to go along with the plan.

• Tap water doesn't taste as good as bottled water.
• Bottled water is safer than tap water.
• Toxic chemicals from the plastic bottles leach into water once the bottles are refilled.

The Great Pacific Garbage Patch

Have you heard of the Great Pacific Garbage Patch, two "islands" of plastic trash floating off the coasts of Hawaii and Japan? Discovered in 1997 by Captain Charles Moore, they are a mix of fishermen's nets, bottles and jugs, toys, nurdles (plastic water bottles turned into beads on their way to be recycled), and other plastic garbage. The flotsam are held

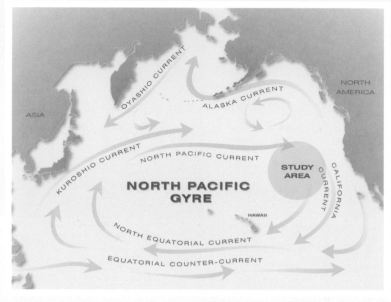

Illustration Credit © 2008 Jean Kent Unatin

together by the North Pacific Gyre, a swirling mix of ocean currents. It was hard to believe the media reports that one of the islands was "twice the size of Texas," so we called Captain Moore directly. He was shipping out from Hawaii back through the garbage patch to the States: "NOAA [National Oceanic and Atmospheric Administration] says we should think of the eastern and western garbage patches as compressors accumulating and spitting out debris onto a super debris highway [that runs] between them. It is held together by ocean currents and is over 3 million square miles (7.7 million square km) in area." Running the numbers, this is about three times as large as Alaska, Texas, and California combined.

The majority of the debris is large plastic objects photodegrading (breaking down by sunlight) into smaller pieces but never completely disappearing. The pieces are obscured by surface wavelets and are difficult to see unless observed directly from above. Up to now, clean-up has been deemed impossible. Eighty percent of the plastic comes from land, not from ships dumping or spilling cargo. They are mostly things such as water and soap bottles that have escaped from local landfills and funneled down rivers into the ocean. Why is the Great Pacific Garbage Patch the final resting place for so much nonbiodegradable garbage? Because the ocean is downhill from everywhere.

- Refilling bottles causes bacteria buildup.
- Bottled water is more convenient.

Let's look at these objections one by one.

Tap Water Doesn't Taste as Good as Bottled Water

Right. Sometimes it tastes better. At least that's the result of our tap water versus bottled water taste test that was held between March and September 2007 in the San Francisco Bay Area; Winthrop, Washington; and Salt Springs, Vancouver. Approximately thirty testers compared water in plastic bottles to the local tap water in blind-taste tests. The results were surprising Every tester in every location preferred the tap water to the bottled water, agreeing on one specific difference: *The tap water tasted fresher than the bottled water; the bottled water tasted stale.* This statement may not hold true across the country, but it might where you live. If you have gotten out of the habit of drinking tap water and don't know why, conduct your own taste test. How does your tap water hold up?

Bottled Water Is Safer Than Tap Water

Tap water is more regulated by the Environmental Protection Agency (EPA) than bottled water is by the Food and Drug Administration (FDA). The results from the multiple daily bacteria tests of tap water must be made public, whereas a public release of tests for bottled water is not required. The Natural Resources Defense Council estimates that 40 percent of all bottled water is just filtered tap water anyway.[13] If safety is your main concern, you may be better off drinking tap water.

Toxic Chemicals from the Plastic Bottles Leach into Water Once the Bottles Are Refilled

Controversy surrounds potential leakage of bisphenol A from #7 plastics (used in some permanent polycarbonate plastic bottles) into water. Bisphenol A is a building block of the plastic and is also considered to be an endocrine disrupter. However, #7 plastic is not used to make disposable water bottles; these are made with #1, or PET (polyethylene terephthalate), plastic. PET is considered to be a stable plastic, although a study by Italian researchers in 2003 did detect some leaching of another endocrine disruptor, DEHP, after nine months of storage in a PET bottle.[14] If you felt confident enough drinking out of the plastic water bottle the first time, you should feel equally fine refilling it and using it once more. The refilled water will be exposed to plastic for a shorter time than the water that was there when you bought the bottle. The best practice: Don't leave water in plastic bottles for too long, don't put plastic bottles through the dishwasher, and don't expose water in plastic bottles to prolonged, direct sunlight.

Refilling Bottles Causes Bacteria Buildup

The water bottle industry discourages refilling water bottles because of bacteria accumulation. "Do not refill" is even printed on some labels these days. When I e-mailed the company to ask why not, they replied, "When one opens any container, microorganisms can be introduced into

Care for a taste?

Taste tests are an ideal way to learn more about the food you eat and increase satisfaction. People enjoy participating and can use what they learn throughout their culinary lives. Tasting parties are easy events to host because they are not about prepared dishes but about ingredients that go into the dish. We feature five different taste tests in this book. Chapter 9 has a salt taste test and chapter 11 tests grass-fed beef versus grain-fed beef, convenience store versus farm-fresh eggs, and honey. This chapter has a tap water versus bottled water test. Try these or create new ones for your family, book group, or dinner club. You'll be surprised at the differences between very simple foods such as salt, honey, eggs, olive oil, and water—differences not noticeable until compared one on one.

the container and begin to grow." It's not the bacteria in water that the bottled water companies are concerned with, it's the bacteria that comes from your mouth, hangs out on the lip of the bottle, and falls back in upon refill and is guzzled down when you drink. I e-mailed the company back and asked how long it would take for these organisms to start growing. What happens if I didn't drink all the water in one day—would I be at risk? Receiving no response, I knew the time had come to confront the question of bad bacteria on my own.

> What if everyone refilled their plastic water bottles once, from the tap, and we cut the amount of oil used and bottles thrown away by half?

OPERATION BAD BACTERIA

In an attempt to establish the evil that lurked within, I hired a San Francisco microbiology lab to run "Operation Bad Bacteria," and test four PET plastic water bottles in various states of short-term use. I also included a stainless steel water bottle that I had been refilling for a year and a half and had never (oops!) washed.

The lab poured sterile water into the empty bottles to count the bacteria or standard plate count. The water bottle I had refilled and reused once had a very low and very safe count of three. The bottle I refilled and drank from daily for more than two weeks had only four. The microbiologist assumed the bottle with the high count of 58 had somehow gotten inappropriately contaminated before testing, but it was still perfectly safe to drink out of. And what about that personal stainless steel bottle—the one that hadn't been washed in a year and a half? Well . . . the microbiologist politely broke

Water Bottle Test Results

SAMPLE	STANDARD BACTERIA PLATE COUNT
Never used; water poured out (plastic)	1
Used once; not refilled (plastic)	58
Used once, refilled, used again (plastic)	3
Refilled for 2 1/2 weeks (plastic)	4
Refilled for 1 1/2 years (metal; never washed)	340,000

the news that it had a case of "bacteria buildup" and pre-scribed a hot water rinse. "[The bacteria count] is high, but it won't kill you," she said. "You could consume the same amount of bacteria eating a raw vegetable or a salad."

This experience led me to the following conclusions. First, reusing bottles at least a few times seems safe, although it is suggested that you wash your bottle with warm soapy water after each use like you would any reusable container. However, during my investigation I also found various reports that demonstrate that even newly purchased bottled water can have very high levels of bacteria. When the NRDC commissioned tests of over 1,000 water bottles from 103 different bottled waters they found that while most bottled water is a good quality, there were some brands that were "spotty."[15] Around one-fourth of the bottled waters tested violated state limits for arsenic or certain cancer-causing synthetic compounds and about one in five of the bottled waters tested contained at least one sample with more bacteria than recommended in industry guidelines. So in the end, perhaps the healthiest option for ourselves and our planet is to use refillable water bottles (stainless steel and aluminum bottles seem good options right now due to concerns over plastic leaching and for ease of cleaning) and to make sure to clean them regularly.

Bottled Water Is More Convenient

My recipe for convenience is familiarity, habit and ease, not necessarily in equal proportions. Something that seems complicated at first can become easy once you get into a habit. For instance, preparing a detailed recipe I have done many years can be more convenient than looking for and learning a new, simpler recipe. What's easiest is often what we are most famil-iar with. Want to change a habit? Allow time to get used to the new thing and stick with it. Don't expect to make the switch overnight. A Ford Motor study showed that for an action to become a habit (such as automatically putting on our seat belt), it must be performed thirteen consecutive times. If you forget to do something once—you have to start counting again.[16]

I went from one-use water bottles, to refilling disposable water bottles, to refilling a stainless steel bottle. After I got used to the new style, it became what I "liked best" (now I just need to get into the habit of washing it.) The same philosophy fits for bringing your own bags to the store. Just leave them in your car and keep trying to remember to take them in. Convenience is relative. Decide what changes you want to make and start practicing.

Bring Your Own Bag (BYOB)

One 15 year-old tree produces 700 bags.

= 700

0   40

In 40 years - save nine trees.

A fifteen-year-old tree produces 700 paper bags[17]

BYOB (bring your own bag) from age 30 to 70

40 years x 52 weeks = 2,080 weeks

Reuse three bags a week x 2,080 weeks = 6,240 bags saved

In forty years, save nine fifteen-year-old trees

Illustration design © 2008 Trevor Hunt.

A Bit of the Bubbly

Sparkling water is easy to serve and really enhances a dinner party—guys, take note. Add additional flair by offering a selection of flavored syrups for guests to mix their own sodas (look for the organic syrups or ones with fewer additives). For the hometown touch, make our Local Honey Sparkler (recipe at the end of the chapter) as a specialty drink or serve a lightly sweet-ened version as a palate cleanser between courses (especially nice between a spicy main course and dessert). Your guests will love this simple, elegant touch.

Sparkling water does add a lot to parties, but how do we get rid of the bottles if it doesn't come out of the tap? Or does it?

A new restaurant trend to eliminate bottled water is emerging around the country. Instead of bottled water, some restaurants offer house-made sparkling water, in spite of a serious reduc-tion in their profits. If a restaurant can purchase bottled water for fifty cents to three dollars a bottle, sell it for five to nine dollars a bottle, and profit $20,000 a year or more, why would they turn down the profit?

At Incanto of San Francisco, one of the first U.S. restaurants to stop serving bottled water, owner Mark Pastore says they have been making their own sparkling water since the day they opened in 2002. (Interesting side note: In 1988, many years before entering the restaurant industry, Pastore worked on the first congressional policy study on global warming.)

> I wanted a business that would serve the community. The life cycle of the sip
> of bottled water is such a waste of resources. So many resources are used to
> make bottles: the glass or plastic, the caps, ink, and paper for labels, and the
> boxes. Moving water in pipes is much more energy efficient than moving it in

trucks and boats, and chilling it directly is more energy efficient than chilling cases of glass and cardboard. Our multiuse bottles have 1,500 to 2,000 uses before they chip or break. Compared with a single-use bottle, the significant energy savings reduces greenhouse gases.

We stepped through an Alice-in-Wonderland-type door into Pastore's secret water room behind the wine cellar. In it was a refillable CO_2 tank and a large commercial filter. "I've done side-by-side comparisons and you can taste the difference; we change the filter every three months." After filtration and carbonation, the water moves to an eco-chic soda fountain tap that dispenses the effervescent elixir into stylish etched clear-glass bottles (still water is also served). Gone are the days of dining when the servers pose that awkward question, "Bottled or tap?" "My servers have worked in restaurants where management held competitions to see who could sell the most bottled water. The [still and sparkling] filtered waters at Incanto are complimentary."

After sipping her first taste of Incanto's house-made sparkling elixir, my dining companion described the experience, "I paused a moment and really thought about the water. Somehow it was much nicer than before. Usually [servers] just put the glass down and I don't think about it. It has always been so mindless—until now."

Eating at Incanto was lovely, but it couldn't eliminate the sparkling water bottles I use at home. I went to the local kitchen store in search of "sparkling water makers" but could only find torpedo-like cartridges that inject the tap water with carbon dioxide. Unfortunately, one torpedo makes only one quart of sparkling water, which means that I'd throw away the cartridges, as they are not recyclable. I still needed another solution.

My journey led to Seltzer Sisters, a sparkling-water business in Redwood City, California, that carbonates and filters local tap water and delivers it in returnable bottles. Seltzer delivery was a big business from the 1900s to 1950s. Seltzer men used horse-drawn wagons to drop off spar-

kling water on doorsteps along Manhattans' Lower East Side. New York City had thousands of seltzer men, and the business was handed down from father to son to grandson. Although most seltzer businesses were on the East Coast, there were some on the West Coast, too. The Seltzer Sisters warehouse captures this rich history like a sparkling-water museum. Large, old-fashioned water-processing machines are spread around the warehouse floor; there is a 1910 water filter that used cheesecloth screens for cleaning. Nearby sits a large, early "carbonator," shaped like a nuclear missile, that cured dry ice into carbon dioxide. An old silk-screening machine used for labeling the bottles proudly displays a "Barnett and Foster

Engineers of London" logo like a badge of honor. The pride in the work and the product was apparent as I walked past all the machines and the old wooden cases filled with silk-screened labeled bottles from New York, Los Angeles, and Chicago. What made the bottles even more special are the automatic-seal valve tops that don't lose carbonation, even when refrigerated for a week. "As more people are made aware of how little of their plastic is recycled, they are starting to look at ways to cut back," says owner Kathryn Renz. There are about five remaining home-delivery seltzer businesses in the country, keeping this waste-free tradition alive with updated features such as high-end filters and ultraviolet light that take out chemicals such as chloramines and bacteria such as cryptosporidium. "Most parents would rather have their kids drinking clean, sparkling water and homemade Italian sodas. If you have ever looked at the ingredients on a soda can and all the chemicals in it, well, it's a wonder millions of people drink it every day."

Kathryn offered me a glass. The water tasted almost sweet because no salt had been added. Commercial sparkling water uses salt to make the bubbles more effervescent. Seltzer Sisters does not add salt because its customers prefer it sodium free. I signed up as a customer and kissed my plastic water bottles good-bye.

Bottled Water Versus Tap Water: Energy Analysis

In 2006, Americans consumed about twenty-eight gallons (106 liters) of bottled water per person per year (nearly one twelve-ounce [350 ml] bottle per day).[18] Because bottled water seems to have become an important part of the daily average diet, let's look at how much energy bottled water consumption requires and how this compares with energy related to total food consumption.

The total amount of energy required to package and transport water, as well as to produce and dispose of the containers, depends on a number of factors, including the type of water (carbonated or not, local or nonlocal), the type of bottle (plastic or glass), and the transportation distance. Depending on the type of bottled water you choose, a one-quart (1-liter) bottle contributes between 0.3 to 1.7 pounds (130 to 780 grams) of carbon dioxide to the atmosphere.[19] For example, drinking one quart (1 liter) of local bottled water each day for a month produces the same amount of carbon dioxide as driving a car twenty-five miles (40 km) or leaving a car idling in the driveway for three hours.[20]

However, unrefrigerated tap water is at least two hundred times more energy efficient compared to bottled water.[21] Thus, switching from bottled water to tap water is a good step toward reducing carbon emissions.

Book 'n' Cook Club Ideas

Recipes for Seasonal Drinks

Spring: Cooltini

Summer: Backyard Bloody
  Mary Bar
  Local Honey Sparkler

Fall: Backyard Persimmon
  Martini
  Pomegranate Molasses
  Sparkler

Winter: Orange Creamsicle

Videos

The Synthetic Story (2006)

Documentary about marine
  debris studies from the Algalita
  Marine Research Foundation.

Water Taste Test

Materials Needed:
  - Three different brands of
    water in plastic bottles at room
    temperature
  - One pitcher of tap water—
    filtered is preferred—at room
    temperature
  - Four glasses per tester

Mark each glass with a symbol
  indicating bottled or tap water.
  Pour water into corresponding
  glasses before your testers
  arrive. Have testers rank glasses
  from best tasting to worst tasting.
  Evaluate and discuss which each
  tester liked best and why.

Small Things Matter

- Encourage your local grocery store to put up reminder signs in the
  parking lot: "Did you bring your bags?"

- Reuse your water bottle at least once.

- Buy water that's bottled in your state or region.

- Rinse out small disposable glass bottles (i.e., soda bottles) and refill
  with tap water. Keep bottles refrigerated for a convenient "drink to go."

- If you don't like the taste of your water, try using a water filter.

- Sign up for a seltzer delivery service, or find refillable CO_2
  cartridges and make your own sparkling water.

- Lobby elected officials to improve the quality of your local water
  system.

Recipes

SPRING

Cooltini

I have catered Acterra's (the environmental organization I work for) April Earth Day Decadent Dinner for many years. We always serve Cooltinis. It's a seasonal drink in early spring, when backyard citrus is still on the trees in the south and west. This recipe comes from my Acterra colleague, Kay O'Neill.

MAKES 1 COOLTINI

2 ounces fresh squeezed lemon juice (preferably organic Meyer lemons)
2 ounces organic vodka
1 ounce Cointreau
Small amount mint-infused simple syrup, to taste
Freshly made ice cubes
Chambord (French raspberry liqueur)
Cooltini ice cube (optional)
Fresh mint sprig (optional)

Combine first four ingredients in a martini shaker and add five ice cubes. Shake hard; the goal is to get shards of ice into the drink. Using a martini strainer, pour drink into a chilled martini glass. Add a dollop of Chambord and a Cooltini ice cube. Garnish with a mint sprig.

COOLTINI ICE CUBES
12 carob "Earthballs" (cellophane-wrapped candy in the shape of little Earths, sold in the bulk bins of natural food stores)
Ice cube trays
Distilled water

Fill ice cube compartments halfway with distilled water. Put one Earthball in the center of each compartment. Freeze until firm. Remove tray from freezer and cover Earthball with water. Freeze until firm.

SUMMER

Backyard Bloody Mary Bar

Celebrate the summer by inviting friends over for brunch and a Bloody Mary Bar. Use your own backyard tomatoes (cherry or otherwise) for the juice. You can even pickle your home-grown green beans or asparagus for garnish.

MAKES 4 BLOODY MARYS

1 cup peeled, seeded, and coarsely chopped tomatoes

2 cups tomato juice

1 teaspoon Worcestershire sauce

Dash celery salt

1 cup organic vodka

Splash green olive juice

Horseradish or wasabi paste

Pickled pearl onions, olives, green beans, asparagus (buy at the farmers market or pickle your own)

Homegrown cucumber or celery sticks

Selection of hot sauces (such as Tabasco, or your local brand)

Black pepper mill

Bottle of Worcestershire sauce

Good quality herbed salt on a plate, to rim glasses

Fresh lime and/or lemon wedges, to rim glasses

Toothpicks

Ice bucket with fresh ice cubes

Blend the fresh tomatoes to a purée and push through a fine strainer (mixture will be thick). Combine the purée, tomato juice, Worcestershire sauce, celery salt, vodka, and olive juice in a pitcher and stir.

Set up the Bloody Mary Bar. Put the horseradish, onions, and olives in fun bowls and stand up the asparagus, beans, cucumbers, and celery in tall, skinny glassware. Open the hot sauces and put out a pepper grinder and a plate of herb salt. Put out tall glasses, stir spoons, and the drink pitcher and let guests season the drink as they please.

Local Honey Sparkler

Honey syrup makes for a truly satisfying, unique soda, and it is a perfect substitute for high fructose corn syrup in drinks. Since honey is made in all fifty states, search out your local brands.

MAKES 4 GLASSES

1/2 cup honey
1 (32 ounce) bottle sparkling water

Honey syrup: Heat honey in a small saucepan over medium heat for about 1 minute. Remove from heat. It shouldn't be that hot; you should be able to put your finger in it. Add 2 tablespoons sparkling water and stir. Put syrup in a glass container and chill for at least 15 minutes.

Pour 1–2 tablespoons of honey syrup into a glass. Cover with sparkling water. Stir. For best results, chill glasses in the freezer for at least 15 minutes.

Variation: The honey becomes effervescent when the sparkling water is added—think honey latte. It is delicious drizzled over ice cream or yoghurt.

FALL/WINTER

Backyard Persimmon Martini

This martini can be alcoholic or nonalcoholic and is a great use for backyard fall persimmons. Distilled alcohol has a larger "ecological footprint" than beer or wine, so purchase organic, if possible.

MAKES 1 MARTINI

1 medium persimmon, very ripe
1 ounce organic vodka (optional)
3 tablespoons apple or pear juice
5 fresh ice cubes
Organic sugar, for rimming the glass (look for fair-trade sugar)
1 or 2 lime wedges
Fuyu persimmon (optional garnish)

Cut the top off the persimmon and squeeze the pulp into a blender, discard the skin. Add vodka (optional) and blend until smooth. Transfer to a martini shaker, along with the juice and ice cubes. Shake hard; the goal is to get shards of ice into the drink. Place the sugar on a plate, rim a martini glass with a lime wedge and twist the glass in the sugar. Using a martini strainer, pour drink into a martini glass. Squeeze in the juice from 1–2 lime wedges.

Optional garnish: cut off a thin piece of Fuyu persimmon and put a small cut in the center bottom. Dust with sugar and slide onto the side of the glass.

Pomegranate Molasses Sparkler

You can buy pomegranate molasses in the ethnic aisle of many grocery stores, but look for a better-quality homemade pomegranate syrup, which is available at some farmers markets.

MAKES 1 DRINK

1 tablespoon pomegranate molasses or pomegranate syrup
1 teaspoon freshly squeezed lemon juice
2 ounces sparkling water
2 ounces fresh pomegranate or apple juice (see note)
Fresh ice cubes
Fresh nutmeg
Fresh pomegranate seeds
Fresh mint sprigs

Combine pomegranate molasses, lemon juice, sparkling water, pomegranate juice, and ice cubes into a martini shaker. Shake hard; the goal is to get shards of ice into the drink. Pour drink through a martini strainer into a martini glass. Grate on a little fresh nutmeg, and sprinkle a few fresh pomegranate seeds into the glass. Garnish with a small sprig of mint.

NOTE: Make your own pomegranate juice by cutting a pomegranate in half and putting it through a hand-press citrus juicer. Use apple juice if you don't have pomegranate juice.

Orange Creamsicle

This drink combines winter-harvested oranges with protein-packed soy milk for a delicious breakfast smoothie. Read the nutritional label on the soymilk and look for organic—some commercial soy milk is made from genetically engineered, monocropped soybeans and processed like junk food.

MAKES 1 CREAMSICLE

1 cup of your favorite organic soy or soy-rice milk
1/3 cup fresh orange or tangerine juice

Combine both in a juice glass and stir.

PART TWO

SOLUTIONS

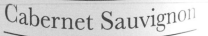

The Summer of Grapes: Local, Organic, Seasonal

I am not a native Californian, but I got here as quickly as I could. My Michigander dad likes to remind me that California is the "land of the fruits and the nuts," and you know, he's right! California grows 50 percent of the fruits and vegetables and 100 percent of the almonds eaten in the United States; it also grows pistachios and walnuts. And it produces most of the grapes, although few of us get to see them grow.

This changed for me when I moved to Portola Valley in 2007, and I could watch grapes grow right outside my window. It's like the Wild West in Portola Valley, a town just a few miles above the San Francisco megalopolis. Families of deer, rabbit, and coyote live here; they pass by my big picture window each day like a traveling Portola Valley zoo. My closest neighbors are horses—Atlas, Daisy, and Cal. It's quiet in Portola Valley. Most of the sound comes from quail and lizards rustling around in the native coffeeberry and rare western leatherwood. They make me jump in surprise as I pass on the dirt trail sidewalks that are lined with coast live oaks. During the summer days, the golden California sunshine beats down on the valley's rolling hills, and the Pacific coastal fog spills over and blankets the hillsides at night. It's the perfect climate for growing grapes.

Grapes are nature's ultimate celebration of the harvest and the bounty of the earth. Fruit like no other, grapes possess great character, allure, and longevity. I've been lucky to spend an evening or two with some seductive wine much older than I am. Grapes embody the essence of what is local, organic, and seasonal; surprisingly, they are grown in every state in the continental United States. Watching them ripen is exciting, connecting us more deeply to the land and the seasons. Whether or not we taste the soil they grew in as we drink, the sheer act of raising the glass is a toast to the land from whence they came.

On evening walks around Portola Valley that summer, I would pass a number of small neighborhood vineyards and I kept tabs on the progress of the grapes. Grape clusters start as poofy bunches of pubescent flowers, looking like flocked artificial Christmas trees tipped onto their sides, and mature into translucent, photogenic orbs. Each evening, the verdurous grapes pulled me in closer, as if summoning me to duty. As a wine drinker with quite a few years' experience, I realized it was time to pitch in and help. I became a volunteer with the fine-wine people of the Portola Valley Ranch. This group of self-described "winos" has been growing and harvesting approximately 1,200 bottles of Cabernet Sauvignon a year since 1981, in a small vineyard that was a part of their homeowners association. This chapter salutes those grapes and many other things local, organic, and seasonal.

Full Circle Food Cycle

To better understand the food system, it helps to view it as a *Full Circle Food Cycle*—three separate components that need to feed into and support each other in order to be sustainable:

1. Production. What are we eating and how is it grown and/or processed?

2. Distribution. How does food get to us once it's grown and/or processed?

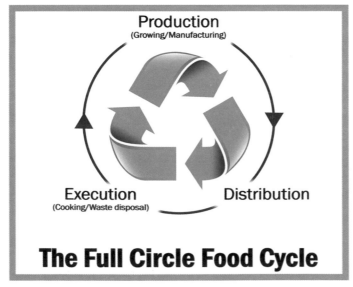

The Full Circle Food Cycle

Illustration credit: © 2008 Trevor Hunt.

3. Execution. What do we do with the food once we have it? That is, how do we cook it, and how does the waste support continued production?

Splitting the food system up this way allows for clarity on what we're dealing with and how we might improve it. Production and distribution are addressed in this chapter—through the eyes of local, organic, and seasonal eating. Execution is discussed in following chapters.

Eating Locally

We are living in the era of the 1,500-mile meal where each ingredient typically travels that distance to get to your plate.[1] Can you feel the vibration of the tires, the rumble of the engine, and the wind in your hair as you sit down to eat? Unripe and unready, our food is picked to travel—eating oil, belching emissions, and leaving us behind in the dust, unsatisfied.

Eating locally grown food is one way to reduce greenhouse gases. According to author Barbara Kingsolver, if everyone in the United States ate only one meal of locally grown meats and vegetables every seven days, 1.1 billion barrels of oil would be saved each week.[2] However, just being a "localvore" in and of itself is not enough to improve the global-warming diet. Fertilizers and pesticides, processing, storage, and cleanup must be factored into carbon footprints, and they can add up to a much greater ecological impact than transportation alone. For instance, it's hard to imagine that lamb grown in New Zealand and shipped to England could have a smaller ecological impact than lamb grown in England itself, but it does.[3] (See Food Miles sidebar page 72.)

To be honest, sometimes this carbon counting makes me crazy. It's complicated to track every kilowatt and gallon involved in the production of our food, and it distracts us from focusing on the real task at hand—learning successful cooking and eating habits. Carbon counting reminds me of the days of calorie counting. Laborious and unappetizing, counting Calories turned the pleasure of eating into a mathematical chore. Carbon credentials are interesting and have their place as tools for food systems change, but please don't make the carbon count your end goal. It's more important to learn how to easily incorporate healthy foods into your diet (and make them taste good so you will eat them on an ongoing basis) rather than how to run the numbers.

Dr. Phil Howard of Michigan State University chose to tackle local eating distribution as his part of the Full Circle Food Cycle. Professor Howard has done extensive research on the changes of ownership and control within our food system and the impact these changes have on human health. With a PhD in rural sociology, Professor Howard has spent an entire career on the study of "eating locally" and has a "deep interest in figuring out how to bring the food system back into the ownership of the small farm so that it benefits the individual again." Unfortunately, industrialism of our food system has failed rural America and eaters everywhere. Howard's studies track the ramifications of this even among the natural foods companies. His Organic Industry Structure chart (see page 74) gives a pictorial summary of "who's eating who" in the food world. If this trend of mergers and acquisitions continues as expected, Howard and his colleagues believe that in a matter of decades the world may be left with just six or so global food realtors controlling our entire food system. Only one of them is expected to be based in the United States. Take a guess as to which one that will be? (Hint: WalMart now controls 20 percent of food sales in the United States.) Says Howard, "What used to be an industry with many

Food Miles

The transport of food around the world is an important part of the industrial food system, but what impact does food transport have on global emissions? Does eating local food really make much difference? To help answer some of these questions, let's look at the concept of "food miles."

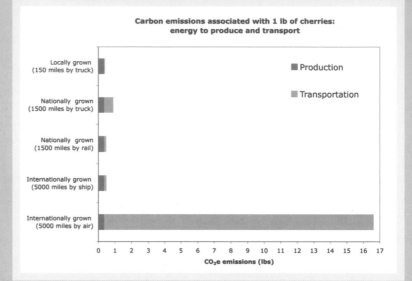

Figure 6. Emissions of CO_2e associated with growing and transport of one pound (0.45 kg) of cherries using four different transportation scenarios that differ by the method (truck, ship, rail, or air freight) and distance (local, national, and international). In all scenarios, the emissions associated with growing the cherries (production) is assumed to be constant.

Food miles refer to the number of miles a food product has traveled to reach your plate. The idea is that the farther away a product is grown from the point of consumption, the greater the number of food miles and transportation-associated emissions. Although the connection between food miles and emissions makes sense, the relationship is actually more complex.

First, the method of transportation (truck, ship, rail, or air) has a large impact on emissions. The most efficient method of transport is by ship, followed by rail, truck, and air.[4] For example, studies have shown that in Sweden, apples shipped from overseas require significantly more energy to get onto the market shelf compared with locally grown apples, especially if they are air freighted.[5]

The other complication regarding food miles is that if reducing emissions is your target, then knowledge of how the food is produced can be as important as how far it's traveled. The methods of food production (for example, farming intensity and the use of fertilizers) can have a large impact on total emissions. A study by the U.K. Department for Environment, Food and Rural Affairs found that it actually took less energy (and produced fewer CO_2 emissions) to grow and ship tomatoes from Spain to the United Kingdom than to grow local tomatoes in the United Kingdom using greenhouses (greenhouses use significant amounts of electricity for light and heat).[6]

A New Zealand study found that importing New Zealand lamb to the United Kingdom was more energy efficient than growing local U.K. lamb due to the U.K. sheep farms' dependence on farm-grown feed (it takes significant energy to grow the feed), whereas New Zealand sheep graze primarily on local grasses.[7]

Although the concept of food miles is not always an accurate assessment of emissions and environmental impact, we should not neglect altogether the idea that locally grown foods generally are associated with fewer emissions compared to imported foods. As an example, let's consider a pound of cherries (See Figure 6). Based on previously published estimates, growing one pound (0.45 kg) of cherries emits about 0.3 pounds (0.13 kg) CO_2 e.[8] The emissions due to transportation are as follows:

- Local transportation by truck emits 0.06 pounds (26 g) of CO_2 e—17 percent of the emissions associated with growing cherries.
- National transport by truck emits 0.59 pounds (262 g) of CO_2 e—175 percent of the emissions associated with growing cherries.
- National transport by rail emits 0.14 pounds (62 g) of CO_2 e—41 percent of the emissions associated with growing cherries
- International transport for Chilean cherries by boat emits only 0.15 pounds (67 g) of CO_2 e—44 percent of the emissions associated with growing cherries, illustrating that transport by boat is quite energy efficient.

However, cherries would probably not survive the two-week trip from farm to market using a boat, so overseas cherries are normally freighted by air, thus emitting 16 pounds (7,410 g) of CO_2 e, or about fifty times the emissions associated with growing cherries. In this case, transportation emissions due to air cargo are 280 times larger than local transportation by truck and even one hundred times larger than transportation by boat. So purchasing a pound of air-freighted cherries is like letting your car idle in the driveway for two and a half hours.

Labeling air-freighted food products according to their place of origin would help consumers make informed decisions about their purchases. If we carry out the food-miles calculation a bit further, we find that if an individual ends up driving twenty miles (32 km) round-trip to a farmers market solely to buy these cherries, the resulting emissions would be similar to purchasing the air-freighted cherries.

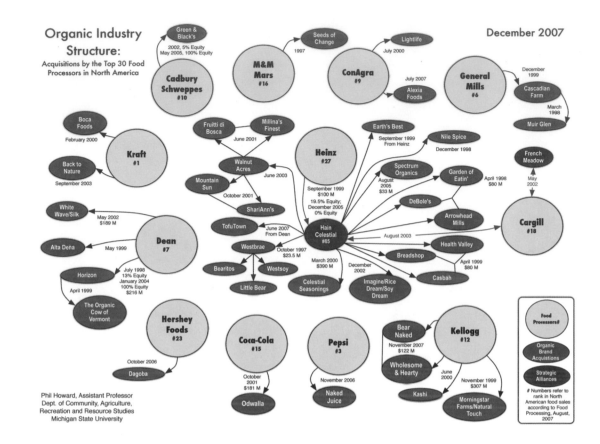

Organic Industry Structure: Acquisitions by the Top 30 Food Processors in North America. December 2007. Phil Howard, Assistant Professor, Dept. of Community, Agriculture, Recreation and Resource Studies, Michigan State University

companies participating could become one where food passes easily between corporations involved in strategic alliances and joint ventures. Then the idea of separate companies would be in name only, with a small handful controlling our food from the field all the way to the supermarket shelf."

It became apparent to Howard that "organics" was being taken over by big corporations in the early 2000s and that small farmers needed a new niche. He wanted to develop strategies to help small- and medium-scale organic farms and he started by asking questions. What did consumers really want to know about their food? In 2006, Howard surveyed one thousand random households from all fifty states and received back an impressively high response rate of 50 percent. People were eager to rank their "most important food concerns beyond health and safety" (health and safety were not surveyed because both are highly regulated on food

> In a matter of decades the world may be left with just six or so global food realtors controlling our entire food system.

labels already). When the results came back, "locally grown" followed by "humane treatment of animals" headed the list.

Dr. Gail Feenstra also took on distribution, looking at ways to bring local foods back to our communities. As a food systems analyst for the University of California, Davis, Feenstra works with their Sustainable Agricultural Research and Education Program. Feenstra has approached the system of eating locally with academic flair. She and her colleagues at the University of California, Santa Cruz, have studied how to bring more local food into colleges, hospitals, schools, and other institutions. She describes her research:

> We interviewed students to find out about demand, and food service directors, farmers, and distributors to find out about supply. We asked people things such as how much local food they buy, how they define local and sustainable, and how they could scale up to use more. There is a lot of uncertainty out there; our research is enabling us to get some real numbers on what is happening and how to improve the system. When food service directors understand their options, they can start collaborative arrangements with other buyers, allowing colleges and other institutions in the region to start buying together.
>
> People, including kids, are craving to know where their food comes from. Supporting local outlets for our food helps us understand what it takes to get food from the farm to our tables. We appreciate food then, not only from the taste perspective, but also from a farm labor and production perspective, and it gives us a different attitude about maintaining agriculture in

Most Local Foods Plate

These foods are grown or produced in many, if not all, of the 50 states:

• Wine • Beer • Cheese • Milk • Honey • Bread • Eggs • Fruits • Vegetables
Regional: • Tomato sauce • Beef • Chickens

Illustration Credit ©
2008 Trevor Hunt.

our community and preventing it from being outsourced. This transfers into policy when voters elect officials who want to maintain community farmland instead of just develop it.

Back at the wine ranch, I was learning my own way to appreciate food from a farm labor and production perspective. In July, the volunteer crew of which I was a part showed up to pick little mini grape clusters off the vines. Our job was to remove every third bunch so the remaining clusters would grow larger. In September we gathered again to cover the vines with black netting and to clip the nets together with clothespins, because everyone likes grapes, including the birds and the gophers. It was hard, tedious, and sweat-inducing work, but it felt good. There was something about being surrounded by the prismatic grapes and chatting with people who were feeding off one another's energy. We were also feeding off the grapes, of course; although harvest was more than a month and a half away, they already tasted sweet. The vineyard was colorfully dotted with slower-growing green grapes next to the more mature purple grapes, whose skins were turning translucent. It's this translucent quality that makes grapes so photogenic. By acting like a photographer's reflector, it absorbs the light and bounces it back, creating a picture-perfect glow.

"In all areas of our lives we cultivate relationships with skilled and trusted professionals, from physician to hairdresser. Should we not be as selective of the farmers who grow our food?"[9]

We should all consider a localvore lifestyle for reasons beyond connection to the land or reduction of greenhouse-gas emissions. Not only does supporting a local food system keep money in the local economy and support the family farmer, humane treatment of animals, food taste, and health, it is one of the best ways to address eaters' number one concern today—food safety. That's the opinion of farmer John Wilcox, owner of Duck Creek Farm on Salt Spring Island, British Columbia. I interviewed John while visiting Salt Spring on a fact-finding mission to learn more about what makes local farms work. Out of necessity, Salt Spring was a "self-supporting" island in the early 1900s, growing and producing enough food to feed its residents. Small artisanal food businesses were sprinkled throughout the island, and Salt Spring was well known for its quality food—large harvests of fruit and pasture-raised lamb. In recent years, the island has depended more on imported goods, but there is a strong group of farmers and citizens working to support a rebirth of growing locally. John is one of them, a sixth-generation farmer, agronomist, and tell-it-like-it-is kind of guy. As we sat around the local pub drinking Salt Spring Golden Ale, John shared some of his stories. "One of the strongest assurances you can have about food safety is farmers showing up at the market each week. Food safety with the big companies is a joke. Tell me the last time you called a large corporation and talked to something other than a machine. You can't find out what's happening—they're too big. Buy from a local farm, and when something goes wrong with your food, come back and tell me straight to my face. If I want to stay in business, you better believe I am going to do something to fix it. That's real food safety."

Eating Organically

From the early beginnings of farming, there has been an intrinsic relationship between agriculture, ceremony, and spirit that has guided humans through the process of growing food. Completely dependent on the whims of nature, farmers brought animals and seeds to be blessed in the church. Seasonal festivals were plentiful, filled with praying for good yields and favorable weather and celebrating the harvest with freshly picked fruits and vegetables and homemade wines. Everyone had a deep connection to the well-being of the farm, and the farm was connected to the spirit.

When searching for what ancient advice or divine guidance early cultivators might have followed about tending to something as complicated as soil, I was surprised to discover that none of the twelve apostles was a farmer, though there were a few fishermen. There are multitudes of analogies in the Bible about sowing and harvesting seeds and much about the harvest of the vineyard, but I found no specifics about tending to the soil. Both the Bible and the Koran mention land stewardship, but only the Torah seems to offer direct advice; specifically on cover cropping and crop rotation:

> Six years you may sow your field and six years you may prune your vineyard
> and gather in the yield. But in the seventh year the land shall have a sabbath
> of complete rest; you shall not sow your field or prune your vineyard. You
> shall not reap the after-growth of your harvest or gather the grapes of your
> untrimmed vines; it shall be a year of complete rest for the land
> (Torah/Lev. 25:2b-5).

In learning how to take care of the soil and grow food, it appears that early cultivators took their cues from nature. Mother Nature's directions are well defined if we only stop and observe them. She offers biodiversity as natural protection from pests and weather conditions; she's set up intimate relationships between animals and plants to feed and refresh each other; she even encourages a finely tuned balance between some of the smallest organisms known—the anaerobic and aerobic microbes in the soil. When modern-day agriculture replicates natural systems, the process becomes regenerative and produces food with deliciously authentic flavor. But industrial agriculture doesn't listen to "God's cues" any longer; in fact, it seems to have taken the spirit entirely out of the picture. Who needs nature when force-feeding chemicals and plentiful fossil fuels take care of everything? By removing our food production system so far away from its roots, society has cast aside an important connection to the meaning of food in our lives. Food shouldn't be just assembly-line widgets that fill up the shelves of our home. Food is our natural communion with the Earth and that is what organic agriculture is all about. More than just the elimination of oil-based fertilizers and pesticides, organic growing represents a symbiotic relationship that humans have with agriculture, where we nourish the soil and the soil nourishes us.

Dr. Christine Jones, an Australian groundcover and soils ecologist with Amazing Carbon, is one scientist who observes nature's cues. Jones is researching how to improve soil and hence improve the food supply. She says the right kind of farming (zero till, using microbial stimulants in place of harsh fertilizers) can make soil healthier and more productive. Crops are getting higher yields and have a higher percentage of protein. Most surprising, the carbon content of the tested soil sometimes increases with soil depth. "In some areas we have found more carbon at 3.6 feet (110 cm) than there is near the surface. This 'deep carbon' is protected from decomposition, which is very exciting. I've never seen this before. We can start rewriting the textbooks!"

Building soil carbon requires green plants and soil microbes such as bacteria and fungi that are responsible for making the carbon stable. Plants pull carbon dioxide out of the air and change it into plant tissues. They also emit some of the carbon through their roots as food for the soil microbes. Microbes change the carbon into humus, a dark, high-molecular-weight, amorphous substance inseparable from the soil matrix. As well as being a great source of nitrogen and plant nutrients, humus can hold from four to twenty times its own weight in water. It is thought to be stable in soil for up to 1,000 years but is easily damaged by cultivation.

Another group of soil microbes discovered in 1996 (mycorrhizal fungi) turns carbon into a gluelike substance called glomalin. Glomalin aggregates organic matter and is said to hold seven times more carbon than humic acid. If all U.S. cropland switched to organic agricultural practices such as composting and cover cropping and built up these soil microbes, 2008 research from the Rodale Institute in Pennsylvania estimates this could mitigate 25 percent of the country's greenhouse-gas emissions. [10]

I spoke with Dr. William Horwath, in the Department of Land, Air and Water Resources at the University of California, Davis, about soil carbon sequestration (the long-term storage of carbon in the biosphere, underground, or the ocean), which he has studied since 1983. He recently directed two field projects (see page 79) looking at the possible benefits of moving from conventional agriculture toward more sustainable and organic agriculture systems. By varying the input of carbon, nitrogen, and water, Horwath has studied the sustainability of three different

Nitrogen: Organic and Synthetic

Farmers often choose synthetic nitrogen fertilizers in favor of organic methods (using cover crops, manure, and compost) because of the ease of application and perceived effectiveness. However, synthetic fertilizers are derived from oil and thus can have significantly higher carbon emissions compared to organic methods.*

The following table compares the nitrogen exchanges for different cropping systems (organic, winter cover crop, and conventional) using two different experimental setups. In the SAFS project, a four-year rotation with six crops was used, and in the LTRAS project, a two-year rotation with three crops was used.

CROPPING SYSTEM	NITROGEN INPUT[1] (kg/ha)	NITROGEN OUTPUT (kg/ha)	SOIL NITROGEN STORAGE (kg/ha)	LOSS OF APPLIED NITROGEN (%)
	SAFS (4 year rotation)			
ORGANIC[2]	1924	933	901	4.6
WINTER COVER CROP[3]	1550	1186	327	2.4
CONVENTIONAL[4]	1827	1339	79	22.3
	LTRAS (2 year rotation)			
ORGANIC[2]	3368	905	685	46.3
WINTER COVER CROP[3]	1500	921	-329	60.5
CONVENTIONAL[4]	2064	1288	-383	56.2

1: Cover crops only in organic and winter cover crop systems. 2: Nitrogen sources—manure and legume cover crop. 3: Nitrogen sources—legume cover crop and reduced (60 to 75%) synthetic nitrogen. 4: Nitrogen source is synthetic.

The results of these studies show that organic methods lose less nitrogen, especially when longer rotations and diverse crops are used, with little difference in crop yields. This demonstrates that effective farming techniques using crop rotation and organic methods can provide a viable and cost effective method of farming in comparison to conventional systems. Even so, one of the challenges for scaling organic methods to feed the soon-to-be 9 billion people on the planet (estimated global population by 2050) is the availability of manure and compost. At present this research suggests that a merger of approaches that includes organic methods and the use of synthetics may be required to adequately meet our global needs in the future.[11]

*NOTE: The transport of manure and compost can be energy intensive. To make organic methods shine, integrated farms with crops and animals are the best solution.

cropping systems: conventional (using pesticides and fertilizers), low-input (reduced pesticides and fertilizers), and organic (no pesticides and fertilizers). The goal of the research was to determine how to maximize the performance of the soil.

The Sustainable Agriculture Farming System Project (SAFS), which was conducted from 1988 to 2000, grew a diverse selection of crops on a four-year crop rotation cycle in an intensively managed plot in California. Crops were chosen to complement one another. For example, low-nitrogen-requiring crops such as safflower were planted with high-nitrogen-demanding crops such as tomatoes to minimize nitrogen losses to the environment. Winter cover crops were planted on the low-input fields (with reduced pesticides and fertilizers) and the organic fields to serve as sources of plant nitrogen, reducing the need for commercial fertilizers to supply nitrogen.

Concurrently, Horwath worked on Long Term Research into Agricultural Systems (LTRAS), which used a two-year crop rotation of tomatoes and corn only. This project was designed to emulate conventional agriculture, using intensive (two-year instead of four-year) rotations and fewer crops in an attempt to achieve the maximum yield of high-value crops such as tomatoes.

The studies found that the intensively managed short rotation of only two crops at LTRAS lost around 50 percent of the nitrogen applied compared to the four-year rotation of diverse crops at SAFS that lost about 10 percent. "The higher crop diversity led to increased cycling and sta-bilization of soil humus and nitrogen, resulting in fewer losses [of nutrients to the environment] compared to the intensive two-year rotation," says Horwath. "The four-year rotation was more similar to natural systems where plants and microbial diversity compete for limited resources, which reduces losses of nutrients to the environment." (See page 79.)

Both studies proved, however, that the simple process of crop rotation alone improved the soil, regardless of which cropping system was used—organic, low input, or conventional. Additionally, the greater the diversity of crops grown and the longer the rotation cycle, the greater the benefits to the soil. Horwath explains:

> Whenever carbon is stored in soil, it is stored with other elements such as nitrogen, phosphorus, and sulfur. The composition of humus is 58 percent carbon, 5 percent nitrogen and about 1 percent each of phosphorus and sulfur. The ratio of carbon to these other elements is 100 carbons to 10 nitrogens to 1 phosphorus and 1 sulfur. Carbon sequestration has many benefits, but it's actually a secondary issue in regard to agriculture, especially in California's Mediterranean climate. Adding more carbon can help the soil absorb and store water more efficiently. It also enhances microbial diversity [which con-tributes to the efficient use of nitrogen] and prevents the loss of nitrogen to the environment.

Global Greenhouse-Gas Emissions

Each year about 40 billion tons of carbon dioxide equivalent are added to the atmosphere as a result of emissions that are human related.[12] Where do these emissions come from? Some greenhouse-gas emissions such as carbon dioxide come

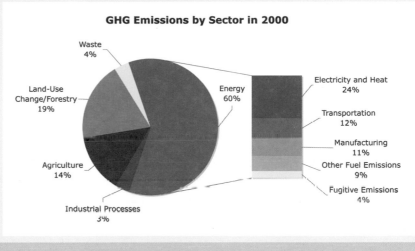

Figure 7. Global greenhouse-gas emissions (CO_2e) for different sectors in the year 2000. The left pie chart indicates the percentage of each sector, with the portioning of the energy sector (60 percent) shown on the right. The data were obtained from the Climate Analysis Indicators Tool (CAIT) Version 4.0. (Washington, DC: World Resources Institute, 2007) and the analysis includes all available greenhouse gases (CO_2, CH_4, N_2O, PFC, HFC, and SF_6). Carbon dioxide equivalent (CO_2e) is used to represent the warming potential of all greenhouse gases (i.e., CO_2, CH_4, N_2O, etc.) in a single value.

from burning fossil fuels that are used primarily to generate energy. Fossil-fuel energy comes from petroleum (42 percent), coal (37 percent), and natural gas (21 percent).[13] Of the 40 billion tons of carbon dioxide equivalent emitted in the year 2000 (see Figure 7), energy generation from fossil fuels represents about 60 percent of the total emissions.[14] This energy generation is mainly used for electricity and heat; manufacturing and construction; and transportation.

The other major contribution to greenhouse-gas emissions comes from land-use change and agriculture. Permanent removal of forests (or deforestation) leads to CO_2 emissions because the carbon stored by trees is released into the atmosphere and is not reabsorbed by the regrowth of new trees. Currently, emissions due to land-use change are largely confined to tropical areas in South America, Africa, and Asia. However, it is the demand by the developed world for wood and other land-based products (for example, meat from cattle and biofuels from sugarcane) that is the driving force in deforestation.

Livestock (especially cows, sheep, and pigs) is the other large contributor to global greenhouse-gas emissions. Cattle emit methane through their normal digestive system and through their manure during decomposition. At present there are an estimated billion-plus head of cattle in the world, and they are responsible for more than 30 percent of the total human-related emissions of methane.[15]

Horwath also discussed how carbon sequestration could supply a temporary financial incentive to farmers looking to set up a low-input or organic cropping system.

> In the low-input system, we gained two to three tons of carbon per hectare over ten years, and in the organic system we gained five tons of carbon. One ton of carbon trades around two to four dollars per ton now, and we hope to see twenty to forty dollars per ton someday. Farmers anywhere can do this, even in states with hotter climates, as long as they put more organic inputs in the soil. It's important to remember there is a limit as to how much carbon we can put into the soil, based on climate. In California, the maximum accumulation happens around five to six years using an intensive carbon input system. Midwestern growers have limits, too; they just reach them at a slower pace because the cooler climate makes their microbes less hungry; however, this leads to the capacity to store more soil carbon compared to warmer climates.

While visiting Salt Spring Island, I also met Michael Ableman, who has a 120-acre organic farm on the island. He also founded the Center for Urban Agriculture at Fairview Gardens, a working organic farm and education center in Southern California. "I've been thinking about climate change in its relation to food and farming a lot lately," he said.

> I think the diversity in organic agriculture will play a big role in how farmers adapt to coming changes; biodiversity both in crop choices and in the broader farm ecosystem will be important. My approach has always been to grow a huge diversity of foods, originally done for economic reasons so that all of our eggs were not in one basket. But without knowing it, I was also creating a system that was inherently stable in regard to climate. Diversity is a form of security in regard to climate because biological systems never stay the same. Case in point: we had incredible heat [in June 2007]; it was 110 degrees F in my greenhouses and 90-plus degrees in the shade—not typical of our northwest coastal region. I watched strawberries literally cooking on the plants while at the same time crops like melons soaked up the heat and thrived. Surprisingly, our spinach survived fairly well, which is strange considering that spinach is a plant that thrives in cool weather. I don't know for sure, but my sense is that it survived because the soil in which it is growing has very high organic matter and acted like a sponge. That "sponge" not only provided enough constant moisture for those plants to drink, but also provided an atmosphere that was cooler. It is the only way that I can explain why that spinach did not go to seed under those very extreme conditions.

What About Taste and Health?

If pleasure is our motivating factor in eating, then taste is the ultimate concern with regard to any of this. Why would an organically grown, global-cooling cuisine taste better and be healthier than foods from a global-warming diet? For the chef's perspective, let's compare soil to a really good sauce. You can have the blandest tasting thing in the world (think tofu) and make it taste good by marinating it and cooking it in a really good sauce (see the recipe for our BBQ'ed Tofu with Lime at the end of this chapter). Growing plants in carbon-rich soil is like simmering them in the best Bordelaise sauce you've ever had. The plants select and pull in all the complex elements found in organic soil in the same way that you select and incorporate ingredients from your spice cabinet. Like a well-stocked kitchen, organic soil has more variety for the plants to choose from.

This same comparison helps when looking at the nutrition density of our food. It's the soil microbes that bring the trace minerals/nutrition from the soil to the plant. The plants utilize the trace elements to build their immune systems in the same way we eat food and take mineral supplements to build ours. In carbon-rich soil, the microbes have been stimulated, so the soil has more to offer to the plants. When the menu includes trace minerals, the plants will order it from the microbes. Then when we eat the plants, we get the benefit, too.

Organic fruits and vegetables taste better than those that are conventionally grown because the plants don't become "bloated" with water like those grown with chemical fertilizers, which cause rapid growth. Slower-growing plants have time to develop thicker cell walls and therefore need to hold less water. The flavors are more concentrated, such as those of dry-farmed wine grapes and tomatoes mentioned in chapter 3. Organic produce also consistently scores a higher brix number (a measure of sugar content) than conventional produce.[16] Though the "whys" for this are still to be studied, some say it is related to the health of the soil and how much carbon it holds. We can enhance these natural sugars in the kitchen with certain culinary techniques. Learn how to do it in chapter 9.

Eating Seasonally

The advent of a 1,500-mile apple and hothouse tomato is confusing. All fruits and vegetables seem to be available everywhere in the United States, all the time. Cutting down on the consumption of jet-set asparagus and sauna-loving strawberries does reduce greenhouse-gas emissions, but why else is it important to eat seasonally? For answers to this question, we look to Mother Nature, who actually gives us hints on what to eat when. Vegetables grown in cooler temperatures usually need to be cooked longer than those that grow in warmer temperatures. It's almost as though Mother Nature is saying, "Spend more time cooking in the winter, dear. You need the heat in your food."

What's in Season When?

FOOD	W	SP	SU	F
apples				•
apricots			•	
artichokes		•		•
arugula		•	•	•
asparagus		•		
avocados	•	•	•	•
basil			•	•
beans (fava)		•		
beans (green)			•	•
beef (pasture-finished)			•	•
beets	•	•	•	•
blueberries			•	
broccoli	•	•		•
carrots	•	•	•	•
cauliflower	•	•		•
chard greens	•	•	•	•
cheeses (fresh goat)		•		
cherries		•	•	
chestnuts				•
collard greens	•		•	•
corn			•	•
cucumber			•	•
dandelion greens	•	•		
eggplant			•	
eggs		•	•	•
fennel	•	•	•	•
figs			•	•
garlic (green)		•		
grapefruit	•			•
grapes (table)			•	
grapes (wine)				•
honeycomb		•	•	•
jicama	•			
kale	•	•	•	•
kiwi	•			•
kohlrabi				•
leeks	•	•	•	•

FOOD	W	SP	SU	F
lemons	•			•
limes	•			•
melons			•	
mint		•	•	•
nectarines			•	
okra			•	•
onions	•	•	•	•
onions (vidalia)		•		
oranges	•			•
parsley			•	•
parsnips	•			•
peaches			•	
pears			•	•
peas (sugar snap and snow)		•	•	•
pecans				•
peppers			•	•
persimmon	•			•
plums			•	
pomegranate				•
potatoes (new)	•	•	•	•
pumpkin				•
quince				•
radishes	•	•	•	•
raspberries			•	•
rhubarb		•	•	
rutabaga	•			•
salmon (wild Pacific, May–Sept.)	•			
squash (summer)		•	•	
squash (winter)				•
strawberries		•	•	
sunchokes (Jerusalem artichokes)				•
sweet potatoes				•
tangerines	•			•
tomatillos			•	•
tomatoes			•	•
turnips	•	•		•
yams				•

W = Winter, SP = Spring, SU = Summer, F = Fall

The majority of this list is based on information from San Francisco Farmers Markets.
To find out what is seasonal in your area, see Book 'n' Cook Club page 88.

Mind you, this is not "hot heat" but "energy heat." Mother Nature reminds us that we need more "energy" in our food in winter, even if we don't live in a cold climate. Unless, of course, we live in the tropics and then we eat the food from that area. So we eat the seasonal foods in the regions we live near, not only because this food has a lower carbon count, but as a way of following nature's cues and getting in tune with our surroundings. Seasonal eating is like getting a tire alignment at the auto shop or a back alignment at the chiropractor. Cars and people work better when they're in tune.

But what vegetables and fruits are in season when? For a quick test, drop them on the floor. If they make a big thud, they are most likely grown in the fall or winter. If they make a muffled thud or a splat, they're most likely grown in the summer. An easier and less messy option is to refer to our "What's in Season When?" guide. Copy and post it on your refrigerator. Knowing what's currently growing will help you with menu planning and grocery shopping.

At first, cooking seasonally might appear limiting, but it's actually the opposite. Seasonal cooking forces us to discover new ways of using familiar foods, inspires us to try new foods, and offers the sweetest, freshest, most "high-vibe" produce at often the best price. Because seasonal vegetables come with heightened, natural flavors, simple cooking techniques are often all that are needed.

The Harvest

Despite the tradition of a November grape harvest, the call to pick the fruit came surprisingly early in 2007. The chairman of the wine committee at Portola Valley Ranch e-mailed an emergency call to action:

> Winos,
> The weather has gone to hell. (The next time Tom [the vineyard manager] tries to leave in October on vacation, I will personally stake him out in the middle of the vineyard.) The emergency harvest grapes we just picked were moderately stressed and many had slight beginnings of mold. We have had three rainstorms so far with at least one more predicted. The vines are shutting down from cold weather and the chance of crop damage from rain is increasing. Let's plan on the main harvest next Saturday, the 20th.

This was the earliest harvest ever for the ranch; never before had there been this type of rain in October. Because Cabernet grapes grow in such dense clusters, too much rain can cause a buildup of white mold. The grapes were also starting to pucker and raisin and had one of their lowest brix (sugar) counts ever—20.6 (22.0 is common). To make up the difference, sugar would have to be added to the wine.

It was a rainy, stressful couple of days worrying about the grapes, but the Saturday when we picked was sunny—a perfect California fall harvest. More than sixty people of all ages showed up that morning with gardening shears, scissors, even large hedge clippers. It was quite a community event. Kids ran around looking for "jackpots"—multiple, large clusters of grapes that grew so tightly together that you couldn't see where the cluster was attached to the vine. It took three boys to harvest one of the jackpots; they squealed with excitement as they showed off their prize. Ten-year-olds were the perfect height for picking the lower grapes; they could get directly underneath the vine and harvest without reaching. The foliage was so lush in places that you could have complete conversations with people on the other side without ever seeing who they were. (Buried behind the vines, I just happened to overhear one harvester whispering about a top-secret sunken ship he had just discovered off the coast of Mexico. It was buried, he said, under sixty-nine feet of silt and was filled with Ming Dynasty treasures.)

After the picking, we gathered for de-stemming. Everyone caught up on community gossip while pulling dense grape clusters out of bins. These weren't like store-bought grapes; they were solid, stiff, purple masses—so much so, that the work was distracting. While half of me focused on the chatter, the other half kept grabbing hold of these thick objects with big, bumpy ridges, over and over and over again. I couldn't have been the only woman bemused by this. Standing there grinning, I recalled the macrobiotic Law of Signatures which says that whatever a fruit or vegetable looks like, that's what it's good for. Following this philosophy, cauliflower is good for the brain, apples are good for the heart, and I now know that Cabernet grape clusters are good for the exact same thing that late-summer zucchini is. Maybe that's why there were so many more men on the wine committee than women.

When the work was done, the harvest was surprisingly pronounced a success. The mold was not as bad as expected, the brix looked fine (21.6 percent), and the yield was up by 10 percent. We shared lunch, uncorked some of the past harvests, and celebrated together at tables decorated with fall foliage: dark red and yellow grapevine leaves. Later that evening, I walked back into the vineyard to congratulate the vines and thank them for the excellent grapes they had grown. Looking out at the turning leaves, I felt a slight sadness at the passing of the season. But then I remembered we had captured that exact moment. It was time in a bottle to be enjoyed years from now, and I smiled.

Book 'n' Cook Club Ideas

Resources to Find Food

Organic and Local Foods
  Guide: http://www.
  localharvest.org/

Farmers markets in your state:
  http://www.ams.usda.gov/
  farmersmarkets/map.htm

Field Trips

Your Local Farm—many farms
  offer public tours. Ask the
  farmers you buy from at the
  farmers market if you can visit
  their farm.

Video Documentaries

The Real Dirt on Farmer John
  (2005)

Ripe for Change (2006)

Recipes

BBQ'ed Tofu with Lime

Backyard Broiled Figs with Goat
  Cheese

A SALAD FOR ALL SEASONS:

Spring: Spring Mix with
  Goat Cheese, Toasted
  California Almonds, and
  Fresh Strawberry Balsamic
  Vinaigrette

Summer: Black Soybean, Roasted
  Corn, and Beet Salad

Fall: Grilled Persimmon Salad
  with Maple-Spiced Walnuts,
  Spinach, and Frisée
  Autumn Tempeh Salad

Winter: Spinach with Pear, Pecan,
  Red Onion, and Artisanal Blue
  Cheese

Small Things Matter

• Shop at the farmers market; ride your bike to get there if you can.

• Buy organic produce that's in season.

• Search out local brands from our "Most Local Foods Plate."

• Sign up for a community-supported agriculture (CSA) box. By
  receiving a seasonal box of produce each week, you create a
  relationship to your local farming community.

Recipes

BBQ'ed Tofu with Lime

A great sauce does for tofu what great soil does for produce—makes it taste really good! Barbecue sauce is produced in many states across the country—support your favorite local or regional brand. The technique of "pressing" removes excess water from tofu and gives it a hearty texture that appeals to meat-eaters.

SERVES 4 TO 6

1 pound organic tofu, firm or superfirm
1 (12-ounce) jar local or regional barbecue sauce
2 tablespoons freshly squeezed lime juice

PRESSING: The night before grilling, slice the tofu into squares, 3/4-inch thick. Cover a baking sheet with a clean dishcloth and lay tofu on top. Cover with another dishcloth and lay something flat, like another baking sheet, on top. Place a couple of pounds of weight on top (cans, jars, bowls, this book) and let sit, unrefrigerated, for 30–60 minutes. Remove tofu.

MARINATING: Combine barbecue sauce and lime juice in a small bowl. Pour 1/4 cup into a medium-size storage container. Put in one layer of tofu, add more sauce, and continue until all the tofu is layered and coated with sauce. Cover the container and let marinate overnight in the refrigerator.

GRILLING: Preheat the grill to medium. Clean the grates and use a paper towel to brush on a light coat of oil. Place the marinated tofu directly onto the grates; grill until dark grill marks appear on the tofu. Save the barbecue sauce for basting. Grill about 15–20 minutes with medium to medium-high heat—high enough to cook the tofu, but low enough to give it time to develop a "meatlike" texture. Check for grill marks by slightly lifting up the tofu. If it needs to cook more, put the tofu back onto the grill in the same position it was, with grill marks touching the grates. If the grill is too hot, your tofu will dry out and burn. Baste the tofu every 5 minutes with reserved sauce.

When done, remove tofu from grill, slice into triangles or sticks, baste with a little more barbecue sauce, and serve.

Backyard Broiled Figs with Goat Cheese

People say they "don't like figs," until they try these tasty treats. Often neighborhood fig trees go unharvested, so cut down on food waste with this super-easy appetizer. Don't wait for a party to make them.

SERVES 4 TO 6

1 pint figs (approximately 10 figs)
5 ounces goat cheese—look for your local or regional brand
Onion jam, or some other sweet/savory jam (optional); look for a local or regional brand

Wash figs and let dry. Coat a small baking tray with oil. Slice a small sliver off each side of the fig, for stability, and cut the fig in half. Place on the tray with a dollop of goat cheese on top. Keep the cheese in a mound; do not flatten. Place the figs under the broiler for 5 minutes, or until browned on the top. Remove from heat, cool slightly, and garnish with onion jam. Serve warm.

A Salad for all Seasons

SPRING

Spring Mix with Goat Cheese, Toasted California Almonds, and Fresh Strawberry Balsamic Vinaigrette

As spring arrives and the goats return to pasture to eat the young grass, their milk changes from dense winter milk to light spring milk. Fresh goat cheese is a perfect way to welcome spring. Enjoy it with strawberries as they too come back into season.

SERVES 4

Vinaigrette
2 tablespoons balsamic vinegar
1 tablespoon apple juice
1/2 cup sliced strawberries, blended into a purée
Salt and pepper to taste
2 tablespoons olive oil

Salad
4 cups mixed baby lettuce
1 cup sliced strawberries
1/2 cup crumbled goat cheese (see Note)
1/4 cup sliced almonds, toasted

Purée the vinegar, juice, and strawberries in a blender with salt and pepper to taste. Slowly drizzle in olive oil and blend until thickened. Toss lettuce with dressing. Divide salad among 4 plates and top with strawberries, goat cheese, and almonds.

NOTE: Got kids? Substitute goat cheese with mild Queso Fresco.

SUMMER
Black Soybean, Roasted Corn, and Beet Salad

Red peppers, corn, and beets are all in season this time of year. Roasting brings out the sugars in vegetables; learn how to do it in chapter 9.

SERVES 8

Salad
1 1/2 cups corn kernels, roasted or grilled and removed from cob
1 (15-ounce) can black soybeans, rinsed and drained*
2 beets, roasted and diced (see recipe page 170)
1 large red bell pepper, seeded and diced
2 green onions, sliced thin
2 tablespoons chopped cilantro

Vinaigrette
3 tablespoons freshly squeezed lime juice
1 tablespoon frozen pineapple concentrate
1 tablespoon toasted sesame oil
1 tablespoon soy sauce
1/2 teaspoon dried oregano
A few drops Tabasco or Sriracha pepper sauce
Freshly ground pepper to taste

Combine the salad ingredients in a large bowl. Mix together ingredients for vinaigrette and pour over vegetables. Mix well. For best results, let salad marinate for at least 1 hour.

* Eden Foods is the only company that sells black soybeans. They are available in natural foods stores. You can substitute black turtle beans.

Grilled Persimmon Salad with Maple-Spiced Walnuts, Spinach, and Frisée

This salad is easy but elegant, perfect for fall and holiday meals. Plus it has "kid appeal." One of my ten-year-old students told me it was the only salad he had ever liked!

SERVES 4

Grilled Persimmons

2 Fuyu persimmons, sliced lengthwise in $1/4$-inch slices

1 tablespoon olive oil

Pinch of sugar and salt

Maple-Spiced Walnuts

3 cups walnuts

$1/2$ cup maple syrup

1 teaspoon cinnamon

1 teaspoon cumin

$1/4$ teaspoon cloves

$1/4$ teaspoon nutmeg

$1/4$ teaspoon ground ginger

$1/4$ teaspoon cayenne

$1/4$ teaspoon cardamom powder

$1/4$ teaspoon salt

Vinaigrette

2 tablespoons sherry vinegar

2 tablespoons Dijon mustard

1 tablespoon honey

1 teaspoon chopped fresh thyme

3 tablespoons walnut oil

2 tablespoons olive oil

Salt and freshly ground pepper

Salad

4 cups loosely packed spinach leaves, washed and dried

2 cups washed and dried frisée with stems trimmed and torn into bite-size pieces

1/3 cup thinly sliced red onion

2 ounces dry Jack cheese, shaved into thin shards (this is the U.S. version of Parmigiano Reggiano)

1/4 cup pomegranate seeds

TO GRILL THE PERSIMMONS: Preheat a grill or grill pan; make sure the grates are clean. Brush persimmon slices with oil, sprinkle with a pinch of sugar and salt, and place on grill. Grill until slightly golden and softened, about 4–5 minutes. Turn over and grill another 4–5 minutes. Set aside.

TO MAKE THE MAPLE-SPICED WALNUTS: Preheat the oven to 350 degrees F. Toss walnuts in a large bowl with maple syrup. Add spices and mix well. Cover a baking sheet with Silpat (permanent parchment paper) or a piece of parchment paper. Spread the nuts out in a single layer. Bake 10–12 minutes, flipping after 5 minutes. Remove from the pan into a large bowl. Store in an airtight container.

TO MAKE THE VINAIGRETTE: Whisk together the vinegar, mustard, honey, and thyme. Slowly whisk in the oils. Season with salt and pepper. Set aside.

In a large bowl, combine the spinach, frisée, and red onion. Toss with dressing and a little salt. Garnish with persimmons, nuts, cheese, and pomegranate seeds.

Autumn Tempeh Salad

Kabocha is considered one of the sweetest squashes; introduce it for more diversity in your produce selection. Tempeh (pronounced TEM-pay) is made from soy and is heartier than tofu. It has a "meatiness" that many people like. This recipe is an adaptation of one by my colleague, chef Carolyn Peters.

SERVES 4

1 $\frac{1}{2}$ pounds Kabocha or other winter squash, cut into 1-inch cubes
1 medium turnip or rutabaga, cut into 1-inch cubes
2 tablespoons olive oil, divided
1 teaspoon salt
1 teaspoon dried rosemary
1 teaspoon dried thyme
1 teaspoon dried sage
1 (10-ounce) package tempeh, any style
2 tablespoons soy sauce
2 stalks celery, diced
Half a red onion, finely diced
$\frac{1}{4}$ cup chopped fresh parsley
2 tablespoons dried currants or raisins

Preheat oven to 400 degrees F. Toss squash and root vegetables with 1 tablespoon olive oil, salt, and dried herbs; place on a baking dish in one layer. Cover with foil and bake for 20 minutes. Remove foil and stir squash. Return to oven uncovered and bake another 15–20 minutes. Check for tenderness. A fork should easily pierce the squash, but it should not be so soft that it's falling apart. Set aside to cool.

While squash is baking, cut tempeh in half and steam for 15 minutes. Remove from the steamer and let cool. Mix together remaining ingredients (soy sauce through raisins and remaining tablespoon oil) in a large bowl. Add tempeh that has been cut into 1-inch cubes. Toss in cooled squash and adjust seasonings. Serve.

Spinach with Pear, Pecan, Red Onion, and Artisanal Blue Cheese

Pecans are local! Trees grow wild in Texas, Oklahoma, Mississippi, Louisiana, and South Carolina, and as far north as southern Iowa and Indiana. Pears are a fitting winter fruit.

SERVES 4

3/4 cup shelled and halved pecans

Vinaigrette
3 tablespoons olive oil
1 tablespoon balsamic vinegar
2 teaspoons Dijon mustard
Salt and pepper to taste

Salad
4 cups washed fresh spinach torn into bite-size pieces
1/4 cup thinly sliced red onion
1/4 cup crumbled local blue cheese
1 pear, thinly sliced

Preheat oven to 350 degrees F. Place pecans on a baking sheet. Bake nuts for 5–8 minutes, until golden brown, not dark brown. Let cool.

Combine the vinaigrette ingredients in a small bowl. Whisk and set aside. Combine spinach, onion, and cheese; toss with dressing. Divide salad among 4 plates and top with pear and nuts.

Variation: Substitute red grapes for pear during the summer and fall.

6

Holy Cow!

L ouis Sukovaty is a hard guy to keep up with. He walks at a quick clip, leading me around Crown S Ranch, LLC, in Winthrop, Washington. Winthrop is in the north-central part of the state in the Methow Valley, a forty-square-mile area with a growing interest in local food production and agriculture.

"The ruminants are incredible—the cows, sheep, goats, and deer who eat grass for food, something humans can't do. With more than one stomach, ruminants have an overly efficient digestive process, exactly what is needed to convert grass to energy." Sukovaty is a third-generation farmer whose farming practices are based on his extensive research in animal husbandry (the way it was done prior to the invention of fossil-fuel fertilizers and chemicals), his engineering background (he is a licensed professional engineer in both electrical and mechanical engineering), and his passion for working with nature.

A number-crunching, wild-eyed rancher, Sukovaty describes himself as an "artisan finisher," taking cattle from 500 to 1,200 pounds. "Weight doesn't matter as much as the 'finish of the animal'—how fat the animal is and whether the marbling will provide a product the consumer wants." Sukovaty says his work on the farm is similar to cooking.

> A big misunderstanding about grass-fed beef is that people think it will taste gamey, but that depends on what you feed them. You can make the flavor

stronger or milder by adjusting their feed. Feed them well and the meat tastes great. Feed them on dry land with only bitter shrubs like Barnaby [Barnaby's thistle] and bitterbrush and the meat will turn out gamey. My fields have a ton of white and sweet clover—what I consider to be ice cream for the cows—and they love it! It gives the meat an almost nutty flavor. Not strong or overpowering, and also not that lardy, fat-tasting meat you get with corn-fed beef.

Americans take beef any way they can get it. The United States is the largest beef producer in the world and one of the largest dairy producers. Unfortunately, conventionally raised livestock are responsible for up to 18 percent of the world's greenhouse-gas emissions and are a substantial part of the global-warming diet. A United Nations Food and Agriculture Organization report entitled *Livestock's Long Shadow* notes that raising and feeding cows by conventional methods uses billions of pounds of fertilizers and billions of gallons of water, degrades the soil, and requires the deforestation of millions of acres of land. Livestock now uses 30 percent of the Earth's entire surface, mostly for permanent pasture.[1] They also create a lot of manure; one cow can excrete 120 pounds of manure daily. Cows, and their manure, produce methane, a greenhouse gas that is twenty-three times better at trapping heat than carbon dioxide. An ideal world of carbon-free eaters might leave meat behind and move toward greener pastures, but with 70 percent of the U.S. population eating meat several times a week, and consumption of beef expected to double worldwide by 2050, meat eating is here to stay.[2] Can we adjust the system to make it work? Better yet, could eating meat possibly make the pastures greener?

In 2007, Cornell researchers studied the "agricultural land footprint" of forty-two different diets to determine how much meat (and other foods) people could eat with a limited amount of land to grow it on. What would the diet of the citizens of New York State be if the state had to grow all

its own food? The diets studied had the same number of Calories and core of grains, fruits, vegetables, and dairy products, but varying amounts of meat (from none to 13.4 ounces daily) and fat (from 20 to 45 percent of Calories). Cornell found that a low-fat vegetarian diet needed less than half an acre (0.4 acre to be exact) per person per year to produce their food, whereas a high-fat diet with a lot of meat needed 2.1 acres. The study showed that environmental efficiency could be obtained eating meat if New Yorkers reduced their daily meat and egg consumption by approximately two-thirds, from 5.8 ounces (the average American consumption) to about 2 ounces per day. [3]

Pasture-Raised, Planned-Grazed Cattle

Crown S Ranch finishes just fifty animals each year. The animals come to the farm in March and leave in November. For ranches that do not grow grass year-round, eating beef could be considered a "seasonal" activity, which starts in late summer when pasture animals begin to be slaughtered. If done right, raising beef is a natural part of a truly sustainable agricultural system, says Sukovaty. "I like to create things and work with the animals. It's great to be out there in the pastures and watch the whole cycle. Cows bred well are such an important part of a healthy ecosystem. They can harvest more per year on an acre of grass than I could if I was growing grain for them." Sukovaty goes on to describe the cycle he loves to watch, calculating figures under his breath.

> Cows come onto a pasture, eat up the grass, distribute cowpats and urinate over everything; basically they mow the pasture and fertilize it. They take only about 50 percent of the nutrient quantity out of the grass they eat, concentrating and depositing what they don't use back onto the pasture. In this process they separate out plant phosphorus and potassium (found in the cowpats) from nitrogen (found in the urea). Clover (a legume) comes in around the cowpats because it loves phosphorus and doesn't need nitrogen (it can fix its own). The grasses, on the other hand, need nitrogen, so they utilize the cow's urine.

Sukovaty says this natural cycle creates a good balance between grasses and legumes—swapping back and forth, keeping pastures healthy and the cycle continuous. Within twenty-four hours of the cows moving onto a new pasture, the first new shoots of grass and legumes pop back up on the grazed pasture. Six weeks later, that pasture is completely regrown, and the Crown S Ranch cows are allowed to return. This cycle goes on four or five times during the season, a self-perpetuating system operated solely by cow power. "That's why cows can harvest more nutrients per year on an acre of grass than I could if I grew corn and fed it to them." After our chat, Sukovaty runs his numbers to exemplify his point. (See chart on page 101.)

Continual grazing of large tracts of land by relatively small numbers of animals wandering around is widely recognized as having a destructive effect. Just as a hammer can be used to build a home as well as wreck one, the grazing and animal impact of large herds of livestock can

Energy, Emissions, and Agriculture

It is estimated that agriculture-related emissions account for at least 20 percent of global greenhouse-gas emissions.[4] This might be somewhat surprising, considering all the attention that is normally focused on transportation and home energy use. However, commercial agriculture and the need to feed more than 6 billion people create significant energy demands and impacts.

In producing corn, for example, energy is required to produce and transport the seeds, prepare the soil (including the production and application of fertilizers and pesticides), till the soil, and plant the seeds. During the growing phase, there is maintenance through further pesticide application or soil manipulation and, of course, irrigation, which can involve significant resources, especially in areas with little rainfall. Once the corn is ready for harvest, machines are used to collect and separate the corn from the stalk. At this point, further transportation and processing are required to ship the corn to stores or feedlots or to convert the corn into one of many corn-based products.

Although growing crops such as corn requires significant amounts of energy, the most energy-intensive sector in agriculture and the one that is also responsible for the largest emissions of greenhouse gases (up to 18 percent of global greenhouse-gas emissions) is from livestock, of which beef cattle are the largest contributor.[5] These estimates represent the entire livestock chain, including CO_2 emissions for transportation and fertilizer production, CH_4 (methane) emissions from cattle flatulence and manure, N_2O (nitrous oxide) emissions from manure and

land management, and indirect CO_2 emissions due to land-use change and the energy associated with growing the food that livestock eat (i.e., corn or soybeans).[6] It should be noted that pasture-raised cattle (or any free-range animal such as bison in the United States or kangaroo in Australia) require much less energy to grow compared to feedlot cattle.[7]

be harnessed to heal land. In fact, managing domestic livestock in a way that simulates the behavior of wild herds of hooved animals in the presence of predators gives humanity a way to restore the health of degraded grasslands and forests over much of the Earth's surface, according to Allan Savory, the founder of Holistic Management International. This wildlife biologist began developing a grazing procedure in the 1960s that gave land managers the tools to not only increase their land productivity but to reverse desertification, an aim that had eluded human understanding since the dawn of agriculture and livestock domestication. Savory teaches that to understand our environment, we have to look at it as a whole and not in pieces. He believes that hooved grazing animals, their predators, soil life (microbes, etc.), and grasses have coevolved and are responsible for keeping the carbon cycle—birth, growth, death, and decay—going on grasslands. The practical work of holistic managers on 30 million acres of land throughout the world clearly supports his belief.[8]

Grasses, unlike trees, do not shed their leaves as part of the carbon cycle, but they do "recycle themselves" through the grazing and trampling of tightly bunched herds of ungulates. Lacking the physiological features of trees that automatically return leaves to the soil surface in fall, grasslands depend on hooved animals to cycle biomass and fertilize and aerate the soil. This is especially important during dry seasons and times of drought when microbes die or become dormant. I chatted with Savory on the phone from his home office in Albuquerque, New Mexico. He speaks like an environmental statesman, offering a broad-based perspective gained from his well-developed ability to follow nature's cues and observe the natural world as patterns of wholes. "I have more hope than ever

Right: Comparison of number of cattle that can be raised on grass versus corn/hay based on experience at Crown S Ranch.[9] This is especially interesting because it contradicts the commonly held assumption that growing cattle on corn/hay feed is a more efficient use of land.

NUMBER OF CATTLE THAT CAN BE FINISHED WITH 1 ACRE OF PERMANENT PASTURE (GRASS-LEGUME MIX) GRAZED	
Calf weight start	600 pounds
Calf weight finish	1,200 pounds
Conservative rate of gain	2.5 pounds per day
Days for cow to reach finish weight	240 days
Feed requirement per day	22.5 pounds per day
Total feed required for each finished cow	5,400 pounds
Reasonable yield per acre per year of pasture	11,000 pounds
Number of cattle that can be finished per acre of pasture	2.037 cows

NUMBER OF FINISHED CATTLE PER 1 ACRE OF CORN/HAY RAISED FROM FEEDLOT FEEDING	
Corn grown per acre	7,840 pounds
Average yield of hay per acre	11,000 pounds
Days for cow to reach finish weight	101 days
Corn fed per cow per day	19.5 pounds
Total corn required per cow	3,144.3 pounds
Hay fed per cow per day (for digestive system)	6.2 pounds
Total hay required per cow	990.2 pounds
Corn required per cow	0.40 acre
Hay required per cow	0.09 acre
Total of corn and hay required	0.49 acre
Number of cattle that can be finished on 1 acre of corn/hay	2.04 cows

before," said Savory. "History shows that the only time humans ever unite is in times of catastrophe. We needed something to unite us [because] there is so much mounting conflict in the world. The only nonhuman thing I can think of that could do this is global climate change. It will unite us in the greatest battle ever fought by humans—the battle to learn to live in harmony with ourselves and our environment." Savory has long held that desertification, biodiversity loss, and climate change are three aspects of the same issue that must be simultaneously addressed by restoring full ground cover and soil health in all environments. It bears mention that when livestock is managed to simulate wild herds bunched for protection from predation, then biological succession advances, plant density increases, water and minerals are effectively cycled, and the amount of sunlight entering the food web through photosynthesis dramatically increases. Using livestock as tools to increase the availability of clean, fresh water available to wildlife, agriculture, and human populations may surprise some, but the evidence apparent in perennial stream and spring flow, drought resistance, and groundwater recharge on holistically managed ranches is convincing.

Planned grazing is a solar-powered system that builds topsoil and sequesters carbon. Unlike factory-farmed meat production, a fossil-fuel-powered system that plows up pasture to grow monocropped fields of shallow-rooted, seasonal grain crops, planned grazing allows for maximum solar gain by intensively managing deep-rooted grasses and forbs (herbs other than grasses). And unlike industrial grazing, where cows that keep returning to the same plants weaken the plants' health, planned grazing rigorously plans and guides the movement of herds from one paddock to another, with recovery periods in between. Cows are allowed to harvest the "teenage" grass (not too young or too old), allowing plants to regrow their root structure between grazing events. The result is greener pastures with extensive root and microbial systems that efficiently transfer carbon from the air to the soil and transform a significant portion of it into the stable forms of humus and glomalin, as discussed in chapter 2.

"Our motto at the farm is 'Better for the Animals. Better for the Environment. Better for You,'" says Sukovaty. "My farming philosophy is to follow nature's cues and utilize all of nature's systems. Taking care of the soil is key, and pastureland is a vital part of a healthy ecosystem. Soil has the ability to store up to 3,500 pounds of carbon dioxide per acre, sequestered as soil organic matter.[10] Farmers vested in improving their soil gain more organic matter and microbes, allowing for better stores of carbon and better grass for cows." A healthy level of microbes

Illustration © 2008 iStock photos.

almost guarantees a good grass crop for Sukovaty, and he depends on the earthworms to tell

Why Is the Cow Sacred?

Since 1500 BC, Hindus have venerated the cow as mother goddess for her ability to give milk, especially during times of drought. Because both mothers and cows supplied milk to children, they were honored for "providing" children to all of mankind. Ancient societies also valued and venerated cow manure, using it as fertilizer, disinfectant, and fuel. Because cows are thought of as God's "useful gift," eating beef remains sacrilegious in certain areas of India.

The role of the cow in sustainable land management is also sacred. Think of cows as masterful healers or expert Shiatsu practitioners walking happily over the back of Mother Nature. Their hooved feet dig in to distribute the manure, aerate the soil, and stimulate the microbes. Like a good massage, they hit all her "spots" and loosen her up. And spelling "moo" backward gives you "oom" (the sacred chant). So what we really have here are four-legged bodhisattvas and master masseuses blessing and tending to our soil, all for free.

him how good of a job he is doing. "Most people think I am a grass farmer—in the 'industry,' cattle farmers are considered grass farmers—but I am really a microbe farmer. I can change sandy, low-organic dirt into a rich, alive soil in about five to ten years with a pasture system. And when a sudden explosion of earthworms finally shows up, I know I am finally getting it right."

Improving Farmland and Fitness

Eliminating meat or reducing and replacing corn-fed beef with pasture-raised beef improves farmland and fitness. "It may not be eating meat that causes us health problems," says author Michael Pollan, "but what the meat eats."[11] A 2006 study by the Union of Concerned Scientists and Dr. Kate Clancy highlights the nutritional differences between grass-fed and grain-fed animals, determining that cattle grown on pasture may produce beef and milk with real health benefits. *Greener Pastures* is the first study of its kind to combine "analyses of the nutritional, environmental and public health benefits of grass-based farming."[12] It addresses what many have intuitively believed for years, that what's good for the environment is also good for animals and humans. *Greener Pastures* shows that grass-fed beef and milk have higher omega-3 fatty acids than that of grain-fed cows, illustrating the nutritional differences between grain and grass. Remember, though, that Popeye "eats greens"; he doesn't "eat browns or eat corn." It is the "green" in the plant that makes the difference. When cows are taken off grass and fed hay in winter, the nutritional differences decrease.[13]

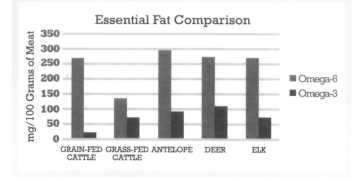

Essential Fat Comparison

Omega-6 and omega-3 fatty acids work in balance with each other to strengthen the immune system and help reduce the risk of heart disease and inflammation. Modern diets favor the ingestion of more omega-6s at the expense of omega-3s. The University of Maryland Medical Center reports that a "healthy diet should consist of roughly two to four times more omega-6 fatty acids than omega-3 fatty acids." The typical American diet tends to contain fourteen to twenty-five times more omega-6 fatty acids than omega-3 fatty acids, and many researchers believe this imbalance is a significant factor in the rising rate of inflammatory disorders, such as arthritis, atherosclerosis, and inflammatory bowel disease in the United States.[14]

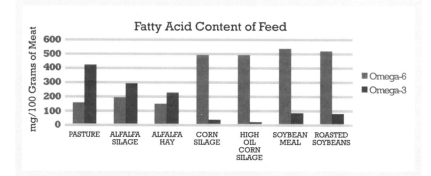

Fatty Acid Content of Feed

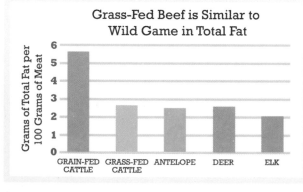

Grass-Fed Beef is Similar to Wild Game in Total Fat

Comparison of fats contained in grain-fed cattle versus grass-fed cattle and the fat content of different types of feed. Fat content of wild game is also provided for comparison. The ratio of omega-6 to omega-3 in grain-fed cattle is approximately 13, whereas the ratio for grass-fed cattle and other wild animals is between 2 and 4.[16]

Grass-fed beef not only has better fat, it has less overall fat, similar to that of wild game. On average, Americans eat more than sixty pounds of beef per year. According to Jo Robinson and www.eatwild.com, replacing grain-fed beef with pasture-raised beef would reduce a person's yearly caloric intake by 16,642 Calories, or enough for the person to lose 4.7 pounds (2.1 kg).[15]

In November 2007, I went to the American Grassfed Association conference to learn more about grass-fed beef. People from all walks of life attended, including farmers, ranchers, scientists, and chefs. The supposed political divide that society puts between the country and city folk didn't matter at the conference, for we were brought together by a greater connection—that of good food and the proper treatment of animals and the environment. While there, I met rancher Will Harris, owner of White Oak Pastures, Inc., in Bluffton, Georgia. He is a polite and proud Southerner with a looong, slooow Georgian drawl (I kept asking him questions just to hear him speak). Harris is a fifth-generation cattleman who has just completed production on a half-million-dollar USDA processing facility on his ranch in hopes of significantly expanding the distribution of his product. (Note: one of the largest obstacles to growth of the grass-fed industry is the lack of processing facilities available to the small rancher.) On the way back from a conference farm tour, Harris took a group of us out to lunch, seven ranchers and me. Interestingly, all the "beef people" ordered vegetarian portabella mushroom sandwiches or fish; no one ordered meat. When asked why they said they don't eat commercial beef, "because of how the cows are raised, what they eat, and how they are processed." Harris explained that cows are fed grain because it is cheap and efficient. "Cows live in total confinement with a high-carbohydrate grain concentrate augered into troughs from trucks; [this type of] feed system is not conducive for handling hay or grass."

Grain-based diets disturb the digestive systems of cows and make many of them sick. If E. coli occurs, the animals are fed antibiotics. Studies show that if cows are taken off grain and fed grass for five to ten days before slaughter, the E. coli is dramatically reduced.[17] Harris continued:

> Feedlots won't take the cows off the grain before slaughter, because they'd need a lot more land for the animals to graze or a completely different feed handling system. It's a logistical nightmare; besides, animals full of synthetic hormones and high-concentrate feed are gaining weight like crazy—three to four pounds a day. If [the feed is] abruptly changed, they lose weight. Cattle are fed subtherapeutic levels of antibiotics pretty much across the board because it helps them gain weight. It's profitable to feed cows antibiotics. The feedlot is all about turning grain into beef.
>
> Ready and continuous access to open pasture is absolutely necessary to allow animals to express their instinctive behavior. This is a basic tenet of animal husbandry. "Animal husbandry" is often diametrically opposed to the "animal science" that I learned in the 1970s. I believe that one reason that my beef tastes good is that the exercise that my cattle can get 24/7 makes athletes of them, comparatively speaking. It is also simply the right thing to do for the animals that I have taken dominion over.

Industry maintains that grain creates the texture and flavor preferred by U.S. meat eaters and is the only thing that can successfully fatten up a cow. Farmer Louis Sukovaty disagrees with both statements. His customers prefer the unique flavor and tenderness of his pasture-raised meats, and his cows finish easily and sometimes even early on pasture, coming in at the exact same weight as the factory farm animals—about 1,100 to 1,200 pounds.

Does this chapter push some of your buttons? If so, please consider this idea. It takes a higher quality soil to grow vegetables than it does to grow pastureland. So, let's outlaw factory-farms and free the cows out to pasture so their feet can dig in to heal the damaged earth. They will carbon-enrich and prep the soil, and once it's ready, it can be switched over to growing more row crops. This gives the world time to get off the global-warming diet, while we learn how to cut down on meat, and cure our addiction to synthetic nitrogen fertilizers. Plus it leaves us with greatly improved soil to grow delicious fruits and vegetables.

Cow Power and Methane Digesters

Feedlots aren't the only places that feed corn to cows. Most factory-farmed dairy cows are also fed a grain-based diet because the higher carbohydrates in corn cause cows to produce more milk.

Albert Straus of California's Straus Family Creamery does it differently. Located fifty miles north of San Francisco, the dairy has been family owned and operated for more than sixty-five years. In 1994, the dairy converted to organic farming and opened Straus Family Creamery, the first organic dairy and creamery west of the Mississippi. The creamery considers stewardship of the land one of its primary goals and is working toward establishing the nation's first GMO-free (genetically modified organism-free) verification system. "I do things that are different," says Straus. "A lot [of the things I do] are new and untested, from organics to methane to GMOs. My parents used to say that I do things that cost a lot of money. But I stick my neck out because that is what I believe in. I try to make a change."

These days, Straus has been spending money and making change with his methane digester, turning animal waste into fuel. Studies show that pasture-raised cows create less—but still ample—methane than grain-fed cows. (Better food = less gas.) Researchers measured results by attaching "methane recovery units" onto the cows.[18] Straus powers his farm by capturing the methane from his 280 cows. The digester creates 600,000 kilowatt hours of electricity per year, saves about 6,000 dollars in monthly energy costs, and supplies 90 percent of the farm's power—re-moo-able energy!

Dairy cows are best suited for creating renewables because their manure is easier to "harvest" than manure from beef cows. Cows are milked two or three times a day at the dairy. The manure collected in the barn during milking is hosed into a machine that separates solids from liquids. Solids are dried to create a mulchlike substance, which is spread on the fields. The liquids flow into a covered pond, where anaerobic bacteria "eat" the manure particles, producing methane, a by-product of the bacteria's digestion. Methane is captured in the pond cover

Top Left: Some of the happy ladies at Straus. **Top Right:** Separating manure solids and liquids. **Bottom:** Methane digester pond.

and then flows through pipes to a combustion engine, where it powers a generator that converts the gas into electricity. Additionally, heat created by the engine can heat water to 180 degrees F (82.2 degrees C). This water is hot enough to be used to clean the barn, heat the house, and reheat the pond waste, thereby creating even more methane to be burned for fuel.

"Using methane gas for power is not new, but it hasn't been used much in recent times," says Doug Williams of Williams Engineering, which set up the digester at the Straus dairy. Williams got his PhD during the first energy crisis in the 1970s, after becoming fascinated with how much energy the world needed and how much we depend primarily on fossil fuels to get it. In response he started studying methane, which has remained his lifelong focus. He continues:

> Methane was commonly used in Paris in 1800s for lighting, before petroleum came along and trumped everything. Vegetable oils and alcohol were also commonly used back then to run diesel engines, but the cheapness of fossil fuel replaced the need for anything else. Methane is just as effective as propane

for heating water or running engines, you just have to adjust the air/fuel ratio differently to make the engine run efficiently. Best of all, when you use a methane digester for manure, it eliminates the smell and even turns that into power!

Methane is making a comeback, but is hasn't been easy. There are over one hundred farm-scale digesters operating at commercial livestock farms in the United States. Although the systems can pay for themselves over time and can power entire farms, dairies have been slow to install them due to the required paperwork and an initial investment—upward of $250,000. Europeans, especially the Swiss and the Germans, are far ahead of the United States in utilizing methane. Their waste systems power cities with the energy harvested from household food and garden scraps mixed with organic waste from industries and slaughterhouses.

Bridport, Vermont, is one of the first U.S. cities where methane digesters are tied directly into the municipal power system. Bridport's Blue Spruce Farm has a thousand dairy cows creating more power then the farm can use, so it sells the excess back to the grid and profits an average of more than ten cents for every kilowatt-hour produced. By partnering with the Central Vermont Public Service Cow Power program, Vermont's largest investor-owned electric utility, Blue Spruce is part of a network of dairy farms supplying energy to more than 4,500 Vermont customers. Five thousand cows on the program's four farms can power approximately a thousand average-size Vermont homes each year.

"The impact a small dairy farm can have on greenhouse-gas savings is significant," says Dave Dunn, the manager of the program. "Our studies show 1,000 cows enrolled in this program can save approximately 3,400 metric tons of carbon dioxide equivalent, which is like taking 750 cars off the road."

The goal of this renewable energy program, which began in 2005, was to create a true connection between supply (farms) and demand (consumers). "Both customers and farmers are really excited about generating energy locally and receiving the side benefits of reduced methane and odor and cleaner air and water. People also like the fact that the end product is safer and more nutrient-accessible as fertilizer for fields." Tapping into a sense of community among Vermonters strengthened the program further. Even with one of the highest premiums in the country, nearly 3 percent of the utility's customers participate, making it one of the most popular voluntary renewable energy programs in the United States.

Organic Raw Milk

On my way home from Crown S Ranch, I stopped at the Methow Valley Creamery in Twisp, Washington. Run by Elise and Ron VanderYacht, the dairy produces organic raw milk from a small herd of pasture-raised, grass-fed cows. Elise brought me a glass of their milk—cold, creamy, and brilliant white. Tasted side-by-side with factory-farmed milk, the VanderYacht's milk tastes incredibly rich with a slight tinge of sweetness. "It's something that kids really like," says Elise. Raw milk is a whole food and creamier than industrialized milk because it is not homogenized or pasteurized. Homogenization breaks up milk fat by forcing it through a very fine filter, keeping it from separating, and pasteurization creates a longer shelf life. Both processes are favored by large dairy farms and are purported to affect the health properties of milk. The Methow Valley Creamery milk quickly fills me up. A little of their milk brings a lot of satisfaction. Substitute creamy raw milk for soymilk in the Orange Creamsicle recipe in chapter 4.

"Tell me about the cows," I ask Ron, a lifelong farmer and rancher who has been in the business for forty years. Ron reminded me of a quiet Ben Cartwright on the old TV show *Bonanza*; he even shares Ben's silver gray curls. The first time Ron traveled the 115-mile (185 km) road from Seattle to Twisp, he and his father arrived on horseback.

> Cows have taught me patience. Cows love to be bored. All they want to do is kick back, eat, sleep, and chew their cud, ten to twelve hours a day. It is so soothing to watch them. Cows have cliques—you see them always hanging out with the same group of cows. The females have babysitters—they take turns leaving their young with each other so they can go out in the field for a while alone. And each cow has a different personality. Our cows are named by their personalities. Look at Diamond Lil out there holding her head up high; she is so shiny and so proud. Airhead got her name because she is just a dizzy, ditsy cow. And Lady, she is very proper. Every cow is totally different.

"And cow tipping," I ask, "what about that? Does it really happen?"

Ron laughs. "Cows can go as fast as a horse, you know. You can't outrun a cow. They do thrive on boredom, but they are not slow. But cow tipping? I can't believe it. I've heard it but never seen it in fifty years. I'm afraid it's just an urban myth."

Book 'n' Cook Club Ideas

Books

Pasture Perfect: The Far-Reaching Benefits of Choosing Meat, Eggs, and Dairy Products from Grass-fed Animals, by Jo Robinson (revised 2007)

Everything I Want to Do Is Illegal, by Joel Salatin (2007)

Video Documentaries

Polyface Farm (MoonStar Films 2001)

Food Sources

- Farmers markets
- Eat Wild Directory of Farmers—eatwild.org
- Natural food stores/ specialty markets

Recipe

Grass-Fed Beef Crostini with Arugula, Green Peppercorns, and Dry Jack

Eggplant with Greens and Pasture-Raised Ground Pork

Lettuce Cups with Grass-Fed Meat (or Braised Tempeh) and Peanut Sauce

Braised Tempeh

Field Trips

Visit your nearest ranch selling planned grazed or pasture-raised animals. No matter what kind of protein you eat—plant or animal—learn who grows, raises, or manufactures the product. Meet them face-to-face if possible.

Small Things Matter

- Cut your meat consumption by 10 to 30 percent or more. Learn how to incorporate "umami" into your meals to take the place of meat.
- Buy grass-fed, pasture-raised meats and dairy products from your region. Ask your butcher where the meat comes from. If he or she isn't carrying local or regional grass-fed and pasture-raised animal products, see if a program can get started.
- Call your local power company and inquire about supporting "cow-generated power" in your area.

Recipes

Grass-Fed Beef Crostini with Arugula, Green Peppercorns, and Dry Jack

Often a small amount of meat is all that's needed to satisfy beef-eating family and friends. Serve this elegant appetizer as part of a cool cuisine menu to create that perfect balance.

MAKES 20 APPETIZERS

1 baguette, sliced into $1/4$-inch-thick slices
$1/2$ cup olive oil, divided
2 cloves garlic, peeled
1 pound grass-fed, pasture-raised sirloin or steak, sliced thinly
1 teaspoon lemon pepper
3 cups arugula or spinach leaves
$1/4$ pound Sonoma Dry Jack cheese, thinly shaved with a vegetable peeler (substitute Parmesan)
1 (3.5-ounce) jar green peppercorns
Salt and freshly ground pepper, to taste

Preheat oven to 350 degrees F. To make crostini, brush baguette slices with oil, rub with raw garlic, and place on a baking sheet. Bake until golden brown, about 10 minutes.

Preheat grill. Rub beef with a little olive oil and season with salt and pepper. Grill until medium rare, remove from heat and let sit 10 minutes on a cutting board.

In a medium-size bowl, toss arugula with 1 teaspoon olive oil and salt. Place 3 peppercorns on crostini. Place thin slices of beef on top of peppercorns. Top with arugula, cheese, and freshly ground pepper.

Variation: substitute capers for green peppercorns.

Eggplant with Greens and Pasture-Raised Ground Pork

Make this dish in the summer when eggplant is in season. Substitute Braised Tempeh for the pork if you don't want the meat. Serve over whole grain noodles or any whole grain.

SERVES 5 TO 6

Chili Paste

2 cloves garlic, minced

3 tablespoons chili paste

1 tablespoon hoisin sauce

1 tablespoon grated ginger root

$^1/_2$ teaspoon ground cardamom

1 tablespoon brown rice vinegar

1 tablespoon Madeira or Marsala

Stir-fry

1 cup stock, vegetable or chicken

3 tablespoons tamari or soy sauce

1 tablespoon real maple syrup

1 teaspoon arrowroot or kudzu

$^1/_4$ cup olive oil

1 pound eggplant, peeled if desired, cut in 1$^1/_2$-inch cubes (about 5 cups)

Pinch of salt

$^1/_2$ pound ground grass-fed pork (or substitute chicken)

Pinch cinnamon

Splash dry white wine or stock

1 bunch greens (dinosaur kale, kale, chard, mustard greens, collards), stems removed and finely chopped, leaves sliced into 1-inch squares (about 2–3 cups)

4 scallions, cut into 1$^1/_2$-inch pieces

1 teaspoon toasted sesame oil

For chili paste, combine all the ingredients in a small bowl and set aside.

For stir-fry, combine the stock, tamari, maple syrup, and arrowroot; set aside.

Heat a wok or large skillet, add oil and heat over high heat until hot but not smoking. Add eggplant and a pinch of salt. Cover and stir-fry until tender, 5 minutes, stirring frequently. Remove from heat and transfer to a large bowl. If pan gets too dry while sautéing, deglaze with a splash of wine or stock.

Return pan to heat and add ground pork and a pinch of salt and cinnamon. Cook until browned. Deglaze the pan with white wine or stock as needed. Transfer the meat into the bowl with the eggplant.

While pork is browning, bring 6 cups of water to boil in a large pot. Add a pinch of salt and the greens. Cook until greens are bright green and tender. Drain. (See Note.)

Return your wok to medium heat. By this time you should have nicely browned bits or a "fond" on the bottom of the wok. This is the good stuff! Add a little wine to the wok while it is heating to loosen up the fond. Add the chili paste; heat for 30 seconds. Add scallions; stir-fry 30 seconds. Stir stock mixture and add along with greens and eggplant mixture. Stir-fry until heated through and thickened. Serve over pasta or grain. Drizzle with toasted sesame oil.

NOTE: When greens are just cool enough to handle, pick out a couple of handfuls and lightly squeeze out excess water. Don't squeeze them "bone dry"; a light squeeze is best. Serving this dish over pasta? Add the greens into the pasta pot 5 minutes before draining the pasta. Drain pasta and greens together.

Lettuce Cups with Grass-Fed Meat (or Braised Tempeh) and Peanut Sauce

Lettuce cups are a good way to use up a variety of backyard summer vegetables, and they are a terrific afternoon snack for the kids. Replace the head lettuce with bite-size romaine or butter lettuce leaves for an up-to-date appetizer.

MAKES 10 TO 12 CUPS

Peanut Sauce

2 tablespoons peanut or almond butter

1 tablespoon freshly squeezed lime juice

2 tablespoons coconut milk

1–2 teaspoons soy sauce

1 teaspoon local honey

Lettuce Cups

Head lettuce, romaine, or butter lettuce

Filling

$1/2$ pound ground beef, pork, or chicken or 1 recipe Braised Tempeh

Salt to taste (optional)

1 tablespoon olive oil

2 stalks celery, diced small

1 small red onion, diced

1 carrot, grated

1 zucchini, diced small

1 jalapeño pepper, minced

1 red bell pepper, diced small

1 tablespoon chopped green chiles

1 ear of corn, kernels removed

$1/4$ cup ground nuts (peanuts, almonds, pecans, walnuts, hazelnuts)

$1/4$ cup sesame soy teriyaki sauce (Soy Vay is good)

2 scallions, sliced thin

$1/4$ cup chopped cilantro, basil, or a combination of both

For Peanut Sauce, mix all ingredients in a small bowl and set aside.

For Lettuce Cups, wash head lettuce and cut off the bottom 2 inches. Start peeling lettuce cups off the top, being careful not to rip them as you go. You may need to trim the sides of the head to loosen the inner leaves, and you may want to trim the cups for a more uniform look. Set cups aside.

For the filling, heat a 12-inch skillet and brown ground meat with salt to taste or prepare Braised Tempeh. Remove from skillet.

Heat skillet again with olive oil. Add celery and onion to skillet. Sauté until translucent. Add carrots, zucchini, peppers, chiles, corn, and nuts. Sauté 5 minutes. Stir in sesame soy sauce, scallions, meat or tempeh, and herbs.

Fill lettuce cups with veggie mix. Drizzle with Peanut Sauce. Roll and eat.

Braised Tempeh

Do you like the above recipes but don't want to use meat? Substitute tempeh, a protein food made from soybeans that is less processed and more "meaty" than tofu. Braising infuses complexity and depth of flavor into mild-tasting tempeh.

MAKES 2 CUPS

1 (8-ounce) package organic tempeh, any flavor
2 tablespoons olive oil

Braising Liquid
1 tablespoon Worcestershire sauce (vegetarian Worcestershire sauce is available)
2 teaspoons soy sauce
$1/4$ teaspoon salt
$1/2$ teaspoon dried thyme
3 cloves garlic, minced
2 teaspoons lemon pepper spice
2 tablespoons stock (vegetable, chicken, mushroom, or beef)
2 tablespoons dark beer (chocolate stout preferred)

Crumble tempeh into small "ground-beef-like" pieces by hand or by pulsing in the food processor. Set aside.

Assemble braising liquid ingredients in a small bowl. Set aside.

Heat a medium sauté pan to medium high heat. Add oil and tempeh. Sauté, stirring often, until tempeh turns light brown and a little crispy around the edges, about 5 minutes. Pour the braising liquid into the pan; immediately cover and shake (like popcorn) to distribute the sauce. After 1 minute, remove cover and stir. Continue cooking until the liquid has evaporated and the texture is crumbly. Adjust seasonings.

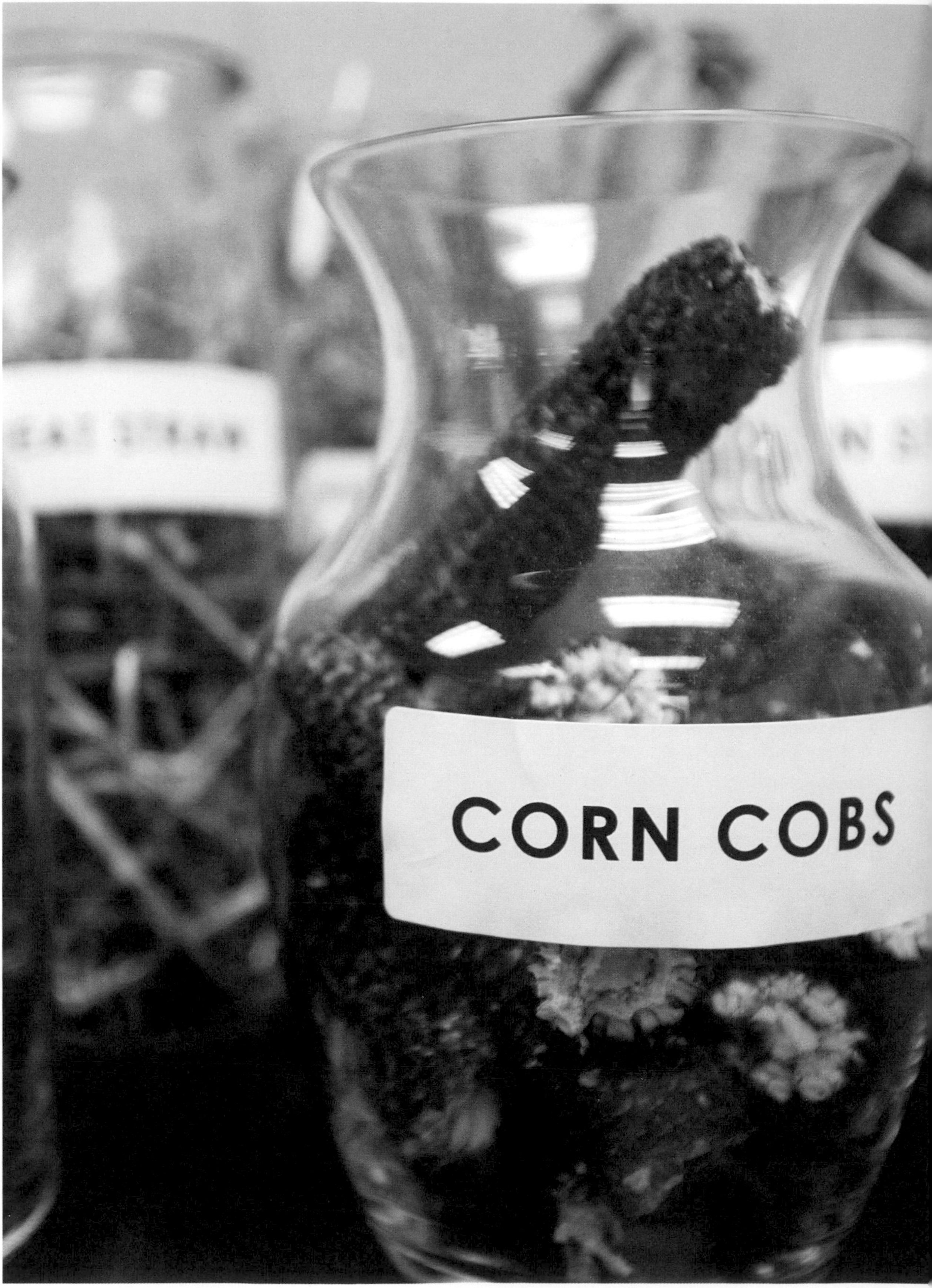
CORN COBS

7

Seven Innovative Recipes for Success

In February 2007, I listened to a Wall Street radio reporter discussing financial opportunities and investment possibilities associated with climate-change solutions. Suggesting many areas where profit and progress could happen simultaneously, he felt that there was great potential to make money on business solutions for global warming. Four days later I turned on the radio again, only to hear the exact opposite. This reporter believed that the country should not invest the money or time adjusting the business sector toward solving global warming because trying to do so will eventually hurt our economy as a whole.

These completely opposite views on the same problem illustrate the ancient Chinese blessing and curse, "May you live in interesting times." Major changes to societal structure are upon us. Will we view the proverbial glass as half empty (getting warmer and more CO_2-enriched with each passing day), or can we possibly see it as half full? Could the solutions to global warming be the best thing that has happened to the culinary world in a long time? Can value found in the global-warming crisis lead us toward evolution rather than pollution?

The following individuals and organizations are innovative risk-takers who are creating value out of the problems that face us. Some are in a "do not try this at home" league of their own, but others are everyday people trying out not-so-everyday ideas. In a world where it is a lot easier to complain about what someone else is doing rather than doing something about it ourselves, we salute their efforts. Inventing our way out of this crisis creates a vision for the future that we will all want to be part of and one that we hopefully will be inspired to help create.

Innovative Risk-taker 1: Kiteship Inc.—Reducing Food Miles One Gust at a Time

"Food miles," the distance that food travels to get to your plate (see "Food Miles" sidebar in chapter 5), is one of the many ways energy is used in today's food system. Trucks move much of the world's goods even though trucking uses up to ten times more energy than trains or barges. Containerships are considered to be one of the most energy-efficient ways to move food, even though ships of this size travel approximately thirteen to thirty feet on a gallon of gas. Think it costs a lot to fill your car's gas tank? Depending on the size of the ship, the fuel needed to move a containership from San Francisco to Japan and back to San Francisco could cost $2 to $3.5 million.

Dave Culp, of California-based Kiteship Inc., chuckles as he gives me that number. A self-described "forward-thinking sailor," Dave has been installing kites on boats since 1978 after getting into high-speed sailing in college. The young engineer became frustrated with engineering challenges of sailboats held back by the "little amount of available horsepower from wind." Sailboats can go only as fast as their sail allows them to; the bigger the sail, the faster the boat. But if the sail is too big, the boat tips over. Culp discovered a way around this: Mount a kite on a boat. "I could put an infinitely large kite on an infinitely small boat and break the speed of light."

The *Emma Maersk*

The *Emma Maersk* is one of the world's largest containerships (she's 1,300 feet [396 m] long, can carry 13,400 semitruck-size containers, and has a 110,000 horsepower main engine). The engine alone weighs more than the largest Coast Guard cutters. *Emma Maersk* makes twenty-four nautical miles per hour—about thirty miles (48 km) per hour—when cruising. She takes twelve days to cross the Pacific, and burns 320 tons per day of bunker fuel—that's thirty feet per gallon (2.4 meters/liter) burned.

A twenty-four-day, round-trip journey in this behemoth will burn 7,680 tons of bunker fuel (that's about 2.4 million gallons [9.1 million liters], enough for a Prius automobile to drive 5,000 times around the Earth, or make 250 round trips to the moon, if there were a road). The fuel bill for this single trip, at $450 a ton, is $3.46 million.[1]

Dave Culp puts one of his kites to the test.

Of course, breaking the speed of light may not be a practical goal, but it does seem that kites offer many benefits to ships. By not requiring masts the way sails do, kites make ships lighter. Because they attach directly to the boat, they do not require ballasts, special reinforcing, and all the additional costs associated with that kind of equipment. Kites travel under bridges and up to loading docks easily and can be easily gathered up and stored in boxes below the deck. And kites can make boats move "really, really fast"—Dave's favorite attribute—because they fly 500 to 800 feet above the boat, where the winds blow much stronger.

Realizing the potential of kites, Culp teamed with his partner, Dean Jordan, and started Kiteship, a small business that designs and installs kites on full-size ships. Hired in 2001 by Larry Ellison at Oracle Corporation, they invented a kite that was a new and completely legal style of spinnaker for yacht racing. Kiteship kept making kites and now holds two Guinness World Records for the largest kites ever made.

These days, Culp and Jordan have set their sails for a greater good. "When we first started the business, fuel didn't cost enough and environmental awareness wasn't high enough to bring kites back to ships," says Culp. "Still, we believed that fuel would someday rise high enough to bring wind power back into shipping—and when it did, kites would be much more cost effective than sails." In preparation, Kiteship designed and prototyped a 13,000-square-foot kite, complete with launching control, recovery, and automated flying system. Ocean cargo and containerships 100 to 500 feet long would require a 15,000- to 50,000-square-foot kite (the size of a football field)—large, but certainly doable, says Dave. "We aim to show how kites can reduce fuel costs of large containerships by 5 to 15 percent." Dave says it would cost a couple million dollars to produce that kind of kite, but it could save $100,000 to $250,000 per trip, and pay for itself after ten to fifteen uses (at early 2008 prices). Using kites would also cut emissions by 15 percent. "Ships—already required to prevent sulfur emissions—must now use much more expensive fuel and install $5–$10 million scrubbers, neither of which ever earns the owner back a dime. When carbon trading comes into place, the savings will become even greater with kites."

Asked what the future holds for Kiteship, Dave says he looks forward to the day when he reads on a food label, "Delivered Under Sail."

Innovative Risk-taker 2: Kaiser Permanente—A Distribution Revolution

Dr. Preston Maring has two green thumbs. One he earned from his home garden and the other from his garden at work, which currently feeds thousands of people in six western states and the District of Columbia. In a time when food systems are consolidating and municipalities and organizations are struggling to bring fresher foods into cities and schools, Dr. Maring, an obstetrician/gynecologist at Kaiser Permanente medical hospitals for thirty-six years, seems to have figured it all out. "With a couple of thousand people and farmers looking to sell, you can set up a farmers market (typically in courtyards or sidewalks) or food-box system almost anywhere." Since 2003, Dr. Broccoli (a nickname given to him by his staff) has been testing his theory with grand success. In 2003, Maring started Kaiser's first organic farmers market in Oakland, California. Now Kaiser has thirty markets, and Kaiser's thirteen San Francisco Bay Area markets make up 10 percent of the 135 farmers markets in the region. Maring markets are popping up everywhere, including one in Watts, a tough, low-income South Central Los Angeles neighborhood. There is also one at the United Motors Auto Factory, near Maring's office. Most of the shoppers at this market are men who happily go home every Friday "with roses and big bags of fruits and veggies for their spouses."

But why stop there? The Kaiser distribution revolution extends far beyond the reach of a farmers market. At hospitals that can't have markets, Maring uses secret distribution weapon number two—the community-supported agriculture (CSA) box. Under this system, boxes of

Dr. Preston Maring poses with his favorite foods.

seasonal fruits and vegetables are dropped off directly to Kaiser staff who preorder on a weekly basis. Maring even sets up CSAs at businesses outside of Kaiser—such as at nearby Oracle Corporation—and helps them source food from local family farms.

When Maring shared the broader health and societal benefits of buying local and seasonal with Chris Mittelstaedt, the founder, CEO, and "Chief Banana" of The Fruit Guys (the fresh fruit vendor for Oracle), Mittelstaedt adjusted his business model to accommodate the cause. He now bundles produce from farmers growing as little as five to ten acres (too small to be their own CSA), and delivers a local Fruit Guys box to Oracle. "My goal," Maring says, "is to drive the local farmers nuts by creating as much business for them as possible. I've come to believe that what people eat makes more difference to their health than almost any other factor. Wherever I can help disparate groups come together so shoppers buy directly from farmers, it is better for everyone."

The biggest floret in Dr. Broccoli's cap, however, is an even greater distribution revolution. A couple of years ago, Maring noticed hospital dieticians writing menus for grapes and asparagus in the middle of winter, causing hospital buyers to purchase them from as far away as South Africa. "When I started talking to farmers about this, they told me asparagus sprouts only when the ground temperature hits 65 degrees F, around the end of February for central California. Kaiser's 6,000 daily patient meals at nineteen hospitals require 250 tons of fresh fruits and vegetables per year. Until we started asking questions, we never realized asparagus doesn't grow anywhere near us in October." Kaiser determined it bought 150 tons of fruits and veggies from California each year and the other 100 tons from farms all over the world. Partnering with the California-based Community Alliance of Family Farms (CAFF), the hospital and the nonprofit group embarked on a six-month study of the sixty-two most commonly eaten fruits and vegetables at Kaiser. Asking questions such as, "How many pounds per month do we use?" and "Where did this come from and how did it get here?" the group discovered that most of the produce was being grown unsustainably on agribusiness farms of 100,000 acres or more. They also discovered that by simply sourcing some of the produce locally, Kaiser Permanente could reduce their carbon footprint by 17 to 20 percent. And it was modest changes in the system that could produce such a large effect, not really big decisions or large sacrifices. For instance, Kaiser now buys California apples when they are in season and gets them elsewhere when they aren't and buys pineapple less often, not necessarily cutting it out all together.

From a food-service perspective, the idea of sourcing local products is a romantic thought at best. Chef, caterer, or commissary, we need dependable deliveries on a regular basis. No one has time in the food business to run to the nearest store when the local onions don't show up. The logistics involved in sourcing from small farms seem nearly impossible without an ever-present possibility of losing one's mind.

Thank goodness this was not the fate of Ralph Rico. Rico has managed Food Service Partners, Kaiser's Northern California food commissary, for more than thirty-one years and hasn't gone nuts yet, even when Preston Maring approached him in 2006 with "local" fever. Maring had secret ideas that would change around Rico's business model, just as it did for The Fruit Guys. Lucky for all of us, Ralph was up for the challenge. "It wasn't really a hard switch to make. The key is setting up your systems for the change. We had a six-month planning period before everything went into effect and it works really smoothly now. We still do menu planning a month ahead of time, but our menus are more seasonal."

When asked what tips or warnings he might have for other large food providers interested in sourcing local food, Dr. Maring answers reassuringly.

> There were certainly bureaucratic issues that needed to be worked out, but the system was basically supportive. People all along the way were willing to help, because by and large, the population cares about themselves and the planet. Not everybody, but most people do. Urban environments of 2,000 people with disposable incomes can easily support one of the two basic systems: a market or a food-box program. It doesn't take anyone special to start a program; it just

takes someone willing to make the phone calls and connections. Most communities have some sort of a farmers market association. Call them and ask if there are farmers looking to get into farmers markets. For a company with a couple of thousand people, bring in four or five vendors, not many more than that, and make sure they all sell something different. Our farmers offer a good product at a reasonable price, and in exchange they are guaranteed no competition.

Innovative Risk-taker 3:
Google–Café 150–International

John Dickman has been googling a lot lately. His mission? To find local farms and artisan producers who can supply quality food for all of Google's international offices. "We do breakfast, lunch, and dinner around the globe," says Dickman, global food service manager for Google.

The Google philosophy encourages employees to try new things and "think out of the box." This extends to Google chefs at main headquarters in Mountain View, California, who, in 2006, started sourcing more local food for Café 150, which today serves more than 400 meals daily. It is just one of the seventeen cafés on Google's main campus, but certainly the one that receives the most press. Café 150 prepares almost everything from scratch, using food that has been grown or produced within a 150-mile radius.

Café 150 puts summer on the shelf to enjoy at a later date.

When the café first opened, employees complained a lot. In November it was, "Where are the tomatoes for my sandwich?" In January they asked, "Where are the strawberries?" And all the time there was the question, "Why does this café never serve shrimp?" As time passed, however, employees got with the program. Coming to work with that "try new things" attitude certainly helped the transition, especially about tomatoes. Even in sunny California, tomatoes are a summer fruit that grow from approximately late April to the end of October. After that,

Apple versus Apple iPod

When we turn on the lights, the energy we are using most likely comes from a coal-fired or natural-gas power plant. Although renewable energy sources are sometimes used, especially hydroelectric power, the majority of electricity produced in the world comes from the burning of fossil fuels. If we understand that energy use, the burning of fossil fuels, and greenhouse-gas emissions are all intimately linked, then it makes sense that anything that requires energy, such as the production, transport, and disposal of a product, is also going to create some greenhouse-gas emissions.

To illustrate this, let's compare an apple, which one can enjoy eating, with an Apple iPod, which one can use to enjoy music. Both items are roughly the same size and weight, but the energy to produce and dispose of them is quite different.[2] We'll start with the apple. We now understand that there is energy associated with growing the tree, including regular irrigation, fertilization, and energy required to harvest and transport the apple to a nearby store or farmers market. There is also energy associated with disposing of the apple, unless you eat every last bite. Take all this energy and add it up, and we then have the energy footprint of an apple. Let's say the result is 1 unit of energy.[3]

We can then do a similar calculation with the iPod, although the calculation is quite a bit more involved. This analysis would start with the energy associated with the mining and production of various metals and minerals required for the electronics, including copper, aluminum, and silicon. Once all the different pieces have been made, we then need to consider the energy to assemble the product, package it, and transport it from its place of manufacture (China) to a store near you. In this analysis, we will neglect both the energy needed to power the product over its lifetime, which for these types of electrical devices is a small percentage of the total energy,[4] and the energy needed to properly dispose of the product.[5]

Based on results from previously published analyses of energy required for computer production, we estimate that the production of an iPod requires between

100 and 500 energy units[6] compared to the 1 unit for the apple. This is not so surprising because an iPod is quite a remarkable electronic achievement (although genetically so is the apple, and it tastes better, too). However, it may be surprising to know that, at least for computers and other electronic devices, the energy required to make the device is about four times

greater than the energy required to operate the device over a three-year lifetime.[7]

The value in such an experiment is to understand that whenever purchases are made, whether it is an apple or an Apple iPod, a bagel or a bicycle, energy was used to produce that product and, as a result, some greenhouse gases were emitted. We call this embodied energy, and, although hidden from sight, it's real and quantifiable.[8]

This also relates to the question of what an individual can do about greenhouse-gas emissions. Although most individuals understand that they have some control over their residential- and transportation-related emissions, most feel they have no control over or connection with the emissions from factories and industry. However, when we understand the idea of embodied energy, this perception changes as we consider that those factories are making products (food and consumer products) for us, the consumers. Estimates in the United States suggest that 80 percent of energy use and greenhouse-gas emissions are a result of consumer demand and the economic activities related to those demands.[9] Significant reduction in carbon emissions can also be achieved both by consuming less and by consuming smarter. Choose products that utilize ecologically intelligent design principles (e.g., "cradle to cradle"[10]), that require less energy to make, that last a long time, and that can be completely recycled and reused after use rather than thrown away.

Google chefs need to use something else for sandwiches. They discovered that grilled persimmons were a good substitute. At first, the employees were shocked and disapproving. By the end of the persimmon season, they were still complaining, except this time it was because they wanted the grilled persimmons back! (See chapter 5 for recipe.) Other winter-survival techniques include canning summer produce. Old-fashioned mason jars sit like trophies along metal shelves, fitting in well with the café décor. Sporting labels such as, "Sneaky Rikki's White Nectarines in Simple Syrup" and "Pickled Summer Squash," the jars are colorful representatives and an exciting reminder of what Café 150 is all about.

Café 150 works with approximately thirty farms, and the chefs post a map of California on their office wall to remind them of the boundaries of their endeavor. At first, some of Google's food distributors had serious reservations about participating, but slowly they are showing up for the challenge. Besides the executive and sous chefs, Café 150 has its own "chef forager," whose sole job is to go out and find food. If he discovers a farm not served by one of his distributors, he gets the distributor to add it to their list. Some foods are easy to find; others are nearly or absolutely impossible, such as shrimp. It took Café 150 eight months to find locally made vinegar—surprising, considering how close the Napa and Sonoma wine country is to the Mountain View headquarters.

Granted, the San Francisco Bay Area has got to be one of the easiest places in the world to conduct a project like this. Dublin, Ireland; Hyderabad, India; and Wroclaw, Poland—now those are different stories, and those are the next cities on Google's list. Dickman continued, "I don't know what to expect, but we are going to try."

> It is going to be difficult. The mindset in corporate food service is to menu plan around cycles and rotations. Buying food in larger lots allows for discounts, so most chefs create a "vanilla menu," which is exactly the same for every café they serve. Google realized we needed restaurant-style chefs who feel comfortable creating "daily specials" rather than a static menu. With the constant changing and variety of local food, every day is a daily special. It's a paradigm shift for some chefs, but once they get into it, they realize it isn't as hard as they thought. The main attribute needed for this style of cooking is flexibility.

Google's first international local café is in Dublin, Ireland. Though one might expect small countries to source their food locally, most use distribution systems similar to those in the United States. Dickman created a back-to-the-future game plan that begins at the nearest farmers market. Talking to the farmers, he learns about the chefs who buy from them. "The Dublin market is great; in the spring they have over thirty farms. I found a couple of chefs selling a product and asked them to cater for the office. Now they work full time for Google."

Innovative Risk-taker 4:
EcoSynergy: Roping in the Wild, Wild West of Carbon Emissions

CORN CHIPS— 12-OUNCE BAG	Grams of Carbon Dioxide Emitted Per Dollar Spent
Grain Farming	1229
Power Generation and Supply	447
Direct Emissions	307
Truck Transportation	229
Vegetable Farming	133
Nitrogenous Fertilizer Manufacturing	99
Oilseed Farming	98
Waste Management and Remediation Services	72
Oil and Gas Extraction	52
Paper and Paperboard Mills	45
Additional Sectors	671
TOTAL FOOTPRINT	3382 grams

Calling all you carbon counters—this one's for you. Do you have any idea what the carbon count is on that box of chocolate chip cookies or that bag of potato chips you're about to eat—and, hey, what about that beer? Time to go to EcoSynergy. These guys can calculate the carbon emitted from producing a peach all the way up to a Prius. Does your company need to go on a low-carb(on) diet? EcoSynergy is for you.

"EcoSynergy is the first company to market an enterprise application for measuring environmental impact, based on work by Carnegie Mellon University," says Aaron Dallek, chief technical officer and co-founder. "It is a peer-reviewed model that measures and calculates the direct and indirect (supply chain) emissions of consumer products, electronics, apparel, autos, and food. Businesses get a more comprehensive and realistic view of their climate impact and learn how they can reduce that impact in the future." Although EcoSynergy does use available data from existing full life-cycle analyses, their primary methods use the Consumer Price Index and national emissions data to establish relationships between emissions and cost. This allows them to help businesses identify where their carbon emissions come from (in their production stream) so that cost effective strategies for reducing emissions can be developed.

Aaron helped me understand how they determine emissions by breaking down a bag of corn chips (see accompanying Corn Chips table) into different emitting sectors. The *grain farming* emissions include the energy required to grow the corn (farm machinery, irrigation etc.), while the *power generation and supply* is primarily the electricity used in the chip-making factory. The *direct emissions* come from the smokestack in the factory, the *truck transportation* includes transport from farm to factory and factory to retail, while the *vegetable and oilseed farming* include the farming emissions associated with the various other ingredients in the chips. *Nitrogenous fertilizer manufacturing* is related to the energy required to make nitrogen fertilizers. *Waste management* is the emissions associated with any waste generated (mostly

BASIC STIR-FRY: 3 WAYS

RECIPES		g CO₂ eq	Assumptions
Base ingredients			
Soy sauce (estimated)	2 tablespoons (28.47 g)	84	$2.00 per pound, sauce = 673 g CO_2 eq/$
White wine	1 tablespoon (14.7 ml)	50	$6.73 per liter, wine = 523 g CO_2 eq/$
Lemon juice	1 tablespoon (14.23 g)	104	$1.16 per pound, fruit = 711 g CO_2 eq/$, 4 times the weight in lemons to get the juice
Vegetable oil	2 tablespoons (28.47 g)	47	$1.10 per pound, sauce = 673 g CO_2 eq/$
Peppers	1/3 pound (151.3 g)	688	$1.93 per pound, vegetables = 1070 g CO_2 eq/$
Broccoli	1/3 pound (151.3 g)	467	$1.31 per pound, vegetables = 1070 g CO_2 eq/$
Carrots	1/3 pound (151.3 g)	209	$0.58 per pound, vegetables = 1070 g CO_2 eq/$
	Total	1649	
RECIPE 1: VEGETABLE STIR-FRY			
Peppers	1/3 pound (151.3 g)	688	$1.93 per pound, vegetables = 1070 g CO_2 eq/$
Broccoli	1/3 pound (151.3 g)	467	$1.31 per pound, vegetables = 1070 g CO_2 eq/$
Carrots	1/3 pound (151.3 g)	209	$0.58 per pound, vegetables = 1070 g CO_2 eq/$
	Total for Recipe 1	3013	g CO_2 eq
RECIPE 2: BEEF STIR-FRY			
Beef (sirloin)	1 pound (454 g)	14043	$6.34 per pound, beef = 2214 g CO_2 eq/$
	Total for Recipe 2	15692	g CO_2 eq
RECIPE 3: CHICKEN STIR-FRY			
Chicken	1 pound (454 g)	3871	$3.30 per pound, chicken = 1173 g CO_2 eq/$
	Total for Recipe 3	5520	g CO_2 eq
NOTES AND ADDITIONAL ASSUMPTIONS			Emissions data is in grams of carbon dioxide equivalent per 2004 purchaser dollars. The price data came from the Consumer Price Index when available, otherwise EcoSynergy used the best available price information to make the above calculation. The price assumption is listed for each ingredient. The emissions per dollar come from the EcoSynergy data base.

Estimates computed by EcoSynergy of the carbon emissions (in grams of CO_2e) associated with growing and producing the ingredients used in the "Basic Stir Fry: 3 Ways" recipe at the end of this chapter. The three stir-fry recipes only differ by their inclusion of beef, chicken, or additional vegetables and yet the emissions for the beef stir-fry is more than 28 pounds (12.7 kg) more than the veggie stir-fry. For reference, a typical car emits about 28 pounds of carbon dioxide in thirty-five miles of driving.

methane emissions), and *oil and gas extraction* is the energy required to get the gas and oil used for farming and production. Finally, *paper and paperboard mills* is the energy associated with the packaging component of making a bag of chips.

EcoSynergy then calculated the emissions for our Basic Stir-fry, comparing a vegetable stir-fry to one with added chicken or beef (recipe at end of chapter). They also calculated the carbon emissions created by the production of this book. (See page 224 in the appendix.)

Innovative Risk-taker 5: StopWaste.Org and Norcal— The Smartest Guys in the Room

When describing the possibilities of organic agriculture on a larger scale, Professor William Horwath of University of California, Davis, said, "Organic agriculture would be the way to go, but we just don't have enough compost in the country to do it." Not enough compost? Compost = trash. How could we possibly not have enough trash when one-third of our household waste is food scraps? Ninety-six billion pounds of food scraps are created in the United States annually, and food leftovers make up the single largest component of the waste stream by weight.[11] Between 1990 and 2000, we got really good at recycling our yard waste, increasing the amount that was turned into compost by 46 percent. The problem is, we never put our banana peels in the bin with it. That's left us reincarnating only 2 to 3 percent of our uneaten food into something other than rotting, useless trash.[12] We are drowning in food scraps; so how can we get more compost?

Food trash is the largest producer of methane in landfills. Like the ponds at the Straus Family Creamery, landfills are anaerobic (without oxygen) environments, the perfect home for methane-producing bacteria. After 1991, all landfills in the United States were required to install methane-capture systems in their permanent storage cells, but because food breaks down in the first seven to twenty-one days of disposal, most of the methane is gone before the waste arrives at its permanent home.

Food waste is a misnomer—it is actually a powerful, untapped fuel source. Watermelons or wood, Mother Nature stores her sunlight and energy in many different types of packages. Some we burn in our cars and others in our stomachs. Calories are the measure of energy stored in food. When humans and animals eat, digestion pulls the stored energy out of the food and turns it into the fuel that powers our bodies. So just because we didn't finish last night's dinner or forgot about that fuzzy food in the back of the refrigerator doesn't mean it can't be used to power something else. Undigested food is a smart, valuable energy source. It is time to give our food scraps the afterlife they deserve.

"When I was a kid, the major concerns around food waste were parents making us feel guilty about the poor starving children overseas when we didn't finish our dinner," says Sally Brown, a research associate professor at the University of Washington. "Now we know that food waste creates harmful greenhouse gases and we have an obligation to identify any potential value within them, or at least minimize any potential harm. If we get the food scraps into a controlled environment, we can harvest them as an energy source."

Germany and Canada are way ahead of the United States in developing large-scale food waste collection systems, but there are a few areas in the United States where programs have begun, such as Seattle, San Diego, and some counties in Minnesota and the San Francisco Bay Area. One of the most successful and largest is in Alameda County, just east of San Francisco. StopWaste.Org has been promoting residential curbside collection of food scraps since 2001. More than 80 percent (approximately 311,000) of the single-family homes in the county have the food-scrap recycling program available to them with an average participation rate of 37 percent. Studies indicate that participating households are diverting about ten pounds of food scraps and food-soiled paper per week by putting it into a yard-waste cart for weekly pickup. The organic mix is transported to a composting facility where it is ground up, mixed, and turned into finished compost that is in demand by landscapers and local farms and wineries.

StopWaste.Org determined that if Alameda County residents and businesses composted all of their food waste (approximately 185,000 tons in 2006), they would save 155,000 tons of carbon dioxide equivalent. That's equal to 33,500 passenger cars not driven for one year, or 17.6 million gallons of gasoline. [13]

But the future of food waste doesn't stop there; plans include implementation of a two-step process for all food scraps, with methane being extracted first, followed by composting. Utilizing technologies and machinery designed in Germany, a new type of anaerobic digester is hopefully coming to a landfill near you. Unlike the wet digesters used on dairy farms that predominantly depend on a liquid fuel source, dry digesters can be used for more solid wastes such as food scraps and even chicken manure. Wastewater and sewage treatment plants have long been using digesters, but designated food-scrap digesters are new. Dry digesters use an acid hydrolysis fermentation process first, followed by an anaerobic process where the methane is harvested. Norcal of San Francisco is a leading waste-systems company working to put these digesters into service. "For every ton of food waste we create, we can save three tons of carbon equivalent," says Chris Choate, vice president of sustainability for Norcal. "We do this by first capturing the methane from a digester, then biodegrading the remains into compost, and finally reducing our transportation as waste facilities can be built closer to cities. Even after digesting the methane, the amount of compost we get in the end remains the same." The dry anaerobic digestion process takes about twenty-one days to complete. Once the leftover waste arrives at the compost facility, it biodegrades in only four weeks, almost half the time it takes compost that hasn't been digested first.

For right now, the glitch in the system is infrastructure. Our systems are set up to take things directly to the landfill, a much cheaper process. "Europe restructured its dumping fees in order to get organics out of landfill, and it works," says Dr. Brown. "Waste that costs thirty-seven dollars a ton to dump in the United States costs two hundred dollars in some places in Europe, so people are going the extra step to recycle it." In order to move the system along, Brown is working with the Environmental Credit Corporation of Pennsylvania. This company identifies projects that sequester carbon and assigns them a dollar value on the Chicago Climate Exchange, currently the only active exchange in the nation that trades carbon for dollars. Brown is working to list some of the digesters on the exchange.

Brown believes that in order to make this all work, the general public needs to know what small things they can do to help. She says most messages and solutions have been about extremes, but people need to hear about simple things they can do on a daily basis such as working with your municipality to support a local composting facility and curb pickup program. "It's little things like putting your orange peels in with your yard waste that can make an enormous difference."

Innovative Risk-taker 6: Coskata, Inc.–Turning Trash into Fuel

So what's for dinner over at Coskata, Inc., tonight? How about Corn Husk, Wheat Straw Succotash, with a Rice Bagasse chaser on the side? That's dinner every night (breakfast and lunch, too), depending, of course, on the daily "catch" for agricultural waste and other trash comprising that day's menu. The dining patrons at Coskata are a discerning group of "bugs" that love the leftovers from nearby Illinois corn, wheat, and soy farms. Daily specials are made from prime ingredients like food-packaging waste, animal fat, plastic bags, diapers, and even tires. When the meal is finished, all that is left is ethanol—produced for one dollar a gallon.

"We heat the waste material into a gas, breaking it down into carbon monoxide and hydrogen," says Wes Bolsen, chief marketing officer and vice president of business development for Coskata, Inc. Bolsen comes to the company from five generations of farming and ranching, and holds an MBA from Stanford. He says that the bugs inhale the gas as food and excrete ethanol.

These "bugs" are nongenetically modified anaerobic microorganisms that live in a bioreactor. The creation of ethanol involves a three-step process: 1) organic matter is turned into a gas; 2) microorganisms consume the gas as food to produce a mix of ethanol and water and; 3) the water is separated from the ethanol. Once the water is recycled back into the manufacturing process, all that is left is 99.7 percent pure ethanol, which can be blended to work in today's flex-fuel vehicles. Coskata gets over 100 gallons of ethanol per ton of dry carbonaceous feedstock.

"The process is environmentally superior to the production of conventional gasoline, because it can reduce carbon dioxide emissions by as much as 84 percent," continues Wes. The only waste created is a small amount of "slag" (1 to 2 percent), a "glassy-like" substance that can be made into construction materials such as bricks or roofing material. Additionally, the Coskata process uses less than one gallon of production water per gallon of ethanol produced, versus the three to five gallons used to produce ethanol from corn, or as much as seven gallons of water used to produce a gallon of cellulosic ethanol using enzymatic processes. Coskata achieves these efficiencies because the water is continually recycled throughout the system, and there is a high conversion rate of material into ethanol by design of the bioreactor, which is where the microorganisms congregate and feast on the input gas. Per Argonne National Laboratory, a nonprofit research laboratory operated by the U.S. Department of Energy, the Coskata process can yield up to a 7.7 net energy balance (the amount of fossil-fuel input required to produce a given amount of liquid-fuel energy output). This compares favorably to the much lower energy efficiency (between 0.9 and 1.3) of corn-based ethanol.[14]

Following nature's cues comes to mind. Just like the anaerobic and aerobic bugs in the soil that use each others' waste products to keep natural agricultural systems balanced and cyclical, humans are beginning to learn the vital lesson of putting our waste to work too.

The first Coskata plant is expected to open in late 2010. I hope the end of this story will show Norcal, StopWaste.Org, and Coskata, Inc., competing for your trash in the future and putting it to use in an environmentally circular and friendly way. It is the Full Circle Food Cycle coming home to roost. Won't that be an exciting world to live in?

Innovative Risk-taker 7: You

My former housemate, Paul Schmitt, is the only guy I ever met whose first action after getting out of bed involved compost. Paul wouldn't make a cup of coffee or check the morning news; he would rub his eyes, put on shoes, go outside, and start playing in the dirt. Paul did have great compost, but I never realized the extent of his craft until I moved to Portola Valley. As a goodbye gift, he gave me a bag of compost. I started pouring it over the plants at my new home, when all of a sudden, I stopped. What was coming out of the bag was astounding. I'd say something cliché like, "I've never seen anything like this before," but *seeing* it wasn't the thing; it was *sensing it.* Paul's soil was alive. Sure, it contained earthworms, but there was so much more than that. Most potting soils are light, dry, and powdery, yet this was moist and heavy, fluffy yet dense. It was a rich chocolate brown color, with a fresh, earthy smell that jumped right out of the bag. The whole thing appeared to pulsate. As I ran my fingers back and forth though the vibrant dirt I realized I shouldn't grow houseplants with this soil, I should grow food. It was a moment of soil-enlightenment. The dirty little love affair I had with soil while writing this book climaxed in a burst of poetic verse: "I want to eat soil, not oil!" Suddenly, I could see all things, like those billions of protozoa, bacteria, and arthropods said to be found in a tablespoon of healthy soil. At last, I got it; I "groked" soil. These were those things; I was holding them in my hands — invisible yet indispensable, so easy to pass over, so key to our health, so *high-vibe.* I peered into the soil, feeling like Horton the elephant in *Horton Hears a Who.* Even though I couldn't see them, I finally knew they were there, and I needed to do something to help.

Here's an innovative recipe for success: try making your own compost, at least until you convince your city or town to do it for you. Reincarnating food scraps is not difficult. The satisfaction derived is terrific, it's fun to do with the kids, the payback is worth it, and, in a crazy world, it just makes sense—a lot more sense than damning your carrot peels and onion skins to years of suspended animation in an anaerobic landfill. When I first started composting, I was scared I wouldn't do it right—but it's actually pretty easy. I started with a compost bin but didn't have yard debris to make it work that well. So I moved to a worm bin which is surprising to me because I am one of those women who doesn't "do worms," if you know what I mean. It's funny to admit that the first animal I have ever owned—for that matter, the first living thing I have ever taken care of, besides a few houseplants—is a worm. But we are all one big happy family now.

Paul's Compost Recipe [15]

Composting can be done anywhere, anytime. It's happening in the wild everywhere, always. Of course, you won't want to do this when it's unpleasant to work outside, but the compost will still work. Composting slows down in the winter and speeds up in the summer. It is common for people in snowy locales to build compost piles in the fall, when the trees contribute their leaves, and leave the pile alone until spring, when the air and soil are warm enough to work. In moderate and hot climates, you can build a compost pile any day of the year.

MATERIALS NEEDED:

- 1 compost bin with lid—minimum 3 feet tall and 3 feet square, a little bigger is better for the compost, but get one that will fit your yard.*
- 1 part kitchen scraps—this can be any food scraps from your kitchen (peels, teabags, coffee grounds, shells, leftovers), except meat and dairy.
- 1 part green garden scraps—any leaves, greens, or weeds from your yard. Don't add any weeds with seeds or runners if you don't want them coming back, especially Bermuda grass, crabgrass, ivy, mint, or anything that is taking over your yard already; also avoid adding thorns from roses, bougainvillea, etc.
- 1 part brown garden scraps—dead leaves, straw, any dead dried plants, even shredded newspaper
- Water—a couple of gallons to moisten the pile at the start.
- Pitchfork.

How Do I Take Care of It?

Start off your compost pile with a bunch of dry stuff, like several handfuls of straw and dry leaves. Then add any kitchen scraps you have on hand, and any trimmings, lawn clippings or weeds from your garden. Top off the kitchen scraps with more leaves, straw, or weeds. As you build your pile, make sure to keep the ratio approximately one part "green matter," food and plant debris such as grass clippings, (the nitrogen) to one part "brown matter," dry leaves and woody plants (the carbon). Every week, water your pile for a minute. If it's really dry, water more. If it is moist already, don't water. The goal is to keep the whole pile as moist as a wrung-out sponge. The outside of the pile will always be a little dry, use your pitchfork to check the inside and see if it is moist enough.

Every two weeks turn your pile with a pitchfork. The goal is to turn the pile inside out, flip the top to the bottom, and mix the whole pile up while you're doing so. While turning it, you'll start to see who's moved in, such as worms, sow bugs, soldier fly larvae, or other organisms doing their composting work. If you notice it's really dry, add water as you're turning it. If it's too wet or stinky or full of fruit flies, add more dry stuff (leaves, straw, shredded newspaper) to each layer as you turn.

* A bin is not necessary for composting, but a lot of people find it helpful for managing the pile. Because almost all bins are plastic, made from petroleum, look for bins made from recycled plastic or mostly recycled plastic. If you are a do-it-yourself type, make one out of scrap wood or wood pallets. The Smith & Hawken Biostack bin is one of the best plastic bins, especially for turning a pile and accessing it daily.

When Is It Ready?

After a few weeks, your pile is going to be a lot smaller than when you built it—that's good! It means the organisms are eating it up and turning it into finished compost. You'll have finished compost when the following happens:

- The pile is smaller than when it started.
- You can't recognize much of what you put in.
- It has no smell or smells like fresh earth.
- It looks darker, close to black (the color of humus).
- It is not hot anymore.

Once your pile is finished composting, remove anything that you don't want in your garden, like a piece of wood that didn't decompose yet, or a corn cob that still looks like a corn cob—put those things in your next compost pile. Take the finished compost and use it as a soil amendment in your garden.

Using Your Compost

Compost can be used the following ways:

- Dug into the soil and mixed with a fork as a soil amendment
- Applied on top of the soil as a side dressing for plants (like mulch)
- Used in potting soil mixes for potted plants and houseplants
- Poured as a liquid fertilizer when mixed with lots of water

Compost improves soil texture, increases the organic matter available in the soil, increases nutrient exchange between plant roots and the soil, and generally brightens up all plants. The unseen life (good bacteria and fungus) in the finished compost rejuvenates plants and soils that have seen better days.

Adding Biocompostables to Your Compost Pile

The use of biodegradable plates, cups, and utensils as alternatives to plastic and polystyrene (Styrofoam) is on the rise. Made from sugarcane fiber, potato or corn starches, the tableware and eating utensils can be composted after use, instead of being thrown into landfill. When composting these products, keep in mind that they can take anywhere from a month to a year to fully degrade. However, it's worth the wait, as it's such a good feeling to compost your plate instead of throwing it into the trash! And the compost will do wonders for your garden.

Our favorite distributor of compostable tableware is a non-profit organization, World Centric, www.worldcentric.org. Check out their Web site to get a flavor for the types of products available today. You'll also get ideas on how to turn your next outdoor function into a compost-generating opportunity.

Book 'n' Cook Club Ideas

On a Budget?

- Buy seasonal fruits and vegetables found at the local farmers market. They often are the most affordable and are always better tasting.
- Reduce meat consumption and use of packaged foods. Eat more whole foods.
- Reduce your food waste— it's free! Eat what you buy and start a compost pile to dispose of the waste.

Recipes

Basic Stir-Fry: 3 Ways

Wind-Powered Zucchini Boats with Cheddar

Main Dish Salad

Roasted Nut and Dried Fruit Mix

Sesame Date Bars

Field Trips

Take a tour of a municipal organic composting facility. Inquire how to start food-scrap composting in your area.

Small Things Matter

- Set up your own "Café 150" for a week or more. Eat only food that comes from within a 150-mile radius of your hometown.
- Start a compost pile or worm bin.
- Search the Web for indoor food scrap kitchen composters.
- Go "carbon neutral" at business conferences and school events. See a list of ways to do it at www.globalwarmingdiet.org.
- Research and support regional carbon offset providers in your area as well as the Chicago Climate Exchange (the first U.S. voluntary pilot program for trading greenhouse gases).
- Start a farmers market at your workplace. Download Dr. Maring's Farmers Market Resource Guide. It describes how the Kaiser markets were started and includes important information on legal issues and permits. http://www.permanente.net/homepage/Kaiser/pdf/46370.pdf.

Recipes

Basic Stir-Fry: 3 Ways

This is a basic but tasty stir-fry recipe. The carbon emissions of this recipe are on page 127.

SERVES 4

Stir-fry Sauce

1 cup vegetable stock

2 tablespoons soy sauce

1 tablespoon dry white wine

1 tablespoon freshly squeezed lemon juice

2 tablespoons cornstarch

1 pound chicken, beef, or vegetables cut into 1-inch pieces

2 tablespoons olive oil, divided

1 pound sliced mixed vegetables (peppers, broccoli, carrots), about 2 cups

Combine first five ingredients and set aside.

If using meat, preheat wok or sauté pan on medium-high heat. Add 1 tablespoon oil and chicken or beef. Stir-fry until cooked through, about 5 minutes. Remove from pan.

Add another tablespoon oil and sliced vegetables and stir-fry, about 5 minutes. While cooking, add 1 tablespoon cold water as needed to "force-steam" vegetables. When vegetable are crisp tender, add stir-fried chicken or beef. Whisk Stir-fry Sauce, making sure cornstarch is mixed in. Add sauce to wok. Cook until thickened.

Wind-Powered Zucchini Boats with Cheddar

Get the kids involved in the solution! Zucchinis are easy to grow and kids can help plant and harvest them as well as make the carrot sails. Broil zucchini to bring out the "sweetness," exactly what kids love.

SERVES 2–4

1 carrot, peeled

2 small zucchini

$1/2$ teaspoon olive oil

Salt

$1/2$ cup grated local cheddar cheese

2 tablespoons freshly grated Sonoma Dry Jack cheese (substitute Parmigiano-Reggiano)

Carrot Sails

Using a hand peeler, peel 8 long carrot slices, pushing down on the peeler to get a wide slice. Fold back and forth accordion-style. Holding the sail lengthwise, secure by inserting a toothpick at the top and the bottom, and then spread out the sail. Set aside.

Wash zucchinis and trim off the top. Cut in half lengthwise. Using a melon baller, scoop a small trough out of the middle of each zucchini. Compost the pulp or save for soup stock. Pour oil into your hands and rub it onto the zucchinis, coating well. Place in a baking dish and sprinkle with salt. Broil for 5 minutes or until lightly browned. Remove from oven. Place cheddar cheese into the troughs and sprinkle with Dry Jack. Put back under the broiler for 1–2 minutes, until cheese is lightly browned, hot, and bubbly. Insert 2 sails for each boat.

Main Dish Salad

"Cool" eating habits focus more on vegetables and less on animal protein. Use animal products to season and enhance vegetables and grains, not as a main dish. Salads give eaters a real shot at reaching the recommended 5 to 9 servings of vegetables a day. Eat a main dish salad for lunch as often as possible. Eat at your desk at work and spend your lunch hour going for a walk instead of looking for food. Ingredient options are endless; keep your kitchen stocked and it never gets boring. Make your salad after the previous night's dinner when it's easier to incorporate dinner leftovers like extra roasted or grilled vegetables and whole grains.

Tips and Tricks for Success

1. PREP THE BASICS. Set your refrigerator up at the beginning of the week to be a "mini salad bar."

• Greens: Keep washed greens on hand or use bagged lettuce (reduce energy used in processing by buying bulk spring mix).

• Protein: Stock ready-to-go baked tofu, hard-boiled eggs, cubed or sliced meats, beans, edamame, Turkey Mole Gomashio (see chapter 10).

2. KEEP IT SMALL. Cut your vegetables into small pieces. Anytime I have a salad of small and grated vegetables along with bigger pieces of broccoli and baby carrots, I always leave the bigger vegetables to the end. Sometimes I don't even eat them. When veggies are small I eat everything! Some eaters prefer larger pieces, however, so discover the cut you prefer.

3. USE EASY VEGGIES. Easy veggies don't take much prep. Radishes, sprouts, snow peas, corn, and peas go directly into your salad from the refrigerator. Beets, carrots, daikon radish, and zucchini can be grated right into a salad. Cucumber and cabbage can be cut with a paring knife and no cutting board, and green onions and celery can be chopped in with kitchen shears.

4. TOP IT OFF WITH WHOLE GRAINS. Sprinkle in leftover grains from dinner.

5. STYLE IT YOUR WAY. Build your salad to fit your preferences. I always like something pickled in mine (pickled products are healing foods in macrobiotics that help with digestion). Make it appeal to *all* your taste buds, a goal of commercial snacks foods. Many snack foods are designed to overstimulate our taste buds so that we eat more. Add sweet to your salad (fresh or dried fruit), as well as salty/sour (cheeses, pickled products, vinegar, gomashio, salted nuts), pungent (pepper flakes, hot sauce, black pepper, hot pepper oil), and umami (meats, tofu with soy sauce, roasted peppers, mushrooms). Here are a few options that keep easily in refrigerator or pantry:

Artichoke hearts
Beans
Canned beets
Capers
Cheeses
Croutons
Fruits
Green peppercorns
Hearts of palm
Leftover pasta (whole grain is best)
Nuts and seeds
Olives
Pepperocinis
Pickled mushrooms
Roasted red peppers
Sauerkraut
Sliced nori sea vegetable
Sun-dried tomatoes

6. PLAN YOUR DRESSINGS: I keep a vinaigrette that doesn't need refrigeration in my desk drawer at work. Don't like fat-free dressings? Use a smaller amount of "the real stuff" along with a squeeze of lemon/lime or a drizzle of your favorite vinegar. Reduce the amount of fat eaten by dipping your fork into the dressing first and then into your salad.

7. GARNISH YOUR SALAD WITH THE CONDIMENT PLATE: The Condiment Plate is "salt and pepper with a college education," and it's a great addition to main dish salads. Learn about it in chapter 10.

Roasted Nut and Dried Fruit Mix

Processed food can take more energy to make than what it gives us in return. Try this whole-foods mix as an answer to the afternoon work blues or a snack for the kids. Keep a sandwich bag in your glove compartment, pannier, or backpack and refill as needed; don't throw out the bag each time. If you have never roasted your own nuts, you are in for a treat. Look for locally grown and/or dried nuts and fruits at the farmers market.

MAKES 3 CUPS

1 cup whole almonds
$^1/_2$ cup walnuts
$^1/_2$ cup pecans
2 teaspoons soy sauce
1 cup dried fruit of choice (raisins, craisins, apricots, strawberries, cherries, dates, plums, persimmons, etc.)

Preheat the oven to 350 F. Place almonds on one baking sheet and walnuts and pecans on another. Roast walnuts/pecans about 8–10 minutes and almonds 10–12 minutes, until lightly browned and fragrant. Remove the walnuts and pecans and set aside. Sprinkle the almonds with the soy sauce; stir to coat. Return to the oven and bake for one minute. Remove and let cool. Combine with dried fruit. Place in little bags for an on-the-go snack.

CHEF TIP:
Why Am I Buying Unripe Fruit?

In order to survive their 1,600- to 2,500-mile road trip, many commercial fruits and vegetables are picked far earlier than one might expect. Harvesting early doesn't allow the natural sugars and flavors to fully develop and the produce to ripen. Like a cake removed from the oven too early, or a wine drunk before its time, unripe produce can't compete. After picking, it is stored in warehouses with controlled temperatures and climates, allowing distributors to ripen them at whatever pace they choose. Fruits and vegetables ripened indoors will never be as flavorful as fruit and vegetables ripened outdoors in a natural environment. Insist on using seasonal produce from local farms for more satisfying meals filled with a natural complexity of flavors.

Sesame Date Bars

This whole-foods, wheat-free snack is great for work or for the kids. Pine nuts used to be a common crop in the United States, until trees were plowed down to grow corn for cow feed. Look for local pine nuts at farmers markets or substitute with fair-trade cashews from small international farms.

MAKES 20 TO 25 SQUARES

1 cup dates, pits removed
$1/4$ cup water
1 (3.5-ounce) fair-trade, organic chocolate bar (optional)
$1/2$ cup pine nuts or cashews
2 tablespoons orange juice
2 tablespoons lemon juice
$1/2$ cup sesame seeds, toasted
$1/2$ cup pecans, lightly toasted and coarsely chopped
$3/4$ cup ground almond meal (See Note)

Preheat oven to 300 degrees F. In a small pot, combine dates and water. Bring to boil, cover, and then turn off heat and let dates soften for at least 5 minutes. Using a knife and cutting board, shave off shards of the chocolate bar until you have 3 tablespoons. Set aside. Combine pine nuts, orange juice, and lemon juice in food processor and blend until well combined. Transfer to a medium-size bowl along with the sesame seeds, pecans, almond meal, softened dates, and their soaking water. Mix with your hands, making sure the dates are broken up and well incorporated. Add shaved chocolate and mix. Mold into 1-inch squares. Bake on ungreased baking sheet for 20 minutes. Let cool on the baking pan.

Variation: Chill bars for a really cool cuisine snack.

NOTE: Almond meal is finely ground almonds found in natural foods and specialty grocery stores.

PART THREE

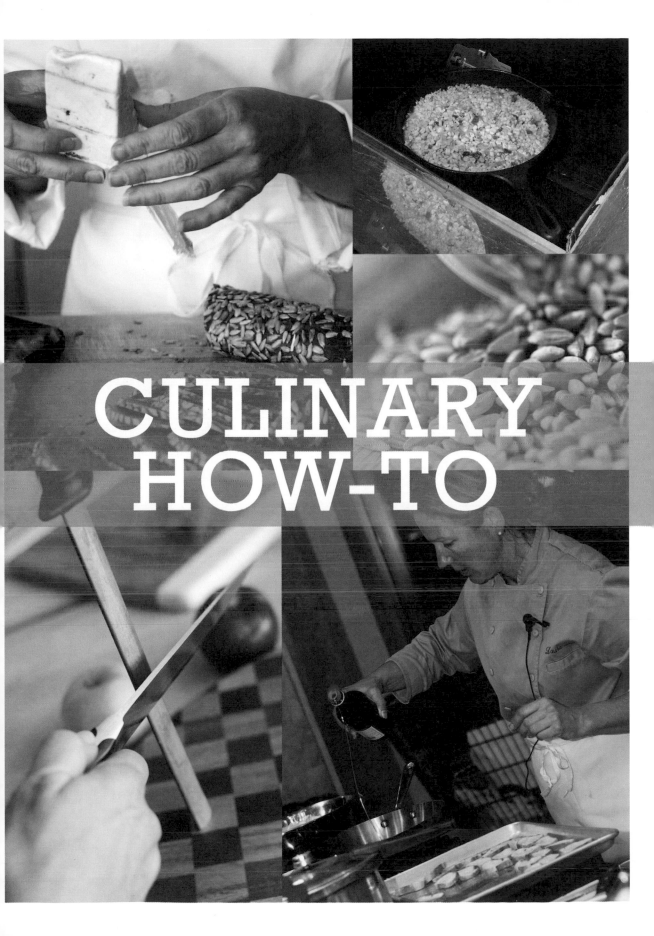

CULINARY HOW-TO

8

America's Changing Palate

Current food trends are extremely favorable for a transition from a global-warming diet to a cool cuisine. The time is now! America's palate is changing, branching out into an exploration of new tastes. We're ready to adventure beyond meat, potatoes, and butter toward higher-flavor, healthier meals. Trends show we want better food and bolder flavors topped with health and variety. We just need to learn how to cook it.

The problem is, few of us have time to cook, and many of us don't know much about doing it. Most Americans still eat dinner at home, but less that one-third of us make our meals from scratch. Instead, we nosh on highly processed take-out foods. We still want real home-cooked meals—we just don't know how to fit cooking into our busy schedules.

Strange, isn't it? We eat three times a day (at least) and yet few of us know how to do it. I'll bet if you played golf three times a day you'd join a club, take private lessons, get periodicals in the mail, and have all the best equipment. So where has the process of cooking and eating escaped us? Those of us who went to elementary school before the 1980s may have learned a few things from the home economics teacher, but chances are good she didn't take many cooking classes either. Some of us learned from our parents, but that practice is not as common as one may think and is limited to what our parents actually knew about the craft. Less than a fourth of my students have ever taken a prior cooking class, which is a shame because cooking is like any other art form—you can do it on your own, but you'll benefit with a bit of training.

Actually, cooking is all about tips, and the more you know, the tastier, faster, more creative and more satisfying your food and cooking will be. The average female spends approximately two hours a day, or 730 hours a year on food shopping, preparation, and eating and the average male spends about 520 hours a year.[1] Divide by 40 and you get two to four months per year of full-time work in the food industry. Our lack of training in the kitchen could be compared to working a new office job with high expectations, no instruction, and four full months devoted solely to figuring out how to use the copier—only worse. At the end of the day, no one at the company expects to chew and swallow your work.

With a little more knowledge of new foods and the cooking techniques that enhance them, we can easily and quickly make foods with bolder flavor and eat a healthy cool cuisine. For example, combine meat, vegetables, and whole grains with easy-to-use ethnic and specialty sauces such as barbecue-lime (see BBQ'ed Tofu with Lime in chapter 5), orange-chipotle-maple (see International Stir-Fry Sauce at the end of this chapter), or lemon-soy (see Green Tea Stir-Fry in chapter 10), and use the meat as a seasoning agent instead of the main part of the dish. Choose "baseline" foods (staples such as meat, grains, produce, milk, and water) that are regionally grown and produced, and season quickly with ethnic sauces and flavor agents such as the Condiment Plate on pages 184 and 185, allowing your taste buds to go traveling while your food stays local.

Cooking like this doesn't need to take more time. It might take a little more money, however, when using higher-quality ingredients, but that's an idea that also might serve us well (as touched upon in chapter 1). Certainly our "pile it high and sell it cheap" food system, as described by rock-star farmer Joel Salatin, isn't satisfying us. Many of us can eat as much as we want. So why is it never enough?

> Cooking is all about tips, and the more you know, the tastier, faster, more creative, and more satisfying your food and cooking will be.

Over the years I have noticed a trend. There are always more leftovers at a catered dinner party than I expect (in spite of good reviews about the food). I've been catering for many years so a lack of portioning experience or bad management can't be the explanation. I've actually started to wonder whether guests are feeding on more than just the food; maybe the people, the excitement and the energy add to their feeling of "fullness"? This has left me questioning the whole idea behind satisfaction. If satisfaction were only about quantity, surely we would have had our fill by now. What if quality plays a more important role than we think?

If satisfaction also involves quality, we would need to learn how to feed our bodies, minds, and souls. Our stomachs

Who Is Emitting?

Enough about international cuisine, which countries are responsible for most of the world's greenhouse-gas emissions? In 2004, the United States had the largest emissions, followed by China and the European Union.[2] Recent estimates suggest that China may have overtaken the United States as the largest greenhouse-gas emitter in the world,[3] which is remarkable because in 1990, China's total emissions were less than half those of the United States. It should be noted that a large percentage of China's manufacturing today is for export to the United States and Europe, and without the demand for those goods, China's emissions (and economy) would be much less.

Insight into the relationship between lifestyle and carbon emissions can be found by looking at per capita CO_2 emissions, as shown in Figure 8. Of the top emitting countries, the United States has the largest per capita CO_2 emissions, at more than twenty tons per year, with Canada and Australia at roughly similar levels. Other developed countries in Europe (such as the United Kingdom, Germany, and France) have about half the total emissions per capita. China's per capita emissions, although rising, are still only about four tons, about five times less than the average American. Overall, these results imply that North Americans and Australians are particularly heavy greenhouse-gas emitters (compared with Europeans) and suggest that significant reductions could be made without major changes to standard of living.

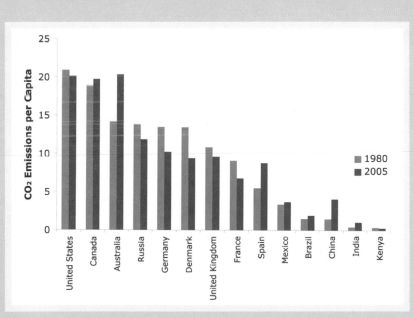

Figure 8. Per capita annual CO_2 emissions in tons per year for a variety of developed and developing countries in 1980 (orange) and 2005 (blue) due to consumption of fossil fuels (petroleum, natural gas, and coal). Data is from the U.S. Dept. of Energy, Energy Information Administration, *International Energy Annual, 2005*.

can be filled with food, but family, friends, and feelings feed our heads and our hearts. Food is just the vehicle that brings us together so we can feed the other parts of ourselves with conversation and connection—the ways that we humans express our "human-ness." When cooking together and sharing food, our meals are prepared with hands of loving grace rather than with hands of indifference. If the energy of the cook goes into the food and the energy of the food goes into the cook, maybe this is what makes all the difference?

Now extend those connections out to the larger community. Get to know and support the local farmers and the people who produce your food and eating becomes a largely connected and deeply satisfying experience. A piece of cheese is just a piece of cheese until you learn the story behind it. After meeting the producers and maybe visiting the farm, that cheese becomes richer. When we eat it, we may think about the farm and how the crops and the cows are doing that day. Experiencing a connection like this makes food more than just food; it becomes a meaningful relationship. By nourishing that relationship, we nourish our entire being and complete the circle of satisfaction. As you learn more about cooking and eating, be open to these deeper lessons. A society that values food only by price will starve. It's the broader connections that we truly hunger for.

These final three chapters offer a hands-on learning opportunity on how America's changing palate and a Cool Cuisine can easily work for you. Whether it's your first "cooking class" or whether you have taken many, please don't let it be your last, because cooking *is* all about tips, and the more you know the tastier, faster, more creative and more satisfying your food and cooking will be.

Recipes

International Stir-Fry Sauce—Orange-Maple-Chipotle

This sauce really lets your taste buds go traveling. Stir-fry it into prepared pasta, vegetables, or meats, or just pour the heated sauce over a bowl of whole grains.

SERVES 4

9 tablespoons vegetable or chicken stock

6 tablespoons orange juice

6 tablespoons tamari

6 tablespoons olive oil

4 teaspoons lime juice

2 1/2 tablespoons maple syrup

1 tablespoon ground coriander

1 tablespoon ground cumin

3 canned chipotle peppers, chopped

4 cloves garlic, finely minced

1/4 cup chopped basil

5 teaspoons arrowroot (or cornstarch)

Chopped basil for garnish

4 ounces goat cheese (optional)

Combine first 12 ingredients (stock through arrowroot). Heat a wok or skillet over medium heat. Whisk the sauce right before adding to the pan, making sure the arrowroot is well dissolved. Pour sauce into the pan and cook until thickened. Pour over grains, vegetables, and meats or stir-fry into pasta. Top with chopped basil and crumbled goat cheese.

Tahini Carrot Daikon Canapé with Black Olive

When all the foods at a party are high in cheese and animal fats, we often leave feeling "not-that-great." Make sure your next party has vegan and raw options, not just for philosophical or environmental reasons, but to create the proper food balance and allow your guests to leave feeling great. This raw appetizer is an explosion of international flavors, requiring no energy to cook it.

MAKES 25 APPETIZERS

1 daikon radish, at least 9 inches long and about 1 inch in diameter (see Note)
$1/4$ cup tahini
1 tablespoon brown rice miso
$1/2$ carrot, peeled, grated, and chopped finely
$1/2$ teaspoon brown rice vinegar
$1/2$ teaspoon brown rice syrup (available in natural foods stores)
$3/4$ teaspoon hot chili pepper sauce (like Sriracha)
1 teaspoon toasted sesame seeds
Cilantro leaves for garnish
15 high-quality black olives, pits removed, quartered

Peel the daikon or scrub with a vegetable brush. Slice into $1/8$-inch rounds. Set aside.

In a small bowl, combine the next 7 ingredients (tahini through sesame seeds). Mix well. Mound $1/2$ teaspoon of the mixture onto each daikon slice. Top with a cilantro leaf and an olive sliver.

NOTE: Daikon radish is a long, white radish that looks similar to a carrot. Although becoming more readily available in grocery stores, it is best to buy them at farmers markets, natural food stores, or Asian grocery stores, where turnover is higher and freshness is more likely.

9

Eat More Vegetables!

If an apple a day keeps the doctor away, think what an added cup of sautéed greens or grilled broccoli might do for you. Vegetables and fruits offer protection from cancer and heart disease, strengthen our digestive and immune systems, and make us feel good. Call it "produce-power." Filled with vitamins, minerals, antioxidants, and phytochemicals, vegetables are a ticket to good health—for ourselves and the planet.

We've been hearing how healthy vegetables are for years, so how come we don't eat more of them? More than three-quarters of us say it's because we "can't get them in fast-food places," or we "can't get them at work." Many eaters just don't like vegetables, which may not be the vegetables' fault. Whether you shop in Portland, Maine, or Portland, Oregon, industrial produce is disappointingly the same: perfect looks, no flavor. Grocery-store red bell peppers are a good example of this—what I call "fertilizer-force-fed-phony food." They're like balloons on steroids, filled with water and red food coloring. No wonder we don't like them.

Another reason we may not eat more vegetables is because we don't cook them correctly. Boil or steam an already waterlogged vegetable and what are you left with? An even more waterlogged vegetable. Boiling and steaming vegetables are completely opposite to another very important cooking tip: *Keep water as far away from vegetables as possible.*

This might be hard to hear, but vegetables and water only go so far together. The ill-fit combination reminds me of a Thanksgiving dinner at one of those "old ex-boyfriend's" parents' home. Twelve of us were gathered around the table, and the room was filled with wonderful smells wafting from the kitchen. Excitement grew as the cooks delicately placed the old-fashioned serving platters around the table, overflowing with holiday favorites. Platter after platter came out of the kitchen until there was no more room on the table, except right in front of me. The final dish was presented, like an exclamation point after a well-spoken speech. I looked down with anticipation and saw a really big bowl of very well-boiled broccoli with a pat of butter on top. Limp vegetables—the exclamation point? I acknowledged the dish, looked out to the crowd, and forced a ravenous smile. The hosts' consideration of my dietary choices did not go unnoticed, but this "vegetarian option" just didn't compete. How did the accepted exclamation point on an amazing holiday smorgasbord ever become a bowl of soggy vegetables?

Keep water as far away from vegetables as possible.

It's really not that surprising; soggy vegetables are everywhere. They've been to a lot of holiday parties I've attended, as well as potlucks and restaurants, too. Most of us boil or steam our vegetables; who's ever told us to do it differently? I should be grateful my herbivorian preferences were honored at that Thanksgiving dinner. What did I want after all? At least it wasn't meat.

What I wanted then is what I want now—a vegetable with integrity, one that can hold its floret up high. I want vegetables with deep flavor and highlighted natural sugars. And so, dear reader, do you. While dry farming (no watering, just rainfall) intensifies the flavor of produce so, too, can cooking in little to no water. Want to eat more vegetables? Learn the cooking techniques that intensify their sugars and flavor.

Vegetables—Just Do It

Cooking is a lot like exercise—just do it. My far-from-altruistic exercise philosophy applies well to cooking. I complain that I have to exercise, and I complain if I don't exercise. But if I don't exercise, I don't feel good, and then I complain again. If I do exercise, I feel great and complain only once. Will power is not the motivating factor here; it's the elimination of discomfort! Why not just exercise and cut my losses?

Healthful cooking habits are no different. Commit to cooking vegetables at least a few times a week. Restaurants and takeout delis don't sell the high-vibe vegetable dishes you can make using produce from local farms and farmers markets. So buy the vegetables fresh and cook them at home. Invest in yourself.

Bringing Out the Sweetness in Vegetables

Eaters are naturally attracted to sweetness. Food historians say that detecting sweetness was how early eaters figured out what was safe to eat. It's an instinctual preference especially seen in children (eaters still learning to eat). All vegetables have a natural sweetness, and our job as cooks is to find it. For example, let's consider the lowly onion. Biting a raw onion makes you wince. But sliced and sautéed, that onion becomes sweet; and the longer it cooks, the sweeter it becomes. Why? Because the high, dry heat caramelizes or "burns" the sugars; it brings out the sweetness and intensifies the flavor, exactly what eaters like! Caramelization begins at 330 degrees F (166 degrees C) and only involves sugar molecules. It does not create the same level of complexity that happens during the Maillard Reaction (a flavor-enhancing meat-cooking technique described in chapter 11), which begins at 250 degrees F (121 degrees C). Still, caramelization does a great job making a vegetable "meatier." Vegetables are caramelized when we sauté, roast, and grill them.

Vegetable-Cooking Techniques

Sautéing

Sautéing quickly cooks vegetables, protein, and sauce in a hot, relatively dry pan. Because little water is added, vegetables experience the high, dry heat needed to enhance their sugars. Though roasting and grilling are best for achieving this sugar-enhancing effect, sautéing runs a close second. It is a common cooking method, but a few tips can teach you how to do it even better. Learn them in chapter 10.

CHEF TIP:

Cooking Vegetables

- *Keep water as far away from vegetables as possible.*
- *Use a high, dry heat to heighten vegetable sugars.*
- *Add salt to caramelized onions only after the onions are cooked (salt brings out the onion juice and slows caramelization).*
- *Use waterless cooking techniques to preserve more vegetable nutrients.*

Roasting

Roasting is one of the easiest, tastiest ways to cook vegetables. You can roast any vegetable with the technique described in the recipes at the end of the chapter. Roasting allows for the variability and flexibility required when cooking seasonally. No matter what produce is available— at the farmers market, in the grocery store, or in your CSA box—you can roast it. This means your shopping list can read "the freshest vegetables" instead of "the limp-looking vegetables that fit my recipe." Roasted vegetables are easy to cut (1- to 2-inch chunks), making preparation a breeze. Soon the vegetables are in the oven, and you are on to another task.

Grilling

Cooking and eating are primal activities made possible, in part, by fire. Grilling connects us to our ancestors and an ancient way of cooking. The word "grilling" first appeared in Virginia in the 1700s when plantation slaves earned the title of "pit master" by refining the craft. In the

CHEF TIP:
Roasting Vegetables
- *Pair and cook vegetables as Mother Nature teaches (hard with the hard, soft with soft).*
- *Chop vegetables into the same size pieces to ensure even cooking.*
- *Pour a little oil directly into your hands and lightly rub the vegetables to coat and then sprinkle with salt. Do this directly on the baking sheet for easy cleanup.*
- *Freshness is the key to enjoying root vegetables such as turnips, rutabagas, and parsnips. Since turnover is lower than other vegetables, give them a "squeeze" test before buying. Fresh vegetables feel firm, with no give or "squeezability."*

Energy Efficiency of Foods

We understand that food contains energy as described by the number of Calories.[1] It also takes energy to make food and that energy can be estimated. The energy efficiency of a food item can then be defined as the total amount of energy required to produce the food divided by the total amount of energy the food contains.[2] Published estimates show that vegetables and grains such as potatoes, rice, and corn have an energy intensity of about 1.2 to 2.5, whereas the energy intensity of meats such as chicken, pork, and beef ranges from 16 to 68.[3] So, in general, it takes significantly more energy to make food from animal products than it does to grow vegetables.

In terms of understanding the impact of food on climate, we note that, in addition to energy, the production of animal-based foods generates significant emissions of methane, an important greenhouse gas. So when we compare different food items, the carbon intensity, or the carbon emissions (associated both with the energy to grow the food and any animal-related emissions) per 100 Calories of food item, is a more accurate method for measuring the impact of food on climate.[4]

Let's compare the carbon intensity of different foods using Figure 9.[5] For example, whereas 100 Calories of corn emits 11 grams (0.024 pounds) of carbon dioxide, 100 Calories of pork emits 308 grams (0.7 pounds). Red meats (beef, pork, and lamb) have the largest carbon intensity; chicken and dairy are more efficient.[6] The carbon intensity of fish products varies; farmed salmon has about the same as most red meat; farmed shrimp has a higher carbon intensity (more than 400 grams (0.9 pounds) CO_2/100 Calories)[7], and other fish, such as herring, have a lower carbon intensity (about 25 grams (0.025 pounds) CO_2/100 Calories). Vegetables and fruits, in comparison, generally have the lowest carbon intensity.

Although issues relating to how products are farmed, processed, and packaged affect these estimates, generally speaking, the carbon intensity of animal products is much higher than that of vegetable products. We also note that these estimates come from analyses of commercial farms, and that organic farms may use less energy and thus produce fewer emissions in growing these foods.[8]

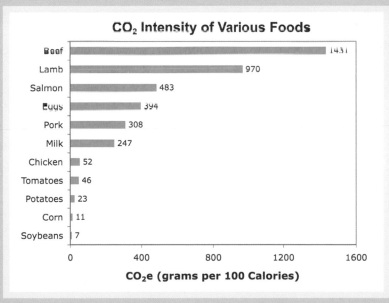

CO₂ Intensity of Various Foods

Food	CO_2e (grams per 100 Calories)
Beef	1431
Lamb	970
Salmon	483
Eggs	394
Pork	308
Milk	247
Chicken	52
Tomatoes	46
Potatoes	23
Corn	11
Soybeans	7

CO_2e (grams per 100 Calories)

Figure 9. Estimates of the carbon dioxide intensity of various food products given in grams of CO₂e per 100 Calories. Calculation includes emissions of methane and nitrous oxide. For example, 100 Calories of milk produces 247 grams of CO₂e, while 100 Calories of potatoes produces 23 grams of CO₂e.

1920s, Henry Ford invented the charcoal briquette from leftover wood scraps and sawdust from his car factory. E. G. Kingsford (a former Ford dealer) bought Henry Ford's briquette invention and started the first large-scale commercial charcoal business, still in operation today. Grills are owned by 81 percent of all households in the United States.[9]

Jamais Cascio, of Open the Future, estimates that grilling one cheeseburger creates an average of 10.7 pounds (4.85 kg) of carbon emissions. This includes the feed to grow the cattle for the meat and the cows for the cheese; the energy for growing produce such as wheat and tomatoes; the energy for processing, storing, and transporting the components, including the bun and the pickles; the energy for cooking the burger; and the methane produced by the cow. If everyone in the United States ate just one cheeseburger a week, Cascio determined that the carbon emissions would be equivalent to the emissions generated by driving 6.5 million SUVs over a year.[10] For the lowest-carbon way to grill, compare the emissions from the top three fuel sources: charcoal briquettes, propane gas, and natural gas (see chart.)

FUEL SOURCE	POUNDS CO_2 EMITTED PER HOUR
Charcoal briquettes made from wood	6.3
Propane Gas	4.2
Natural Gas	3.5

Carbon emissions associated with one hour grilling using either wood-based charcoal briquettes, a propane or a natural gas stove. (NOTE: These estimates were made by EcoSynergy following the procedures outlined in chapter 7.)

Want to really reduce the carb(on)s? Skip the meat and grill vegetables instead. People enjoy grilled vegetables because the high, dry heat perfectly heightens the sugars and makes vegetables more interesting. Grilling is one of the best ways to cook a vegetable, and it makes

CHEF TIP:
Grilling Vegetables
- *Coat vegetables lightly with oil, to prevent them from drying out on the grill.*
- *Using wooden skewers? Soak them in water for at least twenty minutes to prevent burning.*
- *Marinate vegetables for a half-hour or less; after that, the vinegar starts to "cook" them.*
- *People tend to undercook grilled vegetables. Look for bumpy grill ridges before you flip them.*
- *Use tongs to turn or flip vegetables. Piercing with a fork makes the juices drain out, just as it does with meat.*

for delicious leftovers. And you don't have to worry about the cancer-causing heterocyclic amines (HCA) found in blackened muscle meats such as red meat, poultry, or fish; they are not produced when grilling vegetables.[11] There isn't a vegetable that can't be grilled, so move over pepper-zucchini-mushroom-onion-corn repertoire. Say hello to something new and exciting!

VEGETABLE GRILLING GUIDE

All vegetables can be grilled—but here are some of my "off-the-beaten-track" favorites. Slice vegetables approximately 3/4-inch thick. Grill over medium heat, which allows them to cook through but not burn. Enjoy vegetables hot off the grill or incorporate into other dishes.

VEGETABLE	SEASON	PREPARATION	COOK TIME	USE IN
BEETS	Year-round	Use smaller beets. Rub whole with oil and salt. Wrap in aluminum foil. Seal well.	30–45 minutes	Main dish salad, composed salad with goat cheese and greens
BROCCOLI	Year-round, especially October through April	Break up into florets. Quick-blanch 30 seconds, marinate.	8–15 minutes	Vegetable platters for parties, broccoli salads with grilled red onions
BROCCOLINI	Late summer through winter	Coat with oil and salt.	8–10 minutes	Pasta dishes with garlic and olive oil
CARROTS	Year-round	Slice in half lengthwise. Quick-blanch 30 seconds, marinate.	8–15 minutes	Pasta and grain salads, roasted vegetable platter with dip for parties
CAULIFLOWER	Year-round, especially September through January	Break up into florets or slice. Quick-blanch 30 seconds, marinate.	10–15 minutes	Quesadillas (thinly sliced), roasted vegetable platter with dip for parties
FENNEL	October through March	Slice lengthwise. Rub with oil and salt.	15–20 minutes	Roasted vegetable platter with dip for parties, sliced with fish and pork
JICAMA	Year round, especially November through April	Marinate raw 30 minutes.	10–15 minutes	Roasted vegetable platter with dip for parties, in salsa with chopped tomatoes, lime, cilantro, and red onion
LONG BEANS	Year-round, especially September through November	Coat raw with oil and salt. Cook on top of a grill pan.	10–12 minutes	Buckwheat pasta salads, pasta dishes, as a side dish with toasted almonds

What About Blanching—Especially for Greens?

Blanching immerses vegetables quickly in boiling water. The technique doesn't cook the vegetable, but bursts through the vegetables' outside cell wall. Blanching goes against the cooking tip of keeping water away from vegetables, but it is not meant for cooking vegetables, only prepping them for the next stage of cooking. Heat a large pot of water to a boil and add your vegetables for 30 seconds. Then remove them with a hand strainer and transfer them into a container of cold water to stop the cooking. When cool, remove from the water; please don't let them sit and soak. Blanching is best used to prep vegetables for grilling or for cooking greens such as kale, chard, and collards. Certainly you can eat plain blanched vegetables, but many eaters prefer a "meatier" roasted or grilled vegetable. Dress blanched greens as you would lettuce or spinach, add them to stir-fries, or use them as a stuffing for meats and winter squash.

Blanch vegetable pieces in small batches; adding too many vegetables at the same time reduces the water temperature. You need a vigorous boil to quickly burst the cell wall. If you blanch in more than one batch, bring the water back to a boil before adding the next batch.

Antioxi-Who and Phyto-What?

Sautéing, roasting, or grilling bring out secret sugars, but what else is hiding in our vegetables? They may have a whole lot more going on that we have yet to find. Only in the last twenty years have we discovered two impressive plant compounds called phytochemicals and antioxidants. We've heard they are good for us, but often that's not enough to motivate us to eat more vegetables. Learning what these compounds do, however, may make you look at carrots with a little more respect and interest.

From the littlest protozoa to the largest whale, life is about survival. For plants it is no different, except they can't run away from their predators. To compensate, plants have developed an in-

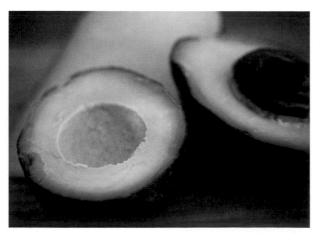

house defense system to protect them from enemies, primarily bacteria and fungi. These defenses come in the form of plant compounds that are bitter, pungent, smelly, or colorful. Examples are caffeine in coffee, solanine in potatoes, saponin in quinoa, capsaicin in peppers, and tannins in tea. Called phytochemicals (plant chemicals), they are used by the plant for protection. It just so happens that by eating the plant, we can benefit from these defense compounds as well.

Cooking Carbon Comparisons

Why don't we microwave all our food? Won't it save more energy? Yes, it will, in some cases, but what an awful thing to do to our vegetables. Microwaving doesn't heighten natural sugars, and it is an "inferior heat source" when compared to roasting and grilling. In the spirit of the "energetics of cooking," we want as close to a firelike energy source as possible to penetrate our food. This is another way the cook can put energy into the food. Leave microwaves for reheating leftovers and disinfecting your kitchen sponge (microwave it after washing the dishes, 2 minutes on high).

COOKING METHOD	POWER SOURCE	WATTS OR BTU PER HOUR	COOK TIME	POUNDS OF CO_2	KG OF CO_2
Steam/Sauté	Electric stove	1,500 watts	15 minutes	.48	.22
Steam/Sauté	Gas stove	8,000 BTUs	15 minutes	.23	.11
Roast	Electric oven	3,500 watts	25 minutes	1.9	.85
Roast	Gas oven	25,000 BTUs	25 minutes	1.2	.55
Slow Cook	Crock-Pot	400 watts	4 hours	2.1	.92
Microwave	Microwave oven	1,000 watts	5 minutes	.11	.05

Comparison of energy and CO_2 emissions associated with various methods of cooking an assortment of vegetables. [12]

In addition to protection, the immovable plant, which had to feed itself, evolved to make glucose (sugar) using readily available carbon dioxide, water, and sunlight. The plant splits water molecules into hydrogen and oxygen—a component of photosynthesis. This dynamic process creates high-energy reactions and free radicals that could be damaging to the plant DNA, so plants produce antioxidants (some plants produce more than others) that balance things out. It just so happens that eating the plant may balance out free radicals in humans too.

Studies have shown that organic produce may have more antioxidants and phytochemicals than chemically grown produce. [13] Treating plants with pesticides and fertilizers could be compared to giving your kids too much money. Because everything is provided, they don't work hard and become lazy. Organically grown plants have to work hard to protect themselves, and they do this by developing strong phytochemicals and antioxidants. The darker the color of the vegetable, the greater the antioxidant content. Filled with so many vitamins, minerals, phytochemicals, antioxidants, as well as compounds we have yet to discover, vegetables are the ultimate example of high-vibe foods. Freshness is important to get the best energy from the plant. To find the freshest vegetables, change your thinking about wanting specific vegetables for a specific recipe; instead, go shopping with an open mind rather than with certain vegetables in mind. Look for

vibrant produce—vegetables and fruits that seem to jump off the counter and say "eat me." They don't need to look picture-perfect, but stay away from yellowed spots and "sagging skin."

Salt

When we start with fresh, seasonal vegetables, all that's needed is a cooking technique that fits their personality (and yours), a little oil, and some good-quality salt. Salt can make all the difference. If you still use traditional canister salt, taste it next to a better-quality salt and you may never use canister salt again. It has a bitter and almost metallic taste. There is a dramatic difference in the flavor of salts that goes undetected without a side-by-side comparison (see How to Do a Salt Test sidebar). Restaurant kitchens use kosher salt, preferring its larger granules, lower sodium content, and lower price. Artisanal salts come in a variety of colors and flavors and offer cooks an additional level of complexity. Experiment and find your favorites.

Real sea salt is grayer than commercial salt because of the sea minerals. Commercial salt is washed to remove the color (and flavor), and an anticaking agent is added to prevent clumping and to help the grains fit through the holes of a saltshaker. People think sea salt is healthier than commercial salt because of its minerals, but you'd have to eat a lot of salt to capitalize on the difference.[14] For

How to Do a Salt Taste Test

INGREDIENTS NEEDED:
Whatever common household salt you use
Kosher salt
1 or 2 artisanal salts

DIRECTIONS:
Start with the kosher or artisanal salt. Put a small amount in one of your hands. Lick the index finger of your other hand, dab it in the salt, and taste. Clean off your hands. Repeat with the common household salt. Follow with another artisan salt, or retry the first one. Optional: cleanse your palate in between tastes with a cracker or a raw carrot.

me, adding sea salt is more about taste and "kitchen alchemy." Salt is a powerful food; in macrobiotics it is considered the most yang (concentrated, forceful) food, compared to yin (spacey, unassertive) foods such as sugar. I use mineral-rich salts as a strengthening ingredient in cooking and as a way to add to the energetics of food. Sprinkle it on with intent when cooking for a sick friend or when looking for an added little "health-kick."

A cook needs to control the salt with his or her fingers, so please liberate your cooking salt from its shaker. Instead, keep little bowls of salt next to your stove; you can crush the granules with your fingers and add them to the pan or dish. Save chunky, hard-to-crush salt for dishes that require a longer cooking time, such as soups and stews, where the salt can dissolve. Once you get a feel for measuring salt with your fingers, the measuring spoons are the next to go (except when baking). Freedom cooking! You are on your way to faster cooking times.

Salt bowls can be uniquely personal and fun to shop for in those interesting artsy stores while on vacation. Even men like finding one for their kitchen. The bowls make good gifts, especially when you include a special salt in the package. Some bowls have lids; others don't. Use either, but keep them small—about two inches in diameter—and wash them before refilling.

Trying to reduce your use of salt? Here's a different seasoning technique. Mix dried herbs with olive oil (and a little salt or not) in a small bowl or a mortar with pestle. Marinate at least an hour, giving the herbs a chance to "moisten up." Grind with the mortar and pestle to get an even better infusion of herbs into the oil. Rub onto the vegetables and bake.

Sharp Knives Needed

If you still say you don't like cooking with vegetables, it may be because your knife isn't sharp. An appropriate-size sharp knife makes cutting vegetables fun; the wrong knife makes it a painful experience. You need an 8-inch or longer chef's knife. Paring knives and other half-size knives won't do. An 8-inch knife allows you to cut faster because you can fit the entire vegetable, such as an average-size onion, beneath the blade. When you cut, the edge bends off to the side. (The tiny microscopic teeth actually bend over.) In order for the knife to

How to Hone a Knife: Hold the steel in one hand, tip facing down and away from you. Hold your knife in the other hand, blade facing down. Tilt the knife in a 20-degree angle away from the steel. Start at the top of the honing rod and at the heel or edge of the knife closest to the handle. Slide the knife along the steel in a downward slicing motion to the tip of the knife; repeat five times on one side then the other, then three times, then two times then single strokes alternating between right and left ten times. Every six months or so, depending on how much you use your knife, sharpen it on a stone or take it to a professional sharpener. Sooner or later, you will have to replace your steel because it will wear out.

remain sharp, it must be kept straight. But sharpening the blade removes steel and can prematurely wear out a knife. Instead, use a "steel" or "honing rod" to realign the edge. *Hone the knife after every half hour of cutting time.* If you cut for fifteen minutes one day and twenty minutes the next, hone your knife after the second day of cutting.

A Final Note

Even with an ongoing effort to be vital and fit, we don't always want to eat healthfully. Enjoy and have fun with your food and remember that health is about balance, not rigidity. Think of your stomach as a compost pile; put in at least 50 percent fruits and vegetables and you will be in good shape to digest whatever else gets added.

Carbon Footprint Label

Food labels list information about the nutritional content of the food, allowing consumers to make informed and healthy decisions about what they eat. Included on many food labels is information about the perceived benefit of the food, how it was grown (such as certified organic), and its place of origin. In the United States, the Food and Drug Administration regulates food labels to ensure they are accurate and useful to consumers.

Since all foods have a carbon footprint (carbon emissions associated with their production and transportation), what if food labels also contained information about the associated carbon emissions? At right is an example of what such a label might look like for a jar of peanut butter. Accompanying the standard nutritional information is the carbon footprint or the CO_2 emissions per serving and for the entire jar. These calculations were made by EcoSynergy, one of our innovative risk takers (chapter 7), who computed the energy to farm, produce, and transport peanut butter. The label also includes a carbon rating between 1 and 10, so that consumers can better choose between high- and low-carbon foods.

Nutrition Facts

Peanut Butter
Serving Size: 2 tablespoons
Servings Per Container: about 14

Amount Per Serving

Calories 200	Calories from fat 10

	% Daily Value
Total Fat 16 g	25%
Saturated Fat 2.5 g	12%
Trans Fat 0 g	0%
Cholesterol 0 mg	0%
Sodium 120 mg	5%
Total Carbohydrates 6 g	2%
Dietary Fiber 2 g	9%
Sugars 1 g	
Protein 8 g	

Carbon Footprint

Per Serving: **118g CO_2e**
Total Carbon: **1648g CO_2e**

Primary location of origin:
Orrville, Ohio

Method of transportation:
Train/Truck

1	2	3	4	5	6	7	8	9	10

LOW   **CARBON RATING**   HIGH

Note: Carbon rating ranges from 1 to 10, with lower numbers being more climate friendly.

Carbon dioxide equivalent (CO_2e) accounts for carbon dioxide and other greenhouse gases.

Labeling the carbon footprint of all food items would help consumers know more about how and where the food is grown and produced and what effect that product has on the environment. However, your best source for knowing more about your food is still establishing direct contact with the farmers who grow it and, if possible, the producers who make it.

Book 'n' Cook Club Ideas

Field Trips

Sign up for a cooking class. Find classes through adult education programs, culinary stores, or the Slow Foods convivium in your area.

Head to the farmers market. Have everyone in your group buy a vegetable they are not familiar with and cook it using any of the three "sugar-enhancing" techniques; roasting, grilling or sautéing. Or buy one vegetable and cook it all three ways to discover which method you like best for that vegetable.

Recipes

Grilled Vegetables with the Best Marinade Ever

Roasted Vegetables—Carrots and Beets

Roasted and Fresh Vegetable Platter with Red Pepper Walnut Dip

Veggie Almond Chili

Collard Greens with Black Olives and Piment d'Espelette

Dijon Green Beans with Roasted Candied Shallots

Video Clips

Learn the right way to cut an onion and hone a knife at www.globalwarmingdiet.org

Small Things Matter

• Find out your favorite preparation method for individual vegetables. Here are some good matches:

Sautéing: celery, carrots, daikon radishes, snow and sugar snap peas, asparagus, greens, green beans

Roasting: beets, leeks, zucchini, whole squashes, whole onions, brussels sprouts, all of the root vegetables (carrots, potatoes, rutabagas, turnips, sweet potatoes, yams)

Grilling: mushrooms, eggplant, peppers, corn, broccoli, fennel, cauliflower, jicama, carrots

Small Things Matter-Continued

- Reduce your sodium intake by reducing your consumption of energy-consuming processed foods and use the salt to cook whole foods instead.

- Buy an 8-inch or larger chef's knife and keep it sharp with a honing rod.

- Using disposables for your next barbecue? Try compostable plates, cups, and utensils. When the party is over, these products can be put right into your backyard compost pile. See www.worldcentric.org for biocompostables.

- Make your oven energy-efficient for roasting vegetables:

  1. Bake more than one thing at a time. Make a complete "roasted dinner" by baking vegetables, grains, and protein dish all together. Be sure to keep space between roasting pans to allow for appropriate heat circulation.

  2. Make sure the oven seals tightly. Even a small gap allows heat to escape. If you can move a dollar bill through the closed oven door, the seal should be replaced.

  3. Save energy and ensure correct baking times by checking temperature with an oven thermometer.

  4. Use a smaller oven when baking a small amount of food. A toaster oven can use a third to half as much energy as a full size oven.

Recipes

Grilled Vegetables with the Best Marinade Ever

Any vegetable can be grilled. At dinner parties, I'll often serve a platter of grilled jicama, cauliflower, broccoli, and carrots along with BBQ'ed Tofu with Lime (chapter 5) and chicken, Orange-Chipotle-Maple Pasta (chapter 8), and Spinach with Grape, Pecan, Red Onion, and Artisanal Blue Cheese (chapter 5) for a great summer dinner.

GRILLED VEGETABLES

1 head broccoli, sliced lengthwise in 2 or 3 pieces
2 carrots, peeled and sliced lengthwise in 3 pieces
1 head cauliflower, sliced lengthwise in 4 to 6 pieces
1 small jicama, sliced lengthwise in 4 to 6 pieces

THE BEST MARINADE EVER
GOOD FOR UP TO 2 CUPS MIXED VEGGIES

$1/4$ cup balsamic vinegar
$1/4$ cup olive oil
$1/4$ cup soy sauce

Slice vegetables approximately $3/4$-inch thick and large enough not to fall through the grates of the grill. Bring a large pot of water to boil. Add the broccoli, blanch 15 seconds and remove to an ice bath. Bring the pot back to a vigorous boil and add the carrots. Blanch for 30 seconds and remove to an ice bath. Repeat with the cauliflower. Remove from cool water and blot to remove the excess water. Place the vegetables (including the jicama) in two 13 x 9-inch pans. Combine the marinade ingredients and stir. Pour over the vegetables and let marinate for 30 minutes, turning every 10 minutes so that all the vegetables have contact with the marinade.

Preheat the grill. Remove vegetables from the marinade and grill over medium heat until crisp tender. Look for the "ridge marks" before you turn and remove from grill. Cooking time varies, depending on the vegetable.

For variety, add favorite herbs and spices to the marinade. For an Asian flavor, add toasted sesame oil and finely chopped lemongrass; for a southwestern flavor, add ground cumin and chopped cilantro; for an Italian flavor, add freshly chopped oregano and basil.

Roasted Vegetables

Roasted vegetables are easy to cook and delicious to eat. Carrots are especially good roasted; they are nicely sweet and kid-friendly. Follow this basic recipe for other vegetables such as fennel, asparagus, potatoes, and summer squash. Look for a little browning to occur on your vegetables, which means the sugars have been heightened.

ROASTED CARROTS

MAKES 4 CUPS

4 carrots, peeled, trimmed and cut in a roll cut (see note)
2 teaspoons olive oil
Good-quality salt to taste

Preheat oven to 375 degrees F. Place cut carrots in a bowl with oil and salt. Rub carrots with your hands, making sure everything is lightly coated with oil. Place onto a baking sheet in a single layer. Bake for 15–20 minutes until carrots are lightly browned around the edges.

NOTE: How to Do a Roll Cut
Place the carrot vertically on the cutting board. Cut a 3-inch diagonal slice off the top of the carrot. Rotate the carrot a quarter turn, and do another diagonal cut through the center, or "eye," of the carrot. Repeat this motion until you reach the bottom, keeping all pieces approximately the same size.

ROASTED BEETS

Most people don't cook beets because they think the process is time consuming. However, baked beets are one of the easiest vegetables to prepare. Roasting beets brings out the sugars; many kids even like them.

MAKES 3 CUPS

3–4 medium-size red or yellow beets or combination of both
1 teaspoon olive oil
Good-quality salt to taste
2 tablespoons water or stock

Preheat oven to 375 degrees F. Twist off the greens and stems from the beets; save for a later use. Trim the tops and bottoms of beets but do not peel. Wash beets under running water with a vegetable brush; shake off the excess water. Pour oil into your hand and rub beets, coating well. Place in a baking dish (see note) with water or stock and sprinkle with salt. Cover tightly and bake about 60 minutes, until you can pierce a fork all the way through the beet. Once you get the hang of this, you can turn off your oven 10–15 minutes earlier and let the beets roast in the remaining heat. When cool enough to handle, rub off skin and slice. Drizzle any beet liquid left over in the baking dish.

NOTE: Though slicing beets makes for faster cooking, baking beets whole keeps in their juices. Look for a covered baking dish that fits the amount of vegetables you usually bake. If it is too large, there will be too much air surrounding the vegetables. I use an 8 x 8-inch covered roasting dish. If you don't have a dish with its own lid, cover any baking dish with aluminum foil, or tightly wrap the whole beets in aluminum foil; but please, rinse the foil and reuse it one more time before recycling it.

Roasted and Fresh Vegetable Platter with Red Pepper Walnut Dip

Serving a roasted and fresh vegetable platter at parties, rather than just all raw vegetables, is a welcome change. Roasted vegetables are a comforting yet healthy option for family and guests and also make great leftovers. Choose vegetables that are in season, display on a platter lined with green chard, and serve with a zesty dip such as Muhammara (roasted red pepper and walnuts). Choose from a combination of the following vegetables, or try roasting whatever vegetable you please.

Roasted Vegetables—choose from the following: Carrots, fennel, asparagus, heirloom potatoes, red or yellow beets, summer squash, baby turnips, mushrooms. (Follow the basic recipe for Roasted Carrots, but increase cooking times for beets, potatoes, and turnips.)

Fresh Vegetables—choose from the following: Sugar snap and snow peas; thin sticks of cucumbers, celery or red pepper; radishes; cherry tomatoes (only serve tomatoes in the summer).

ROASTED RED PEPPER WALNUT DIP (MUHAMMARA)

This is a favorite dip for roasted vegetables that also works nicely as a refrigerated condiment for vegetables and grains.

MAKES 1 1/2 CUPS

2 red bell peppers
2 unpeeled cloves garlic
3/4 cup walnuts
1 slice nine-grain bread
1/2 habañero pepper, seeded and coarsely chopped
1 tablespoon pomegranate molasses
1 tablespoon water
1 tablespoon walnut oil (can substitute olive oil)
1 teaspoon freshly squeezed lemon juice
1 teaspoon balsamic vinegar
1 teaspoon ground cumin
1/2 teaspoon freshly grated ginger
1 teaspoon salt
Pinch ground cloves

Preheat oven to 375 degrees F. Place peppers and garlic on baking sheet and bake for 20 minutes. Remove the garlic and turn the peppers. Cook the peppers until blackened on all sides, approximately 10 minutes more. Remove from oven. Put the peppers in a bowl and cover with a plate. Let cool.

Reduce the oven to 350 degrees F. Put walnuts on baking sheet and lightly toast for 8 minutes. Remove from oven. Remove 1/4 cup walnuts and chop coarsely. Set aside.

When peppers are cool, slit the bottom and pour juice into a food processor. Remove skins and seeds. Add the peppers, remaining 1/2 cup walnuts, bread, and habañero pepper in food processor. Squeeze the garlic out of its skin into food processor. Blend well. Add remaining ingredients and blend well. Transfer to a serving bowl and garnish with chopped walnuts.

Veggie Almond Chili

This chili has a lot of ingredients, but it doesn't take long to assemble. The key to a satisfying vegetarian chili is creating a deep complexity of flavors so people feel like they are eating chili and not vegetable soup. Chili is best cooked the day before, allowing flavors to develop.

SERVES 8

1/3 cup almonds

1 cup emmer grain,* or 1 cup bulgur

2 tablespoons olive oil

1 large yellow onion, chopped

3 cloves garlic, sliced

2 carrots, diced medium

3 sticks celery, diced medium

1 small jalapeño, chopped

1 teaspoon ground coriander

1 teaspoon dried oregano

1 teaspoon smoked paprika

1 tablespoon chile powder

1 tablespoon ancho chile powder (optional but preferable; can use regular chile powder)

1 chipotle chile, finely chopped

2 reconstituted dry or oil-based sun-dried tomatoes, finely chopped

1 teaspoon Dijon mustard

2 tablespoons dry red or white wine

1 (28-ounce) can tomatoes, liquid reserved, or 2 cups chopped fresh tomatoes

6 tablespoons beer (dark is good, such as a chocolate stout or porter)

2 tablespoons molasses

1/2 teaspoon rich-tasting olive oil

2 1/2 cups vegetable stock

1 cup white or yellow hominy, rinsed and drained

1 cup black beans, cooked (canned or homemade. See recipe on pages 28–29)

1/4 cup chopped cilantro

Garnish: Chopped white onion and cilantro leaves, grated cheddar cheese (optional)

Preheat oven to 350 degrees F. Place almonds on baking sheet and bake for 8 minutes, or until light brown. Remove from oven. When cool, finely grind in a food processor.

If using emmer: Rinse emmer and place in a small saucepan with 2 cups of water and a pinch of salt. Bring to boil, cover, reduce heat, and cook 50 minutes. Remove from heat.

If using quick-cooking bulgur: Place 1 cup bulgur in a small baking pan. Boil 2 cups water and pour on top of bulgur. Sprinkle in a pinch of salt. Cover and let sit for 15 minutes, until all the water is absorbed. For more flavor, use 1 cup water and 1 cup stock.

Heat oil in a heavy-bottomed soup pot. Add onion and sauté on medium heat for 5 minutes, until translucent. Add garlic and stir. Add carrots, celery, and jalapeño; stir and sauté for 5 minutes. Add the next 8 ingredients (coriander through Dijon mustard). Sauté for 3 minutes. Add wine and sauté until mixture is almost dry. While cooking, blend half the tomatoes into a purée. Add the beer, molasses, ground almonds, and olive oil. Add both diced and puréed tomatoes. Stir well and lower heat; allow this thick slurry to lightly cook for 10 minutes. Add stock, hominy, emmer, and beans. Cook for one hour on a low heat. Mix in cilantro. Taste and adjust seasonings. Garnish.

*Emmer is an ancient wheat, described as the "grandfather of farro." It is a larger grain than regular wheat and has a distinct richer flavor and meaty-chewy texture—great for chili. I only know one place it grows in the country: Winthrop, Washington. Buy online at www. bluebirdgrainfarms.com.

Collard Greens with Black Olives and Piment d'Espelette

You can use any kind of greens for this recipe, but do consider collard greens. They have such a strong energy—just look at and feel them. I want that energy in my body.

SERVES 3

1 bunch collard greens, washed
3 tablespoons good-quality, sliced black olives
1 clove garlic, minced
1 tablespoon olive oil
$1/2$ teaspoon Piment d'Espelette (a French spice made of peppers)
Salt to taste
1 slice lemon

Wash greens, remove inner rib, and chop finely (if you like eating it). (If you prefer not to eat the rib and stems, think about composting them.) Cut greens into $1/2$-inch slices.

Bring pot of water to boil. Add greens and cook until bright green and tender, about 3-4 minutes. Drain. When cool, gently squeeze out the excess water, but don't squeeze them bone-dry.

In a small bowl, combine the olives and garlic. Set aside.

Heat oil in a large sauté pan over medium heat. Add olives and garlic combination and sauté about a minute, stirring constantly. Add greens, Piment d'Espelette, and a pinch of salt. Stir, making sure all the greens get coated with the oil. (You can pick them up and mix with your hands.) Squeeze in lemon juice and serve immediately.

Dijon Green Beans with Roasted Candied Shallots

Even though green beans are a summer vegetable, they often find their way onto holiday tables. I serve the easy-to-make Dijon Green Beans in the summer by themselves and then dress them up with the Candied Shallots for Thanksgiving dinner. The Dijon sauce tastes great on many vegetables and chicken, so experiment!

SERVES 4

Candied Shallots
2 teaspoons olive oil
20 shallots, peeled
3 cups chicken or vegetable stock, divided
2 sprigs thyme

Dijon Green Beans
$3/4$ pound green beans, stems removed
1 tablespoon clarified butter or olive oil
1 tablespoon Dijon mustard
Pinch of salt
2 teaspoons dry white wine
Freshly ground pepper

Preheat oven to 350 degrees F. For the Candied Shallots, heat the oil in an ovenproof sauté pan over medium heat. Add the shallots and sauté until they are golden brown on all sides. Add 1 cup stock and thyme to the pan and place in the oven. Do not cover.

After 30 minutes, add another cup of stock, stir, and return to the oven. After 30 minutes, add remaining stock. Bake another $1/2$ hour. The whole process takes $1\,1/2$ hours. Watch for the sauce to get thick and syrupy. Turn off oven and prepare the green beans.

Bring a pot of water to boil with salt. Quickly blanch the beans until crisp tender. Drain. In a large sauté pan, heat the butter or oil and whisk in mustard and a pinch salt. Whisk in wine. Add beans and toss in the sauce. Transfer to a serving platter, top with candied shallots and freshly ground pepper. Drizzle with any leftover "syrup" from the shallot pan.

10

Great Grains

The word refined is a compliment when it comes to your sense of style, but for your diet it's another matter entirely. Since 2005, the USDA Dietary Guidelines have encouraged eating whole grains to help reduce risks for heart disease, high cholesterol, and diabetes.[1] "Make half your grains whole," is their way of promoting three one-ounce servings of grains a day from foods such as brown rice, whole-grain pasta, and whole-grain bread.[2] Just as there are many types of fruits (apples, pears, oranges, etc.), there are many types of grains (rice, wheat, quinoa, millet, etc.). And just as there are different types of apples (Pippin, Red Delicious, Fuji, McIntosh), there are different types of rice (short grain, long grain, Black Japonica, jasmine, arborio) and wheat (emmer, spelt, kamut). A common reason people give for not reducing meat consumption is that they don't know what to eat instead. Many people are afraid that there's nothing else *to* eat; and if there were, it would take too much time to prepare, and they wouldn't know how to prepare it anyway because it all looks so *unfamiliar*. Simply said, though, what you eat in place of meat are whole grains. There is a lot of variety and flavor in eating whole grains, and if you are not doing it, you really should try. Preparation and seasoning are remarkably easy once you know a few little tips and tricks.

Food-Auto Comparison

It's clear that food choices have an impact on energy use and greenhouse-gas emissions, but just how important *are* food choices in comparison to other activities, such as driving a car? We'll use the estimates of carbon intensities of different foods to make this comparison.

First, the average American drives about 10,000 miles (16,100 km) per year. Depending on the vehicle's fuel economy, it emits between 1.8 and 5.2 tons of CO_2e per year.[3] Three types of cars were chosen for this calculation (Ford F-Series truck, Chevrolet Cobalt sedan, and the Toyota Prius hybrid sedan) to represent the different classes of today's popular vehicles. Figure 10 shows the CO_2e emissions of each vehicle.

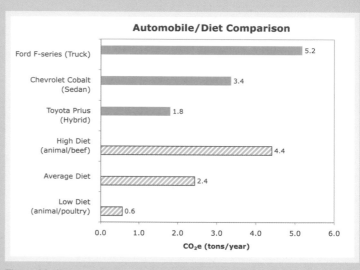

Figure 10. Comparison of the CO_2e emissions associated with driving different automobiles compared with the CO_2e emissions associated with growing and producing the food for three different diets.[4]

Today's U.S. agricultural system provides about 3,700 Calories of food per person per day.[5] From that, we can estimate the amount of CO_2e that is emitted to produce this food because we know the type of food that is eaten (72 percent plant-based and 28 percent animal-based), and we know the carbon intensity of these foods.[6] The result: the average American diet produces about 2.4 tons of CO_2e per year—about the same as driving a car for a year.

Let's see how different eating styles affect carbon emissions. Two diets were chosen to compare with the current U.S. diet (labeled Average Diet, which consumes 28 percent animal-based foods). In the first diet, "High Diet (animal/beef)," the amount of animal-based foods is increased to 38 percent and the type of meat consumed is all beef. In the second diet, "Low Diet (animal/poultry)," the amount of animal product consumed is decreased to 18 percent and the type of meat consumed is all poultry.[7] The results (see Figure 10) show the dramatic effect that changes in diet can have on CO_2e emissions. In fact, the reductions in carbon emissions achieved by modifying one's diet are similar to those achieved by buying a more fuel-efficient car. Thus we can see that adjusting one's diet to include fewer animal-based foods and less red meat is likely to save money and provide health benefits[8] while significantly reducing carbon emissions.

What's the Difference Between Whole Grains and Refined Grains?

White rice is brown rice with its clothes off. Whole grains still wear their bran (fiber-, vitamin-, and mineral-rich outer layer) and germ (antioxidant- and vitamin-rich center). Once the bran and germ are removed, primarily what's left is the starch (endosperm). Whole grains are processed in various ways. Pearl barley is whole barley with most of its bran rubbed off. Bulgur is a cracked and partially cooked form of the whole-wheat berry. Oatmeal is the sliced or flattened form of whole oats. Does this make a difference nutritionally? In a word, "yes."

Quick-digesting carbohydrates, found in refined grains such as white rice and white flour, have come under scrutiny as a surefire recipe for weight gain. Whole grains, however, have complex carbohydrates that are digested and enter the bloodstream at a slower rate than refined grains. This makes whole grains an "energy storehouse" and a steady-burning fuel that keeps insulin and blood-sugar levels more in balance. Studies at the University of Minnesota also show a "synergy" when eating the whole grain. "Research suggests it's the whole food—the whole grain that delivers abundant amounts of antioxidants, vitamins, and phytochemicals—which appears to act together to provide protective effects."[9]

Macrobiotics describes whole foods having an energy, or life force, held within them. This is what the "energetics of food" is all about and what we want to capitalize on when we eat. As food ages or when it is processed, that energy dissipates. A goal for eaters is to get the best energy they can from high-vibe food that is fresh, whole, "drug-free" (no chemical pesticides, herbicides, or fertilizers), and humanely raised. Here, "vibrations" will be the strongest.

Grain Cooking Methods

The world of whole grains is like an exotic country waiting to be explored. At this moment, there are probably more than a dozen different kinds of whole grains in the bulk bins of your local natural foods store. Some of the most common include brown rice (long, medium, and short grain), barley, winter and spring wheat berries, quinoa, millet, buckwheat groats (actually not a wheat or a grain, but it's used as such), kamut, popcorn, wild rice, and spelt, but there are many more. Some are chewy and some are soft. Some cook fast and others slow. Some taste grassy and some taste nutty. Some you will like more than others. Don't just walk by them as they sit in the bulk bin; take a few home and try them out. Maybe you'll find you only like one grain of the entire list. Maybe you like one grain baked but don't like it at all when it is steeped. The best way to discover your favorites is to cook them all (using the different techniques).

Grains and Health

Since 1999, products that contain 51 percent or more whole grains by weight can make the following FDA-approved health claim: "Diets rich in whole-grain foods and other plant foods, and low in total fat, saturated fat and cholesterol, may reduce the risk of heart disease and certain cancers." [10] Here's how these foods help fight the following health problems:

- CHOLESTEROL: Grains, especially oats and barley, are high in soluble fiber, which acts like a sponge to sop up and help decrease cholesterol levels. Soluble fiber forms a gel in water that helps bind acids and cholesterol in the intestinal tract, preventing their reabsorption into the body. Insoluble fiber helps the body eliminate fat.
- CANCER: Whole grains contain key cancer-fighting agents: fiber, antioxidants, and phytochemicals.
- HEART DISEASE: Fiber, especially viscous fiber in whole grains such as oats and barley, lowers overall cholesterol and reduces serum insulin and serum lipids—all factors in coronary heart disease. Furthermore, whole-grain anti-oxidants, vitamin E, plant chemicals such as plant sterols, and phytoestrogens (plant estrogens) may help decrease the risk of heart disease.

Grain Cooking Chart

Different cooking techniques yield different results. The first number on this chart represents the ratio of liquid to grain, the second is the cooking time.

GRAIN	BAKE 350 DEGREES F	PRESSURE-COOK	STEEP	BOIL	YIELD
Rice	water/grain/time	water/grain/time	water/grain/time	water/grain/time	dry = cooked
Short-grain Brown	2:1 60 min	$1^1/_2$:1 45 min	2:1 45 min	8:1 40–45 min	1C = 3C
Long-grain Brown	2:1 55 min	$1^1/_2$:1 45 min	2:1 45 min	8:1 35–40 min	1C = 3C
Sweet Brown Rice	2:1 55 min	$1^1/_2$:1 45 min	2:1 45 min	8:1 30–35 min	1C = 3C
Wild Rice	2:1 60 min	$1^3/_4$:1 45 min	$2^1/_2$:1 50 min	8:1 45–50 min	1C = 2C
Emmer	$1^1/_4$:1 60 min	$1^1/_2$:1 45 min	2:1 70 min	8:1 45–50 min	1C = 2C
Quinoa	2:1 30 min	$1^1/_2$:1 10 min	2:1 15 min	8:1 10 min	1C = 4C
Buckwheat	2:1 20 min	Not advised	Not advised	8:1 12–15 min	1C = 2C
Hato Mugi (Barley)	$2^1/_2$:1 90 min	2:1 50 min	2:1 60 min	8:1 45–50 min	1C = $1^1/_2$ C
Millet	3:1 45 min	$2^1/_4$:1 20 min	2:1 20 min	8:1 25–30 min	1C = 3C

Different cooking methods create variations in the texture of grains. Your job is to find the combinations you like best. For instance, I like to pressure-cook rice and barley (together), or pressure-cook emmer (by itself). I like to bake quinoa and millet (together), and bake buckwheat (by itself). I also like to boil my buckwheat and millet (by themselves). The chart above illustrates four cooking methods for nine grains. Steeping (cooking grains on the stovetop with a water/grain ratio of 2:1) is the most common—and my least favorite method. It produces a more "gummy" end product, and I prefer grains with integrity. Boiling grains (as you would pasta) produces smaller yet individual grains (grains with integrity). Pressure-cooking is a favorite macrobiotic technique because the inward energy of the pressure cooker produces "grains with strength." Baking grains also maintains integrity but not as dramatically as boiling.

Cooking Stages for Whole Grains

Grains can be prepared in a three-stage process, where each stage builds on the previous one. Most eaters will only use stage two, adding other stages as they get more familiar with cooking grains and have the extra time. Be sure, however, to wash the grains before you cook them. Not only does this rinse off the dust, it "wakes them up," as one of my teachers used to say. Grains "fall asleep" waiting to be used; a good rinse refreshes the energy within them. To wash grains, put them in a bowl, cover with water, stir, and then strain. Do this two more times, or until the water is clear.

Stage One: Prep—Choose One Method

Soak: Cover the grain with one inch of water and let it sit for a few hours or overnight. Soaking softens grains and makes them easier to digest. This is an especially good technique when making grains for kids or older adults.

Toast: Toast the raw grain in a heavy, dry skillet (cast iron works well) for a few minutes, until it's light brown and smells nutty. Toasting grains is like toasting bread; it deepens the flavor.

Stage Two: Cook—Choose One Method

Bake: Place the grain and a pinch of salt in a baking pan, and set aside. Bring water or another cooking liquid (don't limit yourself to water; other partial liquids can be used, such as stock or milk) to a boil on the stovetop, then pour it over the grain. Cover the pan and bake at 350 degrees F. (See the chart for cooking times.)

Steep: This is the traditional method that most people call "boil." Cook the grain with liquid and a pinch of salt in a 2:1 ratio (liquid to grain) on the stovetop in a covered pot.

Boil: Bring eight cups of water and a pinch of salt to boil, as if you were cooking pasta. Add the grain and cook according to the chart.

Pressure-cook: A stovetop pressure cooker is needed for this method, and it is a worthwhile investment. Pressure-cooking gives grains a chewy, satisfying texture. Although pressure-cooking shortens the cooking time of some foods, pressure-cooked grains need about the same amount of cooking time as steeped grains. Pressure-cooking is considered one of the strongest "energetic styles" of cooking, making it an ideal technique to use during the winter months.

> "Gomashio changed my life!"—cooking class student

Pop: Hurray! Popcorn is a whole grain; just don't overdo the butter. Season it instead with olive oil or hot pepper toasted sesame oil and brewer's yeast for a lower-fat alternative. Amaranth can be popped as well.

Stage Three: Next-Step Cooking

Stage three gives a second life to leftover grain.

Braise: Braising infuses flavors into a dish with the help of high heat. Heat oil in a large sauté pan. Add grain and sauté over medium-high heat for a few minutes until warm. Pour a prepared sauce into the pan, cover immediately, and shake the pan to distribute the sauce. Cook until the liquid has been absorbed and the pan is almost dry.

Refry: Heat oil in a large sauté pan. Add grain and sauté over medium-high heat for a few minutes until warm. For variety, add onions or chopped vegetables. Or form a patty with leftover grain (like a crab cake) and sauté it in a little oil until warm and lightly browned.

Deep fry: Form a tight patty or croquette with the leftover grain. Submerge it in hot oil and fry until crisp, like a french fry.

Seasoning Lesson 1:
The Condiment Plate

The Condiment Plate is salt and pepper with a college education. It is the key to seasoning grains, pastas, vegetables, and other foods in a quick and easy manner. The technique is simple—cook your food, walk over to your Condiment Plate, and season to your heart's content (or your doctor's guidelines for salt). Keep your Condiment Plate on the kitchen table or a nearby counter, just like the salt and pepper. Don't hide it away or you won't use it. Students have been so enamored of this simple seasoning technique that they have assembled their own plates to give as gifts. The next page lists some of my favorite store-bought condiments. Recipes for homemade condiments are at the end of this chapter.

It's fun to shop for Condiment Plate accessories, such as the plate itself or little jars, because you get to express your own personality in the purchase. Look for a plate that doesn't take up too much room on the counter or table. I like a 9-inch plate because it holds a lot of condiments, but you may do fine with something much smaller. Look for a flat plate; raised sides limit the number of condiments that will fit on the plate and cause the jars to fall into the center of the plate.

The Condiment Plate

Condiments can add salt, flavor, crunch, a nutritional boost, and an overall "kick" to your meals. Sprinkle condiments on everything—vegetables, grains, salads, soups. As you use them, you'll discover favorite combinations. Purchase the small-size bottles that can fit easily on your plate.

Gomashio

This sesame seed and salt mixture can be made at home or bought in the store or online. Find it in the macrobiotic aisle of your natural foods store in different flavors, like garlic gomashio. Make gomashio by grinding seeds or nuts and salt in a food processor or a sirabachi (a Japanese mortar-and pestle-like ridged bowl). Sprinkle it on grains or bagels with cream cheese.

Umeboshi Vinegar

This "vinegar," has a deep, sour-cherry-like flavor, and is made from the umeboshi plum. Although not a true vinegar because salt is used in processing, it can be used as a vinegar substitute or other flavoring agent. Sprinkle on pasta or grains or use it to make a salad dressing. Purported to have great healing properties, umeboshi is considered the "macrobiotic antibiotic" and is also one of the best-kept culinary secrets!

Toasted Sesame Oil

Toasted sesame oil adds a nutty, rich taste to grains and vegetables. It mixes well with umeboshi or soy sauce for a two- or three-taste dressing. Hot pepper sesame oil is also nice.

Soy Sauce and/or Braggs

This is a dark, salty seasoning agent. Most soy is imported; however, Braggs Amino Acids (a nonfermented soy seasoning) is from California. Also known as shoyu or tamari, soy sauce is available in wheat-free and low-sodium options. Sprinkle on grains and pastas. For the best flavor, spend a little more and get a higher-quality, slower-processed, more-artisanal soy sauce.

Eden Shake

This sprinkle combines brown and black sesame seeds with nori sea vegetable. It is available in the macrobiotic aisle of the natural foods store.

Nori Shake/Dulse Shake

Toasted and crumbled in an easy-to-use dispenser, these store-bought sprinkles can quickly enhance your diet with the beneficial minerals found in sea vegetables.

Nutritional Yeast

Available in the bulk bins of natural food stores, yellow-colored nutritional yeast gives a "cheesy" flavor to foods, filling in for the lower-fat content of vegetables and grains. It is a good source of protein and B vitamins. Don't confuse it with brewer's yeast, a more bitter-tasting nutritional supplement that is a by-product of breweries and distilleries.

Flaxseed

Keep whole flaxseed in the freezer and a small amount of ground flaxseed (grind it in a blender) on your Condiment Plate. Flax is high in omega-3 oils and is a good source of added fiber.

Refrigerated Condiments

Farmers markets are a terrific place to pick up premade condiments like olive tapanade, roasted garlic mix, chimichurri, Indian cilantro sauce, and other ethnic-style seasonings. Serve on the side of simply cooked vegetables and grains for an easy dinner.

Other Condiment Plate Options

Be creative. I keep green Tabasco Sauce on my plate. Other options include specialty vinegars, deep-flavored olive oils, and roasted nuts. Buy them in small bottles or transfer them into little jars for easy use.

Seasoning Lesson 2: How to Make a Sauce

Lesson number two in seasoning grains is how to make a simple sauce. Some store-bought sauces taste pretty good, but making your own is easy once you learn the basics, and it empowers you to eat more grains. The sauces don't have to be complicated—no making roux or browning bones. They are quick to prepare and very satisfying to eat.

Most sauces have five basic components: a base, a salt, a thickener, an acid, and seasonings. The base is salted, seasoned, and thickened in different ways, acid "brightens up" the flavor, and seasonings enhance it (both the acid and seasonings are optional additions, as well as the salt). Combine the ingredients in whatever style you choose, with whatever you have in your cupboard. This makes cooking more creative and flexible, and it makes seasonal eating a breeze. It's an ideal way to avoid time-consuming recipes and dependence on specific ingredients. Just go into the kitchen, look around to see what you have, and cook.

Make Your Own Sauce

Choose one ingredient from each option. As you do this, you will learn combinations that work best for you. The recipe makes 1 cup.

BASE (1 CUP)	SALT (TO TASTE)	THICKENER (1 TABLESPOON)	ACID (1 TEASPOON)	SEASONINGS (TO TASTE)
Stock: vegetable, beef, chicken, mushroom, fish	Salt	Butter	Citrus juice: lemon, lime, orange, grapefruit	Herbs and spices—black pepper, basil, minced garlic, freshly grated gingerroot
Cream/milk/coconut milk/soy milk	Soy sauce/tamari	Oil		
	Umeboshi vinegar	Flour	Wine	
Puréed vegetables	Miso	Cornstarch	Vinegar	Spicy hot seasonings—chili sauce, Sriracha, crushed chile peppers, cayenne, harissa or other dried chile pastes
Steeped tea, such as green or black tea	Fish sauce	Arrowroot		
		Kudzu		
Juice				
Verjus (a non-alcoholic wine) or a dark beer such as Chocolate Stout or Porter				Sweetener—sugar, honey, fruit juice concentrate, maple syrup, brown rice syrup, molasses
Combination of the above to equal 1 cup				

SAUCE EXAMPLES

Combination 1: chicken stock, miso, toasted sesame oil and arrowroot, lime juice, grated ginger and garlic

Combination 2: puréed fresh tomatoes, salt, olive oil, red wine, basil, and oregano

Combination 3: vegetable stock, soy sauce, whole wheat flour, white wine, garlic

Combination 4: cream, salt, butter, lemon, pepper

Combination 5: puréed carrots (base and thickener), stock, umeboshi vinegar (salt and acid), rosemary

---

CHEF TIP:
How to Choose a Stock

Stock is a key ingredient in cooking; keep some in your cupboard or freezer at all times. If you buy premade stock, pay attention to the label. Even though stock is mostly water infused with meat, fish, chicken, and/or vegetables, commercial stocks contain emulsifiers, additives, and many strange-sounding ingredients. Avoid stocks with words you cannot pronounce and/or contain the words "flavor" or "flavoring" (which could mean MSG or a host of other unsavory additives). Once you've opened the container, track its freshness by dating the container a week ahead, and make sure to use it by then, or freeze the extra in ice cube trays for future use.

Those Nasty Imported Herbs and Spices

Many herbs, spices, and other seasonings on our Condiment Plate and in our spice drawer are imported: cinnamon from Mexico and Asia, cumin from India and Iran, soy sauce and umeboshi vinegar from Japan. What is a localvore to do?

This book gives practical advice that serves long-term dietary interests, as well as the interests of planet Earth. We encourage buying base foods (meat, milk, produce, water, beans, and whole grains) from the region or country you live in and seasonings from wherever you wish. Avoid an "All-or-Nothing Diet" or the "You're-Either-With-Us-or-Against-Us Diet" mentality. If international seasonings increase your consumption of grains and vegetables, you are headed in the right direction toward a cool cuisine. Besides, most ethnic seasonings are shipped by boat, rather than energy-intensive air freight.

What Herbs Go with What?

- ARTICHOKES: basil, bay, chervil, coriander, dill, parsley, tarragon, thyme
- BEANS: basil, bay, caraway, cumin, dill, marjoram, oregano, parsley, rosemary, savory, thyme
- BEEF: bay, chervil, chives, horseradish, lovage, marjoram, mustard, rosemary, sage, savory, tarragon, thyme
- CABBAGE: bay, caraway, cumin, juniper, mustard, sage, thyme
- CARROTS: basil, chervil, chives, coriander, cumin, dill, fennel, marjoram, mint, parsley, rosemary, tarragon, thyme
- EGGS: basil, chervil, chives, dill, fennel, marjoram, oregano, parsley, sorrel, tarragon
- FRUIT: angelica, anise hyssop, basil, borage, lavender, lemon balm, lemon thyme, lemon verbena, mint
- POULTRY: basil, bay, chervil, chives, coriander, fennel, horseradish, lemon balm, lemon thyme, marjoram, mustard, oregano, parsley, rosemary, sage, tarragon, thyme
- STOCK: bay, chervil, chives, parsley, rosemary, tarragon, thyme

If you are new to combining herbs and spices, there is no hard and fast rule on how to do it—experiment until you find what you like. One way to learn about individual herbs or spices is to add only one to a bland dish such as a pot of rice, mashed potatoes, eggs, or pasta with olive oil. This allows you to pick up the essence of the herb and discover what it really tastes like. Another way to taste an herb or a spice is to mix it into cream cheese or butter, spread on a cracker, and eat. Note: whenever you use dried herbs, crush them first with your fingers or heat them in a pan for thirty seconds—both techniques help release the essential oils.

CHEF TIPS:
Cooking Grains

- *Wake up your grains! Wash them in a bowl, not just in a colander under the faucet. Cover the grains with water, stir, and rinse. Repeat two more times, or until water is clear.*

- *For an easy flavor kick—add chopped onions, sea vegetables, herbs, or spices to your grain pot.*

- *Refrigerating grains dries them out. Keep cooked plain grains (salt is okay, but no vegetables or other additions) on your kitchen counter for one to two days after cooking and use the grain itself like a condiment! Sprinkle grains into soups or onto breakfast cereals or salads. Having room-temperature grains on the counter makes it easy to incorporate them into on-the-go meals.*

- *Salt is optional, but adding $^1/_4$ to $^1/_2$ teaspoon of salt per cup of grain enhances the flavor.*

- *Grains too wet? Transfer the cooked grain to a baking sheet and let cool. This allows excess water to evaporate and maintains "grain integrity" (keeps the grains from clumping).*

- *For cooking liquids, don't limit yourself to water. Cook grains in stock, milk, wine, juice—any liquid offers possibilities. However, don't replace all the water with a new cooking liquid. Replace a small amount at first and then increase as you learn what works best. For example, when steeping a grain (2:1 water to grain), try replacing one cup of the water with one cup of stock.*

- *When baking, replace one-half to one cup of unbleached white flour in recipes with whole-wheat pastry, barley, or oat flour. Make your own oat flour by grinding rolled oats in a blender.*

- *Check the ingredient label when buying whole-grain products. The word* whole *or* 100% *must be used; unbleached flour and cracked wheat aren't whole grains. Also, look for at least 23 grams of fiber per serving.*

- *Chew well. Digestion of whole grains starts in the mouth with the enzyme amylase, which converts starch and glycogen into simple sugars. Macrobiotics suggests chewing each mouthful at least thirty times—try it!*

Book 'n' Cook Club Ideas

Field Trips

Learn about whole grains at a macrobiotic summer camp.

West Coast: George Ohsawa Macrobiotic Foundation.

East Coast: Kushi Institute.

Food Sources

Find whole grains and many unique food products in natural foods stores or at www.goldminenaturalfoods.com.

Find out more about power foods, such as soy sauce/tamari, umeboshi plum, miso, sea vegetables, pickles, and whole grains.

Recipes

Pressure-Cooked Brown Rice and Hato Mugi

Boiled Buckwheat with Hard-Boiled Egg

Baked Millet and Quinoa with Onion and Corn

Winter Emmer Risotto with Roasted Root Vegetables and Rosemary

Spring Barley Risotto with Asparagus, Dill, and Fresh Artichoke

Sunflower, Flax, Umeboshi, Basil Gomashio

Turkey Mole Gomashio

Green Onion Basil Gomashio

Green Tea Stir-Fry with Seasonal Vegetables and Chicken or Baked Tofu

Small Things Matter

• Buy a pressure cooker and start using it to cook grains.

• Build your own Condiment Plate.

• Purchase a small-hole strainer to keep your quinoa and millet from falling through when washed.

• Invest in some quality oils, vinegars, and seasonings and start making your own easy sauces. Don't forget to get the "biologically-more-diverse and-healthier-than-cornstarch" thickeners—arrowroot and kudzu.

Recipes

Pressure-Cooked Brown Rice and Hato Mugi

Hato mugi (Japanese barley) is one of my favorite grains. It is imported, but if it gets you eating more grains and less meat—great. Buy it from your local Asian market or get organically grown online.

MAKES 5 CUPS

1 1/2 cups brown rice
1/2 cup hato mugi (or substitute hulled or pearl barley)
2 1/2 cups water
1/2 teaspoon sea salt

Combine rice and barley in a medium-size bowl. Cover with water, wash and strain. Repeat until water is clear. Add grain, water, and sea salt to the pressure cooker. Bring to pressure, reduce heat to low, and cook on top of a flame tamer (see page 193) for 45 minutes. Remove from heat and let the pressure come down naturally, or put the pressure cooker under the faucet and let cool water bring the pressure down quickly. Serve with Condiment Plate.

Boiled Buckwheat with Hard-Boiled Egg

Buckwheat is a powerful food and considered the most yang (strong) grain. Eat it in the wintertime when you need an extra boost. Boiling buckwheat keeps it light and adding an egg turns it into a nice breakfast. It is sold already toasted.

SERVES 2

8 cups water
Salt
1/2 cup toasted buckwheat
2 hard-boiled eggs, chopped

Bring water and salt to a boil. Add the buckwheat. Boil for 12–15 minutes. Strain. Add chopped eggs. Serve with Condiment Plate.

Baked Millet and Quinoa with Onion and Corn

Baking millet and quinoa helps maintain their grainy "integrity." In the wintertime, substitute carrots or small cubes of root vegetables for the corn.

SERVES 4

1 1/2 cups water
1 1/2 cups stock (vegetable or chicken)
3/4 cup millet
3/4 cup quinoa
1 yellow onion, finely chopped
1 ear of corn, kernels removed
Pinch of salt

Preheat oven to 350 degrees F. Bring water and stock to boil in a small saucepan. Combine millet and quinoa; wash together and strain. Combine grains, stock/water, onion, corn, and salt in a small baking dish. Cover tightly and bake for 30 minutes. Serve with Condiment Plate.

Winter Emmer Risotto with Roasted Root Vegetables and Rosemary

Risotto is the perfect way to introduce eaters to whole grains. They'll enjoy the chewiness of the grain, assisted by the comfort of the cheese.

SERVES 4

Winter Emmer Risotto
1 cup emmer (do not wash)
4 teaspoons butter or olive oil
2 leeks, just the white part, chopped small (about 1 cup)
2 ribs celery, chopped small
1 teaspoon ground sage
1 clove garlic, minced
Pinch of salt
1/4 cup dry white wine
2 1/2 cups vegetable or chicken stock, divided
1/2 cup grated Parmesan cheese (or substitute dry Jack from California if you can find it)
1 tablespoon freshly chopped thyme
Freshly ground pepper to taste

Roasted Root Vegetables

Peeled winter root vegetables (squash, turnip, rutabaga, sweet potato), diced into $1/2$-inch
   cubes (about 2 cups)
1 tablespoon olive oil
1 tablespoon chopped fresh rosemary
$1^1/2$ tablespoons frozen apple juice concentrate
Pinch of salt

For the Winter Emmer Risotto, melt the butter on medium heat in a medium saucepan. Add
emmer and leeks; sauté 4 minutes, stirring. Add celery, sage, garlic, and salt; sauté 1 minute.
Add wine. When pan is almost dry, add half the stock and bring to a boil. Reduce heat and
cover. Cook for $1/2$ hour. Remove cover; pan should be almost dry. Add remaining half of stock
and bring to a boil. Reduce heat and cover. After another $1/2$ hour, remove cover and check
stock level and texture of grain. Continue cooking without a cover, until pan is almost dry. Add in
cheese, thyme, and freshly ground pepper. Transfer to serving platter and garnish with Roasted
Root Vegetables.

For the Roasted Root Vegetables, preheat oven to 350 degrees F. Toss vegetables with olive
oil, rosemary, and apple juice concentrate and sprinkle with salt. Transfer onto a baking sheet
and arrange in a single layer. Bake 20 minutes, stirring halfway through (rearrange back into
a single layer). Increase heat to 375 degrees F and cook for 10 more minutes, or until lightly
browned. Remove from oven and keep warm.

Summer option: Replace winter squash with peppers, zucchini, and basil.

CHEF TIP:
What is a Flame Tamer?

*A flame tamer is a metal heat guard with a handle. It is placed between the pot and
the burner when cooking on the stovetop. Flame tamers allow for slower cooking
times and lower temperatures and are found in Asian markets. They are helpful when
cooking anything that needs a low flame—such as a cream sauce—or when cooking
grains on the stovetop.*

Spring Barley Risotto with Asparagus, Dill, and Fresh Artichoke

Try another type of risotto, this time using pearl barley (not hulled barley), instead of rice. Do not rinse the barley before using. Asparagus and artichokes are seasonal in spring.

SERVES 5

1 cup pearl barley (do not wash)

6 cups water

4 cups stock (vegetable or chicken)

5 teaspoons olive oil, divided

1 medium onion, diced small

$^1/_3$ cup dry white wine

2 fresh artichokes, leaves removed to reveal the heart (or "choke")

3 tablespoons grated Parmesan cheese (or substitute dry Jack from California if you can find it locally)

1 tablespoon cream cheese

2 tablespoons freshly chopped dill

1 tablespoon freshly squeezed lemon juice

$1^1/_2$ cups thinly sliced asparagus stalks and tips

Salt and freshly ground pepper to taste

In the morning, place barley in a medium-size saucepan and cover with 6 cups of water. Let soak 8 hours, or until dinner.

Strain barley, discarding the soak water. Bring stock to boil in a medium saucepan; turn off heat. Heat a large sauté pan over medium heat; add 1 tablespoon oil. Add onion and sauté for 5 minutes. Add soaked barley; sauté 1 minute, stirring constantly. Add wine, artichokes, and a pinch of salt and sauté until pan is almost dry.

Stir 1 cup of the warmed stock into the onion and barley mixture; bring to a boil and cover. Reduce heat to low-simmer and cook 10 minutes or until most of the liquid is absorbed. Continue adding stock in $^1/_2$-cup portions, letting the barley absorb most of the liquid before adding the next. The whole process takes about 40 minutes. Remove from heat. Stir in cheeses, dill, lemon juice, and asparagus. Season with salt and pepper to taste.

Sunflower, Flax, Umeboshi, Basil Gomashio

Place a small jar on your Condiment Plate, and store the rest in an airtight container in the refrigerator for up to 6 months.

MAKES 1³/₄ CUPS

1 cup sunflower seeds
4 teaspoons umeboshi vinegar
1 tablespoon dried basil
³/₄ cup ground flaxseeds
1–1¹/₂ tablespoons salt

Preheat oven to 350 degrees F. Roast sunflower seeds on a baking sheet for 7 minutes. Toss seeds with umeboshi vinegar and return to oven for 2 minutes. Transfer from oven to food processor with basil, flax, and salt. Grind until sunflower seeds are finely chopped, or save power but add in "great energy" by hand grinding with a Japanese suribachi. Sprinkle on whole grains, vegetables, salads, etc.

Turkey Mole Gomashio

This recipe teaches how to use meat as a seasoning, instead of as a main dish. Sprinkle this "gomashio" on top of your fresh-cooked grain and serve with a side salad or vegetable for a complete meal. Mole is a Mexican sauce made with dried peppers, spices, nuts, and chocolate. Find the best quality in Mexican or farmers markets.

MAKES ³/₄ CUP

¹/₂ cup minced organic smoked sliced turkey (about ¹/₄ pound)
¹/₄ cup canned diced green chiles, drained
1 tablespoon minced red onion
1 teaspoon minced garlic
¹/₂ teaspoon dried oregano, crushed with your fingers
1 tablespoon concentrated mole

Combine all ingredients in a small bowl. Mix well. Store in refrigerator for a week.

Green Onion Basil Gomashio

Sprinkle this gomashio on top of grains, vegetables, even chicken, for a delicious seasoning and an "umami" accent.

MAKES 1 CUP

1 tablespoon olive oil

1 bunch green onions, thinly sliced (about 1$\frac{1}{2}$ cups)

1 tablespoon barley or chickpea miso

2 tablespoons chopped basil

Splash of brown rice vinegar or lemon juice

Heat a medium sauté pan and add oil. Add onions and sauté about 30 seconds. Turn off heat. Add miso and cover the pan to let the miso soften a few minutes. Add basil and a splash of vinegar or lemon juice. Stir well, making sure the miso is well incorporated. Store in the refrigerator for 1 week.

Green Tea Stir-Fry with Seasonal Vegetables and Chicken or Baked Tofu

Practice your new sauce-making techniques with this recipe. Chicken and tofu work well together; combining them helps reduce meat consumption. Use a wok for best results. Cutting vegetables into long, diagonal pieces exposes as much of the surface area of the vegetable as possible directly to the wok and assists in caramelization.

MAKES 4 SERVINGS

Choose one of the ingredients below or reduce each amount by half and use a combination:

1 pound boneless, skinless chicken breast, chopped into 1-inch pieces

1 (8-ounce) package baked or fresh tofu, cubed

Marinade for Chicken or Tofu

2 tablespoons dark soy sauce

2 teaspoons freshly grated gingerroot

1 clove garlic

1 teaspoon arrowroot (can substitute cornstarch)

Stir-fry Sauce

1 cup brewed green tea or vegetable stock (base)

2 tablespoons soy sauce (salt)

1 tablespoon brown rice vinegar (acid)
1 tablespoon freshly squeezed lemon or lime juice (acid)
1 tablespoon toasted sesame oil (thickener/fat and seasoning)
1 teaspoon Sriracha (hot pepper sauce) (seasoning)
2 tablespoons arrowroot (can substitute cornstarch) (thickener)

2 tablespoons olive oil, divided
2 teaspoons freshly grated gingerroot (seasoning)
1 clove garlic, chopped (seasoning)
Mixed vegetables, cut on a thin, long diagonal into bite-size pieces (carrots, celery, broccoli, snowpeas; about 2 cups)
1/4 cup ice-cold water as needed
Garnish: sliced green onions, slivered nori sea vegetable

For the marinade, combine marinade ingredients, add chicken and/or tofu and marinate at least 15 minutes and up to 6 hours in the refrigerator.

For the Stir-Fry Sauce, combine all ingredients and set aside.

Heat wok or sauté pan on medium-high heat. Add 1 tablespoon oil, ginger, and garlic; stir-fry 30 seconds. Add chicken and/or tofu, stir-fry until cooked through, about 5 minutes. Remove from pan. Add the last tablespoon oil and sliced vegetables and stir-fry, about 5 minutes. While cooking, add 1 tablespoon cold water as needed to "force-steam" vegetables. When vegetables are crisp tender, add the chicken or tofu. Mix Stir-Fry Sauce, making sure arrowroot is well incorporated. Add sauce to wok. Cook until thickened. Serve over cooked grain. Garnish with green onions and nori. Serve with Condiment Plate.

A Cook's Look– Small-Farmed Beef, Cheese, Eggs, and Honey

Our final chapter looks at using small-farmed and pasture-raised animal products. People continue to eat animals, so animals have to be a part of the solution. Here are a few quick tips and tricks on cooking with them, and ways to be "cooler" when you do.

Beef

The beef industry has spoken—Americans supposedly prefer the taste of corn-fed to grass-fed beef. They also tell us there is no difference in nutritional value between the meats. My research doesn't agree. I hadn't cooked much beef and never taught about beef until writing this book. Then I started feeding grass-fed beef to many taste-testers and students. What did people prefer? Few of my tasters had ever eaten pasture-raised beef before; not many knew the option existed.

People like the taste of meat because it is biochemically complex, and it is the complexity that gives food flavor. Plants and meat have carbohydrates, but meat also has amino acids, which add to the umami, or depth of flavor. Cooking heightens the complexity and enhances the flavor by releasing juices that act like a built-in sauce. Lightly cooked meats with a lot of juice have a lot of flavor; overcooked meats with less juice have less flavor. Browning meat is a specific technique that enhances flavor through a process known as the Maillard Reaction, named after French physician Louis Camille Maillard. He discovered that when meat is seared on heat of at least 250 degrees F (121 degrees C), the sugars and amino acids start changing into new flavor by-products and become even more complex. However, this happens only on the surface of the meat where it gets hot enough for the reaction to occur.

What a cow eats can also affect the flavor of the meat, and grass is a better flavoring agent than corn. Feeding cows grass is like marinating them from the inside out because of substances in the grass that convert to terpenes in the cow's stomach. Terpenes are chemical compounds similar to those found in herbs and spices.[1] At the American Grassfed Association conference I attended in Austin in 2007, they referred to grass-fed beef the way we refer to wine. Dr. William Swecker from the College of Veterinary Medicine at Virginia Tech gave a great example of how grass-fed beef may be sold in the future: "It's a 2008 vintage Angus Hereford cross, finished on orchard grass and alfalfa. Note the subtle hints of cinnamon and apricot. I'll give it a Beef Spectator Rating of 92."

The problems associated with eating meat may not be that we do it, but that we do way too much of it, as discussed in previous chapters. Macrobiotics offers an interesting perspective about eating animals. My teacher, Cornellia Aihara, taught that we take on the energy of the animals we eat. Speaking English with Japanese thrown in around the edges, she would lecture about and act out the different effects. "Person who eats too much chicken," she would say while jutting her head quickly back and forth like a chicken picking up seeds, "becomes very picky." "Person who eats too much cow

Dry Aging Beef

In order to intensify flavor, beef is "dry aged," or stored between 34 and 38 degrees F (1 to 3 degrees C), and in a relative humidity of 70–80 percent, until it "relaxes" and loses a percentage of water weight. This is not to be confused with wet aging, where a carcass is cut into parts and stored in plastic bags (a more common and cost-efficient modern method). When dry-aging grass-fed beef, the temperature must be increased because grass-fed beef has less fat and gets colder faster. If it cools too quickly it can become tough or "cold-shortened." Find out how your grass-fed beef is processed so you get what you pay for. Because of the refrigeration, dry aging is energy intensive and another reason to eat less beef. So save money by eating less beef, and when you do get it, invest in the good stuff.

becomes slow." In all fairness, cows can outrun a horse, as we learned from dairy farmer Ron VanderYacht at Methow Valley Creamery, but he did counter with how much cows love to be bored. Secretly, I blame pockets of traffic on people who eat too much cow. What other possible explanation could there be for everyone driving as a solid mass down the highway, mindlessly bunched together as though they're part of the same herd?

Not knowing much about cooking beef, I invited Steve McCarthy, general manager of Prather Ranch Meat Company of San Francisco, to come to my home and be chef de cuisine for a Grass-Fed vs. Grain-Fed Beef Taste Test in the summer of 2007. Prather sells certified humane-raised and handled animals from small family farms. The ranch is located near Mt. Shasta, California, and has been around since the late 1800s. It was the first ranch in California to be certified humane.

Steve and six other friends came up to my Portola Valley home on the hill for a great sunset and the specific task of eating cow. It was surprisingly hard to find qualified tasters among all my California friends; I needed a team passionate about their beef. "Breeding, feeding, and treating control the flavor of the meat," said Steve. "We have large-framed cows: a Black Angus/ Hereford cross. You have to feed these guys good grass—the kind they like to eat—in order to fatten them up. Some of our cows eat only grass; others finish on barley, alfalfa, and rice for the last three months. A stress-free slaughter is extremely important to the quality of the meat, and so is the dry-aging process, a lost art in this country. Not many people dry-age beef any longer because of the expense. Ours is dry aged for a minimum of two weeks."

After a couple of bottles of really good red wine, such as Peter's deliciously, nonlocal 1990 Chateau Le Tertre Roteboeuf, things started to get silly. "How does it happen with the cows these days," asked Lorna. "Do they still 'do it' naturally or does it happen some other way?" Steve laughs, "AI (artificial insemination) is the buzz word with cows, but ranches do have 'cleanup bulls' that sniff around and make sure all the ladies are taken care of. 'Super bulls' give the sperm—and they are well-known bulls. Up at the ranch there are coffee tables covered with cow magazines and full-page photo spreads of bulls posing next to their name." In unison, the crowd yelled, "Playbull!"

It was a sumptuous evening and interesting dinner party to host. The tasters thought the grilled grass-fed steaks had a more complex flavor, but they managed to eat up every bit of the grain-fed steaks too. The difference in the beef stews was dramatic. The grain-fed stew tasted like vegetable soup compared to the flavor of the grass-fed stew, which was more developed, deep, and complex. (See the judges' responses on page 204.)

Cheese

Cheese won a spot on the Most Local Foods Plate (chapter 5) because there are artisan cheese makers in more than forty-three states, including Alaska and Hawaii.[2] Artisanal cheese is an edible art that offers much more flavor and satisfaction than industrial-produced cheese.

Cheese production falls into three general categories:

1. Factory-produced cheese
2. Artisanal cheese—made in small quantities with minimal machinery
3. Farmstead cheese—produced on the farm where the milk comes from, often from the milk of pasture-raised animals.

Factory cheeses are made in very large quantities with a completely controlled process and a goal of creating a uniform, stable product. Artisanal and farmstead cheeses vary from day to day and must be watched over and tested during aging. Artisanal cheeses highlight the changing of seasons and remind us that cheese-making is really a spring/summer activity done when the grasses are in bloom and animal pregnancies have stimulated milk production. Spring milk is used for light cheeses such as fresh goat chevre. Winter cheeses, such as cheddar and blue, are made from summer milk and aged over the season, or made from the thicker, denser winter milk that comes from less active cows.

Hometown Cheese Platter

Serving cheese from your area is like putting on the jersey of your favorite sports team. Cheese platters are easy to assemble, and the stories behind the cheese and cheese makers are fun to share with your guests. Eaters want to know more about their food, and interest is growing in eating locally. The main items on a cheese platter—cheese, fruit, honey, nuts, and bread—are likely to be grown or produced in or around your home state.

A cheese platter should offer something from each of the following categories:

• Cheese: hard and soft; a mix between cow, sheep, and goat's milk cheeses

• Something sweet: fresh fruit, a fruit paste (like quince paste), dried fruit, honeycomb, candied foods

• Nuts: toasted or seasoned nuts add an extra touch (Nuts can be surprisingly local—see page 206.)

• Crackers and thinly sliced bread: serving both offers a nice variety of textures

The Judges' Response

Grilled Steaks

NONG: "There was definitely a noticeable taste difference between the grass-fed beef and the grain-fed beef. Grass-fed was juicier and reminded me of the taste of farm-raised beef that I grew up eating. The grain-fed beef had less taste—you needed steak sauce."

PETER: "Grain-fed beef had a very up-front beefy taste without much depth. I would call its texture firm. The 'grass-fed alfalfa and barley-finished' steak was succulent and savory with a flavor that seemed to develop as you chewed it. It seemed almost buttery."

CHARLES: "The grass-fed beef was soft, juicy, and you couldn't tell where one strand of meat began and one ended. I needed dental floss after eating the corn-fed beef."

Slow-Cooked Beef Stew

LORNA: "The corn-fed beef stew tastes like cardboard and the [grass-fed beef] like stew. They are night and day; [like] gourmet and fast food. The depth of flavor makes the sauce and vegetables so much better; everything benefits."

from left to right: Lorna Hunt, Robin Gallo, Nong Vang, Charles Elliotte, author, Steve McCarthy, and Peter Neal.

Making Sense of the Terms

- Certified Organic—a term regulated by the USDA. Food is produced without using most conventional pesticides, fertilizers made from synthetic ingredients or sewage sludge, bioengineering, or ionizing radiation. Animals are given no antibiotics or growth hormones. Before a product can be labeled "organic," a government-approved certifier inspects the farm to be sure standards are being met. Handlers and processors are certified, too.

- Grass-Fed—a voluntary standard in the United States for *marketing* grass fed meat. It states that "grass and/or forage shall be the feed source consumed for the lifetime of the ruminant animal, with the exception of milk consumed prior to weaning. The diet shall be derived solely from forage and animals cannot be fed grain or grain by-products and must have continuous access to pasture during the growing season."[3]

- Certified Humane-Raised and Handled—a term regulated in the United States by the nonprofit organization Humane Farm Animal Care. Animals are allowed to engage in their natural behaviors and are raised with sufficient space, shelter, and gentle handling to limit stress. They are not fed added antibiotics or hormones. Processors must comply with the American Meat Institute Standards, a higher standard for slaughtering farm animals than the Federal Humane Slaughter Act. The USDA verifies the inspection process.

- Pasture-Raised—a nonregulated term in the United States characterized by animals raised outside on pasture, harvesting a significant amount of their own food. Pasture-raised differs from "grass-fed" in that animals can be fed grass without being on pasture.

- Grass-Fed, Grain-Finished—a nonregulated term in the United States. Cows are fed grass until the last three months or so, when they are fed grains such as barley, alfalfa, rice, or corn.

- Natural—a nonregulated term coined in early 2008. The USDA is considering a definition of "hormone and antibiotic free."

See www.greenerchoices.org/eco-labels to keep up-to-date on terms and labels.

SEASONAL SWEETS FOR THE CHEESE PLATE

Spring/Summer: honeycomb, berries, plums, cherries, backyard figs

Fall: Fuyu persimmons, apples, pears, honeycomb, quince paste

Winter: citrus fruits, dried fruit, candied nut mix, candied ginger

Designing a Cheese Plate

SERVE IT UP

Cheese is lovely when served on ceramic, granite, or wood. Odd shapes are more interesting than the standard store-bought fare. Look for free granite pieces at local stone shops that commonly throw them out as scrap. They will often have uneven, rough edges that add to the presentation.

SIZE MATTERS

Cheese cubes are passé. Allow your guests to see what the cheese wheel looked like by leaving whole pieces. Labeling cheese is a nice touch. You can neatly cut out and display the label that came with the cheese, or use erasable store-bought labels. I prefer making my own labels, attaching them to place-setting holders and "desk-photo" clips that can be matched to the theme or style of the party.

CUTTING THE CHEESE

Table knives or paring knives don't work well to cut cheese. Invest in a "real cheese knife." There are different styles to choose from, and many are too short to be effective. Make sure the knife blade is long and sturdy enough to cut through dense pieces of cheese. If you serve

Local Nuts Come from Everywhere (Not Just from California)

Almonds—*California*

Hazelnuts—*Oregon and Washington*

Peanuts (technically a legume)—*southeastern, southwestern, and mid-Atlantic regions of the United States*

Pecans—*many of the southern and southwestern States. The major production is from Georgia, Texas, and New Mexico. Other big producers include Arizona, Oklahoma, Alabama, and Louisiana*

Pistachios—*California*

Walnuts—*mostly California but also Oregon, Washington, Pennsylvania, Michigan, Utah, Iowa, and Maine*

individual slices of cheese instead of whole pieces, choose a cut that highlights the unique shape of the cheese and garnish each piece with a dollop of compote or fruit paste.

EXPRESS THE ARTIST WITHIN

Cheese plates benefit from variations of texture and height of the ingredients, as well as a free-flowing look of abundance. Free the accompanying nuts, dried fruit, crackers, and bread from individual bowls or baskets. Instead, sprinkle these items onto colorful cloth napkins draped around the cheese platter or directly onto the tablecloth.

Eggs-*tra* Special Farm-Fresh Eggs

Eating a farm-fresh egg is like eating a piece of good chocolate; it has a rich flavor and a creamy, full body. These days, grocery store eggs remind me more of plastic Easter eggs from the drugstore than real eggs from happy chickens. As our animals move away from natural habitats and feeds, the quality of life for the chickens decreases and the quality of egg decreases. Flavor and nutrition also suffer, just as in beef. Pasture-raised eggs can contain as much as ten times the omega-3 fatty acids (from the grass),[4] 10 percent less fat (the grass, again), and 40 percent more vitamin A (probably the grass too) than eggs from factory hens.[5]

I call pasture-eggs "green eggs" because chickens have a much smaller carbon footprint than cows do.[6] Less fertilizer is used to grow their feed, chickens don't produce much methane, and there is less total waste because we consume a greater portion of the animal as food. We eat only 300 to 400 pounds of the average 1,200 pound cow. We certainly don't throw away three-quarters of the chicken.

Eggs also found a spot on the Most Local Foods Plate because small-farmed egg production occurs in all fifty states. Don't just read about green eggs in books; get real ones from pasture-raised, small-farmed, local chickens. Look for them at farmers markets or ask your neighbors if they know of a hidden source.

Technically, eggs have seasons too: spring, summer, and fall. These are the "lightest" times of year (chickens lay according to the amount of daylight). These are also the times when the really lucky chickens (who live on farms with portable chicken coops) get to peck on plants and peck bugs out of cow patties. If you can find these eggs—buy them! The addition of plants and bugs give eggs the most complex flavor.

In an attempt to discover if seasonality and taste differences could be detected between factory-farmed and small-farmed eggs, we conducted the "Best Eggs vs. Worst Eggs Taste

Test" throughout 2007. Laying the "best eggs" were the feathery girls from Valhalla Farms in Woodside, California (one of my client's backyard coops). The "worst eggs" came from a local liquor store that also sold milk, packaged burritos, and eggs as hangover relief. Four taste tests occurred throughout the year: early March, late April, July, and November. Testers compared competing sets of hard-boiled eggs, scrambled eggs (with only added salt), and soufflés.

The color of the yolks was the most noticeable and ongoing difference between the eggs. Store-bought eggs have very light yellow yolks, whereas the Valhalla Farm yolks were a deep orange. Color is determined by what the chicken eats. The color fades as eggs age; the fresher the egg, the darker the yolk. The Valhalla eggs were commonly described as "creamier, denser, buttery, and more eggy." However, when subjecting both sets to a soufflé competition, the performance was unexpectedly equal, producing soufflés similar in height. This may have been due to the age of the chickens—see pullet eggs on next page.

The Egg Judgers' Comments

On the Valhalla Farm Eggs

"I may never be able to buy a store-bought egg again." "Creamier." "Buttery." "Less pleasing in appearance, but better taste." "Thicker." "Like a real egg." "Grassy."

On the Liquor Store Eggs

"No color in the yolk." "Smelled like sulfur." "Tough and homogeneous." "Bland."

The July taste test was highly anticipated as this was the height of the season. When the results showed the least noticeable differences, I asked my client if anything was different. It turns out that they left town right before the taste test, which left the chickens eating only chicken feed—no kitchen scraps. The "height of the season" is irrelevant because most backyard chickens aren't following cows around eating out of their patties; they are housed in nonportable chicken coops (to keep them safe from predators, and your garden safe from the chickens) and fed a similar diet year-round. So kitchen scraps (rather than bugs and plants) make the biggest difference in the taste of these eggs. Though the flavor may not be as dramatic as eggs from farms with cows, it is much better than eggs from factory-farm chickens. Further, the "energetics" found in meat and eggs from factory farms is barbaric. If the energy of the food goes into the cook, I shudder at the thought of consuming anything that comes from a factory farm.

Questions for Egg Farmers

Looking for a new egg source? Here are questions to ask the farmer:

1. How many chickens do you have?

2. What do they eat? The color of the yolk depends on the diet of the hen. It is best to feed chickens organically grown grains, legumes, grasses, worms, and insects, and most small farmers serve greens and kitchen scraps as well. The larger small farms include organic pellets, corn, and soy. Conventional farms feed their chickens commercial pellets and corn, soy, and cottonseed meal grown with pesticides and herbicides, or that may have been genetically modified.

3. Are antibiotics used with your chickens? Chicken feed is often laced with antibiotics, especially for chickens that live in confinement.

4. Where do your chickens live? How long do they have access to fresh pasture during the day?

5. Do you have any pullet eggs? Chickens produce their best eggs in the first thirteen weeks of their egg-laying life. Known as pullet eggs, they are smaller than what eaters have been conditioned to think is best. As a chicken ages, egg size increases and quality decreases. Large and small eggs from the same chicken have the same amount of egg "material," but large eggs are said to have more water.

Solar-Cooked Green Egg Omelet

Want a truly Green Egg Omelet? Cook small-farmed eggs in a solar oven. A typical family of four consumes about 1,000 kilowatt-hours per year using an electric range and oven combination, releasing an estimated 1,600 pounds (720 kg) of carbon dioxide.[7] Solar ovens bake an emission-free cuisine, seasoned by the rays of the sun. What is it about food cooked by fire or sunshine? The flavor seems deeper and the experience more satisfying; a good example of the "energetics of cooking" in action.

Solar ovens use reflective panels that direct sunlight through a glass top into the well-insulated black box or "oven." As the sun moves through the sky, the cook adjusts the oven's position so the rays remain centered on the dish. Lower-end, commercial solar ovens cook at around 225 degrees F (107 degrees C). Higher-end ovens can reach 400 degrees F (204 degrees C).

Solar oven made by Dave Coale.

I tested out carbon-free cooking with an oven borrowed from my friend David Coale. He built it out of a cardboard box, leftover insulation, and aluminum foil. Black paper clamps (like the ones in your desk that you don't know what to do with) held the whole thing together. It was a surprisingly effective stove for a cardboard box. I made chocolate chip cookies, Corn and Brown Rice Pilaf, and a Truly Green Egg Omelet. In a world where everything is high-tech and fast, watching the eggs slowly cook by sun power was exciting and fulfilling, and it just made sense. I savored every bite. There's just something special about an omelet kissed by the sun-lit lips of God.

"Solar cooking fights global warming and empowers third-world women at the same time," says solar cooking expert Don Larson, from Common Ground Organic Garden Supply and Education Center, in Palo Alto, California. "There has been a successful campaign in lesser-developed countries to market solar ovens as a convenience item—freeing women from having to seek firewood and providing them a smoke-free cooking appliance. Solar cooking also brings us a little closer to the great outdoors. My favorite dishes are freshly baked dinner rolls, lentil and bean soup, and my solar-roasted garlic—absolutely the best."

Full-Bodied Honey

Honey is another seasonal food, harvested from late spring to early fall when the flowers are in bloom and looking for love. It's the flower that determines the color and flavor of honey; lighter honeys such as sage and citrus are mild, whereas darker honeys such as avocado and eucalyptus are stronger in taste. Buckwheat is one of my favorites. I like a full-bodied honey, just like my olive oil and my men.

Honey is produced in all fifty states,[8] making it an exciting addition to our Hometown Cheese Platter (this chapter) and Most Local Foods Plate (chapter 5). There are more than 300 unique kinds of honey in the United States and many are regionally based, such as the famed Tupelo honey from the Tupelo gum trees of northwest Florida.[9]

Honeycomb is a terrific addition to your next cheese plate; the sweetness of the honey complements the tartness of the cheese. Guests are surprised and delighted to see honeycomb. Many don't know what it is, and there is often a "Wow—this is amazing" kind of response. Honeycomb wax is completely edible, although there are slight variations in color, depending on how dirty the bees' feet are. Bees have dirty feet because pollen is sticky and they pick up a lot of dust while they're out working. When the season is right, buy your hometown honeycomb at farmers

markets or specialty stores (check the label for where it comes from) and show off some "local flavor." Remove the honeycomb from the package and place it directly on the cheese plate; no preparation is needed. Don't have honeycomb? Just drizzle honey directly onto cheeses such as blue and goat.

Beeswax is also used to make the French dessert *canneles,* which is nicknamed the "walking crème brûlée." The wax serves as a liner for the cake mold and as an edible crust that complements the soft custardlike center.

A Bit about Bees

In her forty-five-day life, a worker bee makes about one-twelfth of a teaspoon of honey. Approximately 2 million flowers are visited to make a pound of honey, and the average hive makes eighty pounds of surplus honey each season. When humans remove the honey, it motivates the bees to produce more in preparation for winter. There are three types of bees: the queen, whose full-time job is to lay the eggs; the male drone, whose only job is to mate with the queen; and the female workers, who make up 99 percent of the hive and do ALL the housework including feeding the males! Where is the justice?

Eaters and cooks are dependent on bees. Bees are like the kitchen crew that never gets a break and no one ever thanks. Every third bite we take is attributable to managed honeybees, wild bees, and other pollinators.[10] Dr. Claire Kremen, University of California, Berkeley (environmental sciences policy and management professor and 2007 MacArthur genius grant recipient), says that crops such as melons, watermelon, squash, kiwi, and pumpkins are completely dependent on pollinators. "Other crops like almonds, avocados, peaches, cherries, and apples are almost fully dependent on animal pollinators. We don't know what's going on with

Crop Dependence on Bees

ESSENTIAL/GREAT	MODERATE	LITTLE
melon	strawberries	citrus (seedless)
kiwifruit	cottonseed	tomatoes
pumpkins	apricots	peppers
squash	peaches	beans
watermelon	citrus (seeded)	
almonds	nectarines	
avocados	safflower	
bushberries		
plums		
cherries		
apples		
cucumbers		
alfalfa seed		
sunflower		

Many crops are critically dependent on bees for pollination. The table shows different fruits and vegetables and their reliance on bees.

the honeybee and why they are exiting in large numbers. Global warming could produce additional unknown effects, both on wild and managed bees. Animal pollinators are responsible for pollinating 35 percent of the caloric mass of our diets and 75 percent of the crop types. People will always come up with a way to get the food, even if they have to hand pollinate it, but then those foods become luxury items for the wealthy. Imagine cooking without those crops."

Billions of bees are disappearing lately due to a crisis termed "colony collapse disorder" (CCD).[11] The global-warming diet's abuse of pesticides and herbicides and the resulting loss of native habitat due to practices such as monocropping are being considered as potential causes. However, small organic farms such as Marshall's Farm Natural Honey, north of the San Francisco Bay Area, aren't experiencing the problem like the commercial bee farms.

Owner Spencer Marshall started raising honeybees in his backyard in the 1970s. Today, he and his wife, Helene, keep beehives around the San Francisco Bay Area. During a visit to the farm, Spencer pulled out a bee-covered frame from one of the hives, dulling the bee's natural response with a puff from his hand-held smoker. A solid tap to the ground knocked off all the bees, and he let us dig into the honeycomb cells in pursuit of royal jelly, a special food fed only to the queen. It tasted bitter, but with a remarkably unique and alluring flavor. "You can have a strong hive in good shape with lots of honey, and all of a sudden the bees are gone," said Marshall. "Pesticides seem to disorient the bees. Maybe it makes them senile . . . they just fly away." Dr. Kremen believes farm management practices may influence the diversity and abundance of native bees. "Organic farms have healthy wild bee communities and wild bees actually enhance the honeybee pollination. The value provided by the native bees is an argument in favor of protecting and/or restoring natural habitat."

Compare your local honeys to commercial honey and determine which you like best. Helene explains the differences between large- and small-scale farmed honey. "Commercial honey tastes the same because it gets mixed all together in a large vat with water and heated so it can move through the processing pipes. Marshall Farms uses no pumps, pipes, filters, heat, or water—it's real honey."

Honey Taste Testers
Large- and Small-Scale Responses

Various students and friends compared five of the Marshall honeys. The difference in color and taste were noticeable. Pumpkin Blossom (a rarer honey, due to the low nectar content of pumpkins) was a favorite. Here are some of the testers' responses:

- Pumpkin Blossom: "Nicely different." "Tastes like pumpkin." "Like Muscat wine."
- Greystone Herb Garden: "Complex." "Fruity, floral."
- Sage: "Mild." "Bland." "Slightly herbal."
- Marin Wildflower: "Springtime."
- California Blackberry: "Tart." "Very berry."

The Ozone Hole: A Lesson for the Future

The history of ozone depletion provides parallels to global warming today and offers insight and inspiration on how to move forward.

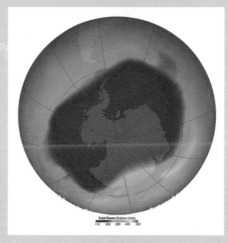

In the 1980s, ozone depletion was being described as the most important environmental issue to face the planet. Ozone in the upper atmosphere provides a critical protective layer between all biological life and the very high energy and damaging ultraviolet light from the sun. In 1985, the discovery of the Antarctic ozone hole became a symbol, both real and frightening, for how humans can inadvertently alter their environment in ways that can affect all life. (The accompanying graphic shows a satellite view of the Antarctic ozone hole in September 2006. Blue and purple indicate low ozone values.) Within a few years of this discovery, it was confirmed that chlorofluorocarbons (CFCs), a class of chemicals entirely manufactured by humans, were destroying large amounts of ozone.

With strong scientific backing and little resistance from industry, international action to reduce the use of ozone-depleting substances moved swiftly. The Montreal Protocol (1987) agreed to reduce ozone-depleting substances using a step-by-step approach that allowed developing countries more time to convert their technologies. Today, CFC production is almost completely phased out, and with the decline of CFCs in the atmosphere, we expect to see a gradual recovery in global ozone and a filling in of the ozone hole during the next fifty years.[12]

Today's story of ozone depletion suggests a *happy ending*, provided that we continue to follow the steps outlined in the Montreal Protocol. If controls on ozone-depleting gases had not been enacted, global ozone levels by 2050 would have been up to 30 percent lower than today, with accompanying rises in cataracts, skin cancer, and damage to animals and crops.[13]

While global warming is scientifically a completely different issue, there are parallels. The science relating to climate change has become solid over the last decade. We understand that rising levels of greenhouse gases are responsible for most of the recent warming, and that if we don't reduce emissions, temperatures will continue to warm. We also realize that solutions exist today that can reduce our emissions without compromising our quality of life. If we follow the same model used for ozone depletion and work together as a society, then we can also imagine *a happy ending* to the issue of global warming.

Book 'n' Cook Club Ideas

Videos

Modern Meat (2002)

The Natural History of the Chicken (2001)

Pollen Nation (2007)

Recipes

Spanish Backyard Potatoes

Slow-Cooked, Grass-Fed Beef Stew

Scrambled Tofu

Truly Green Egg Omelet

Field Trips

Search your grocery store for the cheese and honey produced closest to your area.

Visit a local animal farm producing beef, milk, eggs, and/or cheese.

Visit a local apiary. Find them at www.honeylocator.com.

Go on a canneles ("walking crème brûlée") hunt to local French bakeries. Ask if they use real beeswax to make the dessert.

Food Sources

Small-farmed eggs are found primarily at farmers markets—but ask around. If your neighbor has chickens, babysit or dogsit in exchange.

Grass-fed beef is starting to be sold at farmers markets. If you buy it from a grocery store, ask where it comes from.

Small Things Matter

• Stuck buying eggs at grocery stores? Ask for eggs from "happy chickens." The distribution system for local eggs is poor but we can change it by insisting on better-quality eggs.

• Do you want to raise chickens? Eggs-cellent! Check online for a local "chicken owners support group" such as Silicon Valley Chickens (in the San Francisco Bay Area). They help people start and manage their chicken coops.

Recipes

Spanish Backyard Potatoes

There are so many different kinds of potatoes; grow them yourself or look for varieties like Carola, Charlotte, Katahdin, Huckleberry, and Ozette at farmers markets. The farmer at my market grows fourteen different varieties.

SERVES 6 TO 8

2 pounds fingerling potatoes (or other unique varieties you can find)
2 tablespoons olive oil
Pinch of salt
2 tomatoes, diced
1 tablespoon chopped fresh oregano
1 teaspoon smoked Spanish paprika
$1/2$ teaspoon cayenne
1 teaspoon ground cumin
1 tablespoon red wine vinegar
3 scallions, thinly sliced
1 avocado, diced

Wash potatoes, place in medium saucepan, cover with water, and boil until almost soft, about 15 minutes. Drain.

When cool enough to handle, cut potatoes into 1-inch cubes. Heat oil in a 10-inch nonstick skillet over medium-high heat. Sauté potatoes with a pinch of salt until golden. Add tomatoes and sauté 1 minute. Add oregano through vinegar and sauté 3–4 more minutes. Plate and garnish with scallion and avocado.

Slow-Cooked Grass-Fed Beef Stew

Because it has less fat, grass-fed beef benefits from a long, slow cook.

SERVES 6

1 pound boneless chuck roast, cut into 1$\frac{1}{2}$-inch chunks

1 teaspoon salt

1 teaspoon freshly ground pepper

1 large onion, chopped

4 carrots, peeled and cut into 1-inch chunks

3 ribs celery, cut into 1-inch chunks

1 parsnip, turnip, or rutabaga (whichever one is freshest), peeled and cut into
   1-inch chunks

2 cups organic beef stock

5 cloves garlic, sliced

1 teaspoon chopped fresh rosemary

1 bay leaf

1 cup dry red wine (don't use anything that you don't like the taste of)

3 tablespoons tomato paste

3 tablespoons whole-wheat pastry flour

1 cup frozen peas

1 (16-ounce) package pasta, cooked (Encourage biodiversity! Try pastas made from a
   grain besides wheat.)

CHEF TIP:
Cooking with Grass-Fed Beef

Grass-fed beef has more natural flavor so keep seasoning light! Often a simple coating of salt and pepper with maybe a little bit of herb or spice is all that is needed. Learn to work with and bring out the unique flavors; don't cover them by over-seasoning.

Grass-fed beef has less fat so keep cooking short! Lower-fat, grass-fed meat needs less time to cook; some sources suggest a third less time than grain-fed beef. For best results, use a meat thermometer. Cook steaks hot and fast and serve them medium rare, or sear at a higher temperature (achieving the Maillard Effect) and finish up by using a lower heat. The Crock-Pot (longer cooking time but lower heat) is ideal for cuts such as brisket or chuck. Slow cooking breaks down muscle tissues and enhances the complexity of flavors.

Sprinkle the chuck roast with salt and pepper. Heat a sauté pan and sear the beef over medium-high heat, about 5 minutes until brown on all sides. Transfer to a 5- or 6-quart slow cooker.

Sauté onion in the same skillet until softened, about 3 minutes. Stir while sautéing and loosen up the brown bits (fond) from the pan. Transfer to the slow cooker along with the next 9 ingredients (carrots through tomato paste). Mix and push everything into the liquid. Cook 4–5 hours on high or 7–9 hours on low.

After 3 hours of cooking, check the liquid and remove $1/2$ to 1 cup of it, depending on how much you have. If your ingredients are still covered with liquid, remove more than just 1 cup. You want everything slightly or almost covered with liquid. Refrigerate what you remove. In an hour or two, remove the cooled liquid from refrigerator and skim off the fat. Mix $1/4$ cup of this liquid with the flour and set aside. Reserve the remaining cooled stock for another use.

About 30 minutes before serving, remove an additional $1/4$ cup of the hot liquid from the slow cooker and combine with the flour/stock mixture. Add back into the Crock-Pot and stir. Add the peas. Cover and cook until slightly thickened, about 30 minutes. Serve over noodles.

CHEF TIP:
Replace Beef Stock with Chocolate Stout

Cut down on beef consumption by replacing or halving beef stock with chocolate stout in soups, sauces, and stews. Beer is brewed in all fifty states, giving it a place on the "Most Local Foods Plate" (chapter 5). Comparing beer to wine and spirits, beer may have the lowest ecological footprint. [14]

Scrambled Tofu

Not everyone eats eggs, so when you host a brunch, serve Scrambled Tofu as a side dish. Egg-eating and non-egg-eating friends like it. Make it the day before and just heat up in the morning.
SERVES 4

1 pound firm tofu
3 tablespoons olive oil, divided
1 medium onion, diced small
1 red bell pepper, diced small
1 teaspoon tumeric
1 teaspoon ground cumin
$1/2$ teaspoon ground mustard
1 teaspoon garlic powder
$1/2$ teaspoon smoked paprika
Pinch of cayenne
$1/2$ teaspoon ground thyme
4 teaspoons nutritional yeast
1 teaspoon umeboshi vinegar (optional)
$1/2$ teaspoon salt
Freshly ground pepper
1 fresh tomato, seeded and chopped
1 or 2 green onions, chopped

Slice the tofu into squares, $3/4$ inch thick. Cover a baking sheet with a clean dishcloth and lay tofu on top. Cover with another dishcloth and lay something flat, like another baking sheet, on top. Place a couple of pounds of weight on the baking sheet (cans, jars, bowls), and let sit, unrefrigerated, for 30–60 minutes.

Crumble the pressed tofu into curdlike pieces into a bowl and set aside. Heat a large sauté pan with 1 tablespoon oil. Add onions and cook until they start to turn brown, about 5 minutes. Add the red pepper and sauté another 4 minutes. Remove from pan. Assemble spices (tumeric through thyme) in a small bowl. In the same sauté pan, heat the last 2 tablespoons of oil over medium-high heat, add the spice mix, and sauté for 30 seconds. Add the crumbled tofu, stir well to distribute the spices, and sauté 5 minutes. Stir in the sautéed onion and red pepper, nutritional yeast, umeboshi vinegar, salt, and pepper. Taste and adjust seasonings. Plate and garnish with chopped tomatoes and green onions.

Truly Green Egg Omelet

Green egg omelets use eggs from local chickens, cheese from local cows, and vegetables harvested from your own backyard or farmers market. Add in whatever is in season: zucchinis, tomatoes, peppers, herbs . . . . "Truly" green egg omelets are solar cooked.

SERVES 1 OR 2

2 or 3 fresh eggs from happy chickens

3 tablespoons grated cheese—your favorite local variety

Pinch of smoked paprika

$1/2$ teaspoon chopped canned chipotle pepper, or another hot pepper substitute

1 tablespoon chopped parsley

5 fresh cherry tomatoes, cut in half or quarters

2 tablespoons chopped red onion

Salt and freshly ground pepper

Preheat your solar oven to 300 degrees F or more.

Crack eggs into a bowl, add remaining ingredients, and whisk together. Transfer to a lightly oiled black cast-iron skillet (no cover needed) and place in oven. Rotate the oven every 20–30 minutes, keeping the omelet in direct sunlight. Bake until set, 30–45 minutes. Baking times will vary due to the size of your skillet and how hot your oven is.

Epilogue — The Secret

Global warming is one of the most pressing issues of our time and this book has only touched on the ways our food system is contributing to and helping to solve the problem. Far from a final word on a subject with no predictable outcome, we sincerely hope it serves as a starting point for a continued and lively discussion.

Our food choices have an equal and possibly greater impact on global warming and the environment than our transportation does, for the bad as well as the good. Adapting agricultural, manufacturing, distribution, eating, and waste practices to be more in tune with nature is the next step toward a solution.

Food is energy, energy is power, and food is powerful! Humans have the strength and ability to change the entire food system just by what we eat each day and by what we do with the waste when we are done.

One of the most positive effects we can have on the environment begins on our dinner plate, but climate is far from the only reason to eat food that supports small family farms, sustainable agriculture, and traditional animal husbandry. We eat this way because it benefits our communities and brings us closer together. It also gives us tastier and healthier food. By incorporating more of it into our diets, we may even come to understand that growing and cooking food is a loving act and that the most satisfying dishes are those prepared with love.

Education and balance are key, however, because "if it ain't fun, it don't get done." Let's inspire people into a tasty food revolution they want to be a part of and not push them away with expectations to do everything perfectly—that is the secret.

We are guaranteed to have an effect because food is power. In fact, food is more powerful and can have an even larger effect than politics can. As unfortunate as it is in today's society, many of us don't like being involved in politics, but all of us like being involved with food. Everyone may not vote, but everyone eats.

So let's gather in the kitchen tonight and cook . . . shall we?

Together we can make a great meal—and a great difference.

Appendix

TOP 10 CARBON EMISSIONS ASSOCIATED WITH PUBLISHING A BOOK		
INDUSTRY	%	g CO_2e
Power generation	30.9%	1,098.58
Paper mills	17.9%	635.06
Truck transportation	8.2%	292.19
Book publishers	4.8%	172.26
Waste management services	4.1%	147.53
Books printing	2.3%	83.22
Oil and gas extraction	2.1%	76.14
Air transportation	2.0%	70.81
Wholesale trade	1.4%	50.54
Petroleum refineries	1.4%	49.43
Other	24.8%	882.21

LIFECYCLE BREAKDOWN OF SELLING A BOOK TO THE CONSUMER		
LIFECYCLE	%	g CO_2e
Publishing and Manufacturing	48.1%	3,558
Delivery	9.2%	677
Wholesale	7.6%	564
Retail	35.1%	2,597
Carbon Intensity of Book Publishing: 296 g CO_2e per U.S. dollar		
Price of Book to Consumer: $24.99		
Book's Estimated Carbon Footprint: 7,397 g (16.3 pounds) CO_2e		

Offsetting This Book's Carbon Emissions

The carbon emissions associated with publishing this book were generated in the processes of publishing, manufacturing, delivery, and retail sales. Based on estimates obtained from EcoSynergy Inc. (chapter 7), the total carbon emissions came to about sixteen pounds (7.4 kg) of CO_2e per book, or forty-four tons of CO_2e for the first run of 6,000 copies. For comparison, the average American is responsible for generating about twenty tons of CO_2e per year.

We then purchased carbon offsets to mitigate these emissions. The simplest example of a carbon offset is the planting of trees. For example, if a person wanted to offset the emissions associated with their personal air travel during a year, they could pay an organization to plant a certain number of trees that would absorb the carbon associated with their flights. Various methods for offsetting carbon exist today, such as turning methane into energy (in landfills and on dairy farms), sequestering carbon (in forests, grasslands, or the ocean), or producing renewable energy (through solar and wind power, for example).

We chose Carbon Farmers of America as one of the mitigators to offset the emissions generated from production of this book, and Cool It to offset author travel for research.

Carbon Farmers of America (www.carbonfarmersofamerica.com)

Carbon Farmers of America trains, equips, scientifically monitors, and provides ongoing support to member farmers across the United States to rapidly create new, high-organic-matter topsoil. The organization pays farmer members for every ton of carbon dioxide they capture in new topsoil, and markets and sells the carbon offsets to the public. Each ton of carbon dioxide removed from the atmosphere represents approximately 1,000 pounds (450 kg) of soil organic matter. Carbon Farmers is conducting a joint study with Cornell University of New York (and Dr. David Pimentel) to establish what rates of soil carbon can accumulate under planned grazing and aggressive strategies to increase soil organic matter.

Cool It (www.acterra.org)

The Cool It campaign (hosted by the environmental organization Acterra) sells renewable energy certificates, which offset carbon emissions by supporting new wind and solar power. Acterra is an environmental organization based in Palo Alto, California, that brings people together to create local solutions for a healthy planet.

Further updates on our efforts to reduce the emissions associated with this book can be found at our Web site: www.globalwarmingdiet.org.

Carbon Offsets

A carbon offset is a payment you can make to a third party to remove or offset your own carbon emissions from the atmosphere. If you wanted to offset the emissions associated with flying from Los Angeles to Atlanta then you could pay someone to plant trees that would absorb (over a few years) your one ton of emissions. This would make your flight carbon-neutral.

However, not all carbon offsets are equally effective in reducing emissions. What would happen if the trees you had planted for your flight offset were to burn down? Yep, all your carbon goes back into the atmosphere. Critics of carbon offsets not only challenge the validity of certain types of programs, but they also suggest the "pay to pollute" mentality that carbon offsets may encourage is counterproductive to stimulating real change. While this may be true in some cases, well-designed carbon-offset projects, when managed in an honest and open manner, can promote practices such as renewable energy or enhanced carbon uptake that really do reduce emissions.

While recognizing the debate on carbon offsets, we have chosen to use them for the energy associated with publishing this book only after as many steps as possible were already taken to reduce emissions.

Endnotes

CHAPTER 1

1. D. Pimentel and M. Pimentel, *Food, Energy and Society,* 3rd ed. (Boca Raton, FL: CRC Press, 2008).
2. G. Eshel and P. A. Martin, "Diet, Energy and Global Warming," *Earth Interactions,* 10 (2006), 1–17.
3. D. Pimentel and M. Pimentel, "Sustainability of Meat-Based and Plant-Based Diets and the Environment," *American Journal of Clinical Nutrition,* 78 (2003), 660S–63S.
4. M. Jacobson, *Six Arguments for a Greener Diet: How a More Plant-Based Diet Could Save Your Health and the Environment* (Washington, DC: Center for Science in the Public Interest, 2006).
5. R. Heinberg, "Threats of Peak Oil to the Global Food Supply" (Dublin, Ireland: FEASTA Conference, *What Will We Eat When the Oil Runs Out?,* 2005), http://www.richardheinberg.com/museletter/159, accessed Jan. 29, 2008.
6. Pacific Institute, "Bottled Water and Energy: Getting to 17 Million Barrels" (Oakland, CA: Pacific Institute, 2007), http://www.pacinst.org/topics/integrity_of_science/case_studies/bottled_water_energy.html, accessed Feb. 11, 2008.
7. J. Dukes, "Burning Buried Sunshine: Human Consumption of Ancient Solar Energy," *Climatic Change,* 61 (2003), 31–44.
8. U.S. Department of Agriculture, "High Fructose Corn Syrup: Estimated Number of Per Capita Calories Consumed Daily, by Calendar Year," Table 52 of Sugar and Sweeteners Yearbook Tables (Washington, DC: Economic Research Service, USDA, 2008), http://www.ers.usda.gov/briefing/sugar/data.htm, accessed Feb. 11, 2008.
9. T. Jones, "Using Contemporary Archaeology and Applied Anthropology to Understand Food Loss in the American Food System" (Tucson, AZ: Bureau of Applied Research in Anthropology, University of Arizona, 2004), http://www.communitycompost.org/info/usafood.pdf, accessed Jan. 29, 2008.
10. Eshel and Martin (2006).
11. EnviroSax, "Plastic Bag Facts–USA" (Torrance, CA: Envirosax, 2007), http://usa.envirosax.com/pages/plastic-bag-facts.php, accessed Jan. 29, 2008.
12. A. Drewnowski, et al., "Disparities in Obesity Rates: Analysis by ZIP Code Area," *Social Science and Medicine,* 65 (Dec. 2007), 2458–63.
13. C. L. Ogden, et al., "Prevalence of Overweight and Obesity in the United States, 1999–2004," *JAMA: Journal of the American Medical Association,* 295 (2006), 1549–55. See also National Center for Health Statistics, "Prevalence of Overweight and Obesity among Adults: United States, 2003–2004." (Hyattsville, MD: Centers for Disease Control and Prevention, Department of Health and Human Services, 2007), http://www.cdc.gov/nchs/products/pubs/pubd/hestats/overweight/overwght_adult_03.htm, accessed Jan. 29, 2008.
14. R. Conniff, "Counting Carbons," *Discover* (Aug. 2005), 54–61.
15. We took the average carbon emissions from the range given by J. Cascio, "Cheeseburger Footprint" (San Francisco, CA: Open the Future, 2007), http://www.openthefuture.com/cheeseburger_CF.html; accessed Feb. 12, 2008.
16. A. Lappé and B. Terry, *Grub: Ideas for an Urban Organic Kitchen* (New York: Jeremy P. Tarcher/Penguin, 2006).
17. U.S. Department of Health and Human Services, "Citing 'Dangerous Increase' in Deaths, HHS Launches New Strategies against Overweight Epidemic. Study Shows Poor Diet, Inactivity Close to becoming Leading Preventable Cause of Death" (Washington, DC: HHS, 2004), http://www.hhs.gov/news/press/2004pres/20040309.html, accessed Jan. 29, 2008.
18. IPCC, *Climate Change 2007: The Physical Science Basis: Contribution of Working Group 1 to the Fourth Assessment Report on the Intergovernmental Panel on Climate Change,* S. Solomon, et al., eds. (Cambridge: Cambridge University Press, 2007), Fig SPM.3, http://www.ipcc.ch/ipccreports/ar4-wg1.htm, accessed May 8, 2008.
19. P. Jones, "Global Temperature Record," Climate Research Unit Information Sheet (Norwich: University of East Anglia, 2007), http://www.cru.uea.ac.uk/cru/info/warming/, accessed Oct. 30, 2007.

20. A couple of papers on fingerprints can be found at http://www.nature.com/nature/links/030102/030102-3.html and a climate fingerprints hot map at http://www.climatehotmap.org/, accessed May 1, 2008.

21. The Grosser Aletsch Glacier in Switzerland, the longest glacier in the Alps, has retreated 8,500 feet (2,600 m) since 1980, and the Rongbut Glacier, which drains the north side of Mount Everest into Tibet, has been retreating 65 feet (20 m) per year over the last few decades. In 2006, the Swiss Glacier survey of 85 glaciers found 84 retreating and 1 advancing. Similarly, of the glaciers in the Italian Alps, only about a third were in retreat in 1980, while by 1999, 89 percent of these glaciers were retreating. In 2005, the Italian Glacier Commission found that 123 glaciers were retreating, 1 advancing and 6 stationary, http:glaciology.ethz.ch/messntz/glacierlist.html, accessed May 1, 2008.

22. On the Pacific island of Tonga, the sea level appears to have risen about 0.3 inches (8 mm) a year over the last fifteen years. Although this may not seem like much, during times of storms, low-lying islands are expected to see an increased threat of flooding within the next few decades. Sea level rise is not constant, and depends on local variations in ocean temperature and winds. Further information on Pacific Islands and sea level can be found at http://www.bom.gov.au/pacificsealevel/index.shtml, accessed May 1, 2008.

23. C. Parmesan and G. Yohe, "A Globally Coherent Fingerprint of Climate Impacts across Natural Systems," *Nature*, 421 (2003), 37–42.

24. Deforestation has two impacts on climate. First, because trees take up carbon dioxide, their removal ultimately acts to increase CO_2 levels in the atmosphere and this leads to warming of the planet. However, deforestation also makes the land surface more reflective to sunlight (when trees are present, the surface is green; after trees are cut, the surface is gray or white), and this by itself would cool the planet. Further details on deforestation and its impact on climate can be found in chapter 2.5 of the IPCC report. IPCC, *Climate Change 2007: Impacts, Adaptation and Vulnerability: Contribution of Working Group II to the Fourth Assessment Report on Climate Change,* M. L. Parry, et al., eds. (Cambridge, Cambridge University Press, 2007).

25. So, if carbon dioxide concentrations are 280 parts per million (ppm), then out of a million air molecules, 280 would be carbon dioxide.

26. IPCC, Solomon, et al. (2007).

27. Using the IPCC *Special Report on Emissions Scenarios,* 2000, found at http://www.ipcc.ch/ipccreports/sres/emission/index.htm, one can use the "business as usual" A1FI scenario to project how carbon dioxide will change over the coming century.

28. IPCC, Solomon, et al. (2007), adapted from Fig FAQ3.1

CHAPTER 2

1. D. Montgomery, *Dirt: the Erosion of Civilizations* (Berkeley: University of California Press, 2007).

2. T. Jones, "The Scoop on Dirt," *E: the Environmental Magazine,* 17 (Sept./Oct. 2006), 26–39.

3. C. Jones, "Carbon, Air and Water: Is That All We Need?" *Managing the Carbon Cycle: The Katanning Workshop: 2007,* http://www.amazingcarbon.com/Workshop%20Papers.htm, accessed Jan. 29, 2008.

4. Montgomery (2007).

5. Ibid.

6. M. Jacobson, *Six Arguments for a Greener Diet: How a More Plant-Based Diet Could Save Your Health and the Environment* (Washington, DC: Center for Science in the Public Interest, 2006).

7. Ibid.

8. Ibid.

9. M. Jacobson, "From a Global Warming Diet to a Greener One" (*The Anniston Star,* 2006), http://www.annistonstar.com/opinion/2006/as-columns-0915-0-6i14x2459.htm, accessed Dec. 7, 2006.

10. Montgomery (2007).

11. Fossil fuels are a nonrenewable resource, and limited reserves exist on our planet. Estimates vary as to how many years each energy source will be readily available at an acceptable economic cost, and range from ten to fifty years for oil, thirty-five to eighty years for natural gas, and one hundred to two hundred years for coal.

12. T. Searchinger, et al., "Use of U.S. Croplands for Biofuels Increases Greenhouse Gases through Emissions from Land-Use Change," *Science,* 319 (Feb. 2008), 1238–40.

13. P. Singer and J. Mason, *The Way We Eat: Why Our Food Choices Matter* (Emmaus, PA: Rodale, 2006).

14. C. Bacon, "Confronting the Coffee Crisis: Can Fair Trade, Organic and Specialty Coffees Reduce Small-Scale Farmer Vulnerability in Northern Nicaragua?," *World Development,* 33 (2005), 497–511.

15. Montgomery (2007).

16. Jacobson, *Six Arguments,* (2006).

17. T. Jones (2006).

18. C. Feller, et al., "Charles Darwin, Earthworms and the Natural Sciences: Various Lessons from Past to Future," *Agriculture Ecosystems & Environment,* 99 (Oct. 2003), 29–49.

19. The data on Mauna Loa constitute the longest record of direct measurements of carbon dioxide in the atmosphere. Data from the Scripps Institute of Oceanography are in blue and from NOAA in red. An updated (every month) figure from NOAA can be seen at: http://www.esrl.noaa.gov/gmd/ccgg/trends/co2_data_mlo.html.

20. IPCC, *Climate Change 2007: The Physical Science Basis: Contribution of Working Group 1 to the Fourth Assessment Report on the Intergovernmental Panel on Climate Change,* S. Solomon, et al., eds. (Cambridge: Cambridge University Press, 2007).

CHAPTER 3

1. C. Rosenzweig and D. Hillel, "Potential Impacts of Climate Change on Agriculture and Food Supply," *Consequences,* 1 (Summer 1995), http://www.gcrio.org/consequences/summer95/agriculture.html, accessed May 1, 2008.

2. L. Ziska, "Evaluation of Yield Loss in Field Sorghum from a C3 and C4 Weed with Increasing CO_2," *Weed Science,* 51 (2003), 914–18.

3. The use of tree rings, ice cores, coral reefs, and even historical records such as the time of grape harvest all provide information about the past climate. Information from the NOAA paleoclimatology division provides a good introduction. http://www.ncdc.noaa.gov/paleo/paleo.html, accessed May 8, 2008.

4. The last ice age was caused by a decline (2 watts/m²) in the surface radiation budget due to orbital variations and feedbacks associated with carbon dioxide and ice sheets. See chapter 6 of the 2007 IPCC report and references therein for details. IPCC, *Climate Change 2007: The Physical Science Basis: Contribution of Working Group 1 to the Fourth Assessment Report on the Intergovernmental Panel on Climate Change,* S. Solomon, et al., eds. (Cambridge: Cambridge University Press, 2007), http://www.ipcc.ch/ipccreports/ar4-wg1.htm, accessed May 8, 2008.

5. These data come from the Vostok ice-core temperature reconstruction. You can look at the raw data yourself if you are curious to see how temperature has changed over the last 400,000 years, http://cdiac.ornl.gov/ftp/trends/temp/vostok/vostok.1999.temp.dat, or for a good plot of temperature and carbon dioxide over the last 650,000 years, see Figure TS.1. from the 2007 IPCC report. IPCC, Solomon, et al. (2007).

6. Union of Concerned Scientists, *Agriculture: Growing Concern: A Global Warming Impacts Video"* (Union of Concerned Scientists, 2007), http://www.climatechoices.org/impacts_agriculture/, accessed Aug. 24, 2007.

7. Decadal averages of observations are shown for the period 1906 to 2005 (black line) and blue-shaded bands show the range for simulations from five climate models using only the natural forcings due to solar activity and volcanoes. The red-shaded bands show the range from fourteen climate models using both natural and human forcings. Forcings refer to processes that will act to either warm or cool the planet such as changes in the sun's radiation or changes in the concentration of a gas like carbon dioxide. Forcings can either be natural (e.g., volcanoes that act to cool the planet, or increases in the sun's radiation that would warm the planet) or human-produced (e.g., increases in carbon dioxide that will warm the planet, or increases in aerosols that will cool the planet). IPCC, Solomon, et al. (2007), adapted from Figure SPM.4.

8. These results were produced using fourteen different climate models from international research groups in support of the 2007 IPCC report (Solomon, et al). Further and related details can be found in the FAQ chapter under FAQ 8.1: "How reliable are the models used to make projections of future climate change?" and FAQ 9.2: "Can the warming of the 20th century be explained by natural variability?"

9. S. Postel, *Pillar of Sand: Can the Irrigation Miracle Last? A Worldwatch Book.* (New York: W.W. Norton, 1999).

10. R. Heinberg, "Threats of Peak Oil to the Global Food Supply " (Dublin, Ireland: FEASTA Conference, *What Will We Eat When the Oil Runs Out?*, 2005), http://www.richardheinberg.com/museletter/159, accessed Jan. 29, 2008.

11. S. Kipe, "An Economic Overview of Horticultural Products in the United States" (Washington, DC: U.S. Department of Agriculture, Horticultural and Tropical Products Division, 2004), http://www.fas.usda.gov/htp/Presentations/2004/An%20Economic%20Overview%20of%20HTP%20-%20(08-04).pdf, accessed May 1, 2008.

12. M. Rosengrant, et al., *Global Water Outlook to 2025: Averting an Impending Crisis* (Washington, D.C.: IFPRI and IWMI, 2002).

13. J. Cribb, "Can Australian Soil Science Save the World?" (National Conference of the Australian Soil Science Society, 2006).

14. The IPCC was established in 1988 through the United Nations Environment Program and the World Meteorological Organization to assess the risk of climate change caused by human activities. This international body produces reports every five to seven years that are written by climate change experts from around the world. The IPCC *Climate Change: Fourth Assessment Report* was released in 2007 and can be found at http://www.ipcc.ch/ipccreports/assessments-reports.htm, accessed May 8, 2008.

15. The development of emission scenarios and their storylines is an interesting and somewhat complicated exercise, as described in the IPCC *Special Report on Emission Scenarios* found at http://www.ipcc.ch/ipccreports/sres/emission/index.htm, accessed May 8, 2008.

16. Figure 5 comes from the summary for policy makers from the 2007 IPCC report Solomon, et al. (2007).

17. IPCC, Solomon, et al. (2007).

18. Ibid.

19. IPCC, *Climate Change 2007: Impacts, Adaptation and Vulnerability: Contribution of Working Group II to the Fourth Assessment Report of the Intergovernmental Panel on Climate Change*, M. L. Parry, et al., eds., (Cambridge: Cambridge University Press, 2007).

20. J. C. Zuckerman, "An Uncertain Harvest," *Plenty*, (April/May 2007), 44–53.

21. L. H. Ziska, et al., "Quantitative and Qualitative Evaluation of Selected Wheat Varieties Released Since 1903 to Increasing Atmospheric Carbon Dioxide: Can Yield Sensitivity to Carbon Dioxide Be a Factor in Wheat Performance?" *Global Change Biology*, 10 (2004), 1810–19.

CHAPTER 4

1. A good summary of the observed twentieth-century changes and the predictions for the twenty-first century are given in the IPCC Fourth Assessment Report: Summary for Policymakers section of the report. IPCC, *Climate Change 2007: The Physical Science Basis: Contribution of Working Group 1 to the Fourth Assessment Report on the Intergovernmental Panel on Climate Change,* S. Solomon, et al., eds. (Cambridge: Cambridge University Press, 2007), http://ipcc-wg1.ucar.edu/wg1/wg1-report.html.

2. B. L. Preston and R. N. Jones, "Climate Change Impacts on Australia and the Benefits of Early Action to Reduce Global Greenhouse Gas Emissions" (2006), http://www.csiro.au/files/files/p6fy.pdf, accessed Oct. 31, 2007.

3. Level 5 restrictions include no watering of lawns, limited watering of established gardens on certain days and during certain times, and no filling of pools unless certain other water saving measures have been taken. The Web site of the Brisbane City Council http://www.brisbane.qld.gov.au contains more information about Brisbane's water situation, accessed May 8, 2008.

4. At present, there is debate within the scientific community about the connections between tropical cyclones and global warming. While some studies show an increase in the intensity of tropical cyclones over the past few decades, others attribute this to observational techniques and

instrumentation. Two good sites devoted to the science are http://www.usgcrp.gov/usgcrp/links.
hurricanes.htm and http://www.gfdl.noaa.gov/~tk/glob_warm_hurr.html.

5. IPCC, Solomon, et al. (2007).
6. T. Kosatsky, "The 2003 European Heat Waves," *Euro Surveillance 2005,* 10 (2005), 148–49.
7. P. A. Stott, et al., "Human Contribution to the European Heatwave of 2003," *Nature,* 432 (Dec. 2, 2004), 610–614.
8. B. Wuethrich, "How Climate Change Alters Rhythms of the Wild" *Science,* 287 (2000), 793–95.
9. C. Gjerdrum, et al., "Tufted Puffin Reproduction Reveals Ocean Climate Variability," *Proceedings of the National Academy of Sciences,* 100 (2003), 9377–82.
10. J. Larsen, "Bottled Water Boycotts: Back-to-the-Tap Movement Gains Momentum," *Eco-Economy Updates* (Earth Policy Institute, 2007), http://www.earth-policy.org/Updates/2007/Update68.htm, accessed May 8, 2008.
11. E. Horng, "Ditching Bottled Water to Go Green," (ABC News, 2007), http://abcnews.go.com/WN/GlobalWarming/story?id=3351812&page=1, accessed Jan. 25, 2008.
12. S. Casey, "Our Oceans Are Turning into Plastic . . . Are We?" *Best Life: Your Guide for Better Living* (2007), http://www.bestlifeonline.com/cms/publish/health-fitness/Our_oceans_are_turning_into_plastic_are_we_2c.shtml, accessed Jan. 25, 2008.
13. E. D. Olson, "Bottled Water: Pure Drink or Pure Hype" (New York: Natural Resources Defense Council, 1999), http://www.nrdc.org/water/drinking/bw/bwinx.asp, accessed Sept. 25, 2007.
14. V. Standley, "Picking Plastic? The Green Guide Cracks the Codes," *AScribe: The Public Interest Newswire* (2006), http://www.ascribe.org/cgi-bin/behold.pl?ascribeid=20050127.113349&time=12+56+PST&year=2005&public=1, accessed Jan. 25, 2008.
15. Olson (1999).
16. P. Stec, "Buckle-Up Bug Campaign, Ford Motor Company." As told to L. Stec in Portola Valley on Sept. 28, 2007.
17. D. Marty, "Empowered Shopping: Tips from the Green Side of the Aisle," *E: the Environmental Magazine,* 8 (May/June 2007), 54–55.
18. International Bottled Water Association, "Beverage Marketing's 2006 Market Report Findings," (2007), http://www.bottledwater.org/public/Stats_2005.doc, accessed Jan. 25, 2008.
19. The report by N. Jungbluth, "Comparison of the Environmental Impact of Tap Water vs. Bottled Mineral Water," (Swiss Gas and Water Association, 2005) was used in these calculations, http:www.esu-services.ch/download/jungbluth-2006-LCA-water.pdf, accessed Jan. 25, 2008.
20. This calculation assumes that 4.2MJ of energy is used to produce one liter of bottled water (plastic bottle and domestic water) (Jungbluth 2005) and that a car uses 0.3 gallons of gas per hour when idling (Natural Resources Canada, Office of Energy Efficiency: http://www.oee.nrcan.gc.ca/transportation/personal/idling.cfm?attr=8), accessed May 1, 2008.
21. A. Carlsson-Kanyama, et al., "Food and Life Cycle Energy Inputs: Consequences of Diet and Ways to Increase Efficiency," *Ecological Economics* (2003), 293–307. See also Jungbluth (2005).

CHAPTER 5

1. R. Pirog and A. Benjamin, "Checking the Food Odometer: Comparing Food Miles for Local Versus Conventional Produce Sales to Iowa Institutions" (2003), http://www.leopold.iastate.edu/pubs/staff/files/food_travel072103.pdf; accessed Jan. 25, 2008.
2. B. Kingsolver, *Animal, Vegetable, Miracle* (New York: Harper Collins, 2007).
3. J. E. McWilliams, "Food That Travels Well," *New York Times* (Aug. 16, 2007), http://www.nytimes.com/2007/08/06/opinion/06mcwilliams.html?_r=1&oref=slogin, accessed Jan. 25, 2008.
4. IPCC, *Aviation and the Global Atmosphere: A Special Report of IPCC Working Groups I and III in Collaboration with the Scientific Assessment Panel to the Montreal Protocol on Substances that Deplete the Ozone Layer,* J. E. Penner, et al., (Cambridge: Cambridge University Press, 1999).
5. A. Carlsson-Kanyama, et al., "Food and Life Cycle Energy Inputs: Consequences of Diet and Ways to Increase Efficiency," *Ecological Economics* (2003), 293–307.

6. Great Britain Department for Environment, Food and Rural Affairs (DEFRA), *The Validity of Food Miles as an Indicator of Sustainable Development: Final Report Produced for DEFRA* (Didcot, UK: AEA Technology Environment, 2005), http://statistics.defra.gov.uk/esg/reports/foodmiles/default.asp, accessed Jan. 25, 2008.
7. C. Saunders, et al., "Food Miles: Comparative Energy/Emissions Performance of New Zealand's Agriculture Industry," Agribusiness and Economics Research Unit (AERU), Lincoln University research report number 285 (2006), http://www.lincoln.ac.nz/story_images/2328_RR285_s9760.pdf, accessed Jan. 25, 2008.
8. We used Carlsson-Kanyama's (2003) "Food and Life Cycle Energy Inputs" to estimate the energy required to grow cherries.
9. J. Braun and D. Hillman, "The Federal Food and Farm Bill," *The Snail*, 2 (Summer 2007), 15.
10. T. LaSalle and P. Hepperly, *Regenerative 21st Century Farming: A Solution to Global Warming* (Kutztown, PA: The Rodale Institute, 2008), 3.
11. Data and interpretation provided by Dr. William Horwath, from the Department of Land, Air and Water Resources, University of California, Davis.
12. Carbon dioxide equivalent (CO_2e) is used to represent the warming potential of all greenhouse gases (i.e., CO_2, CH_4, N_2O, etc.) in a single value.
13. U.S. Department of Energy, Energy Information Administration, *Emissions of Greenhouse Gases in the United States 2003* (Dept. of Energy, 2005), http://tonto.eia.doe.gov/FTPROOT/environment/057303.pdf, accessed Jan. 25, 2008.
14. The data used for this figure come from the Climate Analysis Indicators Tool (CAIT) version 4.0. (Washington, DC: World Resources Institute, 2007). Available at http://cait.wri.org/, accessed Jan 25, 2008.
15. H. Steinfeld, et al., *Livestock's Long Shadow: Environmental Issues and Options* (Rome: Food and Agricultural Organization of the United Nations, 2006), http://www.fao.org/docrep/010/a0701e/a0701e00.htm, accessed Oct. 30, 2007.
16. M. Pollan, *The Omnivore's Dilemma: A Natural History of Four Meals* (New York: Penguin Press, 2006).

CHAPTER 6

1. H. Steinfeld, et al., *Livestock's Long Shadow: Environmental Issues and Options* (Rome: Food and Agricultural Organization of the United Nations, 2006), http://www.fao.org/docrep/010/a0701e/a0701e00.htm, accessed Oct. 30, 2007.
2. Ibid.
3. S. Lang, "New Study Reopens Debate: Are Omnivores Better for the Environment Than Vegetarians?" *Cornell Chronicle* (Cornell University, 2007), http://www.organicconsumers.org/articles/article_7575.cfm, accessed Feb. 14, 2008.
4. While varying estimates of agriculture-related emissions exist, this estimate is based on the contributions from livestock (16–18 percent) and plant-based agriculture (less than 5 percent) and serves as a lower bound.
5. H. Steinfeld, et al. (2006).
6. The term livestock generally refers to any domesticated animal such as cattle, sheep, pigs, and chickens that are raised for food or fiber. The estimates of livestock-related, greenhouse-gas emissions from the U.N. Food and Agriculture Organization show that the largest share of CO_2 emissions comes from land-use changes associated primarily with deforestation caused by demand for feed grains and grazing land.
7. D. Pimentel and M. Pimentel, *Food, Energy And Society*, 3rd ed. (Boca Raton, FL: CRC Press, 2008).
8. See Holistic Management International, http://www.holisticmanagement.org, for further information on the scale of this farming practice.
9. These results come from personal communication with Louis Sukovaty at Crown S Ranch. His estimate of corn/hay-fed cattle yield per acre is from M. Pollan, *The Omnivore's Dilemma: A Natural History of Four Meals* (New York: Penguin Press, 2006).
10. P. Hepperly, "Organic Farming Response to Climate Change," *Pesticides and You*, 27 (2007), 14–19. (This study was completed using row crops and not pastureland.)
11. Pollan (2006).

12. K. Clancy, *Greener Pastures: How Grass-fed Beef and Milk Contribute to Healthy Eating, Food and Environment* (Union of Concerned Scientists, 2006), http://www.ucsusa.org/food_and_environment/ sustainable_food/greener-pastures.html, accessed Sept. 5, 2007.
13. Mott Group, "Pasture-Based Livestock Research," *Programs and Activities of the C.S. Mott Group* (Michigan State University, 2007), http://www.mottgroup.msu.edu/ProgramsActivities/Pasturebased LivestockResearch/tabid/893/Default.aspx, accessed Feb. 14, 2008.
14. University of Maryland Center, "Omega-3 Acids" (2007), http://www.umm.edu/altmed/articles/ omega-3_00316.htm, accessed May 23, 2008.
15. J. Robinson, "Health Benefits of Grass-Fed Products," Eatwild.com, http://www.eatwild.com/health benefits.htm, accessed Feb. 11, 2008.
16. J. Robinson, *Why Grassfed Is Best: The Surprising Benefits of Grassfed Meat, Eggs, and Dairy Products.* (Vashion, WA: Vashion Island Press, 2000).
17. T. L. Stanton and D. Schutz, "Effect of Switching from High Grain to Hay Five Days Prior to Slaughter on Finishing Cattle Performance," (Colorado State University, 2000), http://ansci.colostate.edu/files/ renut/2000/pdf/tls002.pdf, accessed Feb. 14, 2008.
18. H. A. DeRamus, et al., "Methane Emissions of Beef Cattle on Forages: Efficiency of Grazing Management Systems," *Journal of Environmental Quality,* 32 (2003), 269–277.

CHAPTER 7

1. Dave Culp of Kiteship supplied this information.
2. This type of calculation is called a cradle-to-grave analysis, where the full life cycle of the product (development, design, production, and disposal) is considered in terms of environmental impact.
3. Estimates of the energy required to grow an apple are 8 MJ (megajoules, where 1 MJ = 10^6 joules) per kg. A. Carlsson-Kanyama, et al., "Food and Life Cycle Energy Inputs: Consequences of Diet and Ways to Increase Efficiency," *Ecological Economics* (2003), 293–307.
4. For such electronic devices with an average consumer lifetime of about three years, the energy to power the device is probably only about 20 percent of the energy needed to make the device. E. Williams, "Energy Intensity of Computer Manufacturing," *Environmental Science and Technology,* 38 (2004), 6166–6174.
5. Many countries including the United States and Canada have laws prohibiting electronic components going into landfills because of toxic residues that may leach into the groundwater, so a company must dismantle, recycle, and dispose of this device properly. For more information about the chemicals used in the electronics industry and what happens to the products after use, see the Silicon Valley Toxics Coalition Web site at http://svtc.etoxics.org/, accessed May 8, 2008.
6. Our estimate uses the energy analysis of Williams 2004 who estimates the energy required to produce a personal computer. We then scaled these estimates either by weight or by cost for an iPod classic (weight 140 grams; price $250). These estimates have a large uncertainty based both on the validity of our assumptions and also the analysis of Williams.
7. E. Williams (2004).
8. This experiment is not intended to criticize the Apple iPod, but rather to convey the idea of embedded energy and life-cycle analysis, where a product's interaction with the environment is measured from cradle to grave. It should also be noted that although the estimate of energy required to make the iPod may seem high, the iPod is quite energy efficient in comparison to other electronic devices. In addition, it is also recognized that Apple as a company has a fairly progressive environmental policy for all their products (http://www.apple.com/environment/).
9. S. Bin and H. Dowlatabadi, "Consumer Lifestyle Approach to U.S. Energy Use and the Related CO_2 Emissions," *Energy Policy,* 33 (2005), 197–208.
10. The concept of cradle to cradle was popularized by William McDonough and Michael Braugart in their book *Cradle to Cradle: Remaking the Way We Make Things* (New York: North Point Press, 2002) and suggests that design emulates the principles of nature where nothing is wasted, but everything is recycled and put back into the system for another use. The classic example is an apple tree, which appears to dump its waste of leaves and fruit every year, but ultimately this waste goes back into nature as food and habitat for other plants and animals.

11. U.S. Environmental Protection Agency, "Waste Not, Want Not: Feeding the Hungry and Reducing Solid Waste through Food Recovery" (Washington, DC: US. EPA, 2007), http://www.epa.gov/epaoswer/non-hw/reduce/wastenot.htm, accessed Feb. 14, 2008.

12. Food Policy Institute, "Food Waste Management," (State University of New Jersey Rutgers, 2002), http://www.foodpolicyinstitute.org/research/waste.html, accessed Sept. 3, 2007.

13. U.S. Environmental Protection Agency, "Waste Reduction Model (WARM): Web-based Calculator," (Washington, DC: U.S. EPA, 2006), http://epa.gov/climatechange/wycd/waste/calculators/Warm_home.html, accessed Feb. 14, 2008.

14. Coskata, "Advantages of the Coskata Process," http://www.coskata.com/ProcessAdvantages.asp, accessed May 1, 2008.

15. From Paul Schmitt, master composter, Palo Alto, California.

CHAPTER 8

1. K. Hamrick and K. Shelley, "How Much Time Do Americans Spend Preparing and Eating Food?" *Amber Waves* (USDA Economic Research Service, 2005), http://www.ers.usda.gov/AmberWaves/November05/DataFeature/, accessed Feb. 12, 2008.

2. U.S. Department of Energy, Energy Information Administration, *International Energy Annual 2005*, http://www.eia.doe.gov/iea/, accessed Nov. 1, 2007.

3. Initial estimates reported by the Netherlands Environmental Assessment Agency show that in 2006 China overtook the United States as the largest emitter of greenhouse gases. For details see: http://www.mnp.nl/en/dossiers/Climatechange/moreinfo/Chinanowno1inCO2emissionsUSAin secondposition.html, accessed May 8, 2008.

CHAPTER 9

1. North Americans commonly think about food energy in terms of "Calories." By definition, a calorie of energy is actually quite small, so common practice is to refer to Calories in multiples of 1,000 or as kilocalories (kcal). It is also common practice to use the term, Calorie (with an uppercase 'C') to mean kcal, which we follow in this book. We note that most other countries report food energy in kilojoules, where 1 Calorie = 1kcal = 4.18 kilojoules (kJ).

2. The energy required to produce the food incorporates all aspects of growing, including farm machinery, irrigation, production, and application of fertilizers and pesticides.

3. In this case, energy intensity is defined as the ratio of energy required to produce the product divided by the amount of protein energy in the food. See D. Pimentel and M. Pimentel, *Food, Energy and Society*, 3rd ed. (Boca Raton, FL: CRC Press, 2008).

4. The calculation of carbon intensity includes the emissions associated with energy used to grow the food item, and any methane emissions associated with animal products. Nitrous oxide emissions due to fertilization of cropland have not been accounted for in this analysis and thus these calculations serve as a lower range for these intensities.

5. Figures for each food item come from estimates of Pimentel and Pimentel (2008). The input energy associated with each food item has been converted into CO_2 emissions based on U.S. national emissions and energy-use statistics in a manner similar to that described in Eshel and Martin (2006). The agriculture-related methane or nitrous oxide emissions are also included through a conversion into CO_2 equivalent using the procedure of G. Eshel and P. A. Martin, "Diet, Energy, and Global Warming," *Earth Interactions* 10 (2006), 1–17. See also U.S. Department of Energy, Energy Information Administration, *Emissions of Greenhouse Gases in the United States 2003* (Dept. of Energy, 2004), http://tonto.eia.doe.gov/FTPROOT/environment/057303.pdf, accessed Jan. 25, 2008.

6. There are significant uncertainties in these estimates depending on both the method of growing the food and on the methodology of calculating the emissions. For example, Pimentel (2008) finds that energy inputs may be reduced by up to 50 percent or more for free-range beef and sheep. Comparisons with other published estimates of energy intensity can differ by less then 20 percent up to 200 percent or more as described by Carlsson-Kanyama (2003).

7. The relatively large emissions from some fish products reflect the relatively large energy demands of long-distance voyages required for fishing particular species.

8. At present, studies offer differing conclusions regarding the energy and yield differences between conventional and organic agriculture, although consensus is found on the improved soil health and water quality associated with organic agriculture. See P. Maeder, et al., "Soil Fertility and Biodiversity in Organic Farming," *Science*, 296 (2002), 1694–1697; C. Forster, et al., "Environmental Impacts of Food Production and Consumption: A Report to the Department for Environment, Food and Rural Affairs (DEFRA)" (Manchester Business School, 2006), http://www.defra.gov.uk/science/project_data/ DocumentLibrary/EV02007/EV02007_4601_FRP.pdf, accessed Oct.31, 2007; and J. Ziesemer, "Energy Use in Organic Food Systems" (Food and Agriculture Organization of the United Nations, 2007), http://www.fao.org/docs/eims/upload/233069/energy-use-oa.pdf, accessed Oct. 31, 2007.

9. J. Silverman and J. Schwartz, "Barbecue DVD," *American Eats* (History Channel, 2006).

10. J. Cascio, "Cheeseburger Footprint" (Open the Future, 2007), http://www.openthefuture.com/ cheeseburger_CF.html, accessed Feb. 12, 2008.

11. A. Weil, "Healthy Cooking Techniques?" Dr. Weil's Q and A Library (Weil Lifestyle, 2007), http://www. drweil.com/drw/u/id/QAA400186, accessed May 1, 2008.

12. Energy estimates were obtained directly from manufacturers when possible or through EcoSynergy estimates. Conversions to CO_2 emissions were from the Energy Information Administration (2006).

13. D. Asami, et al., "Comparison of the Total Phenolic and Ascorbic Acid Content of Freeze-Dried and Air-Dried Marionberry, Strawberry, and Corn Grown Using Conventional, Organic, and Sustainable Agricultural Practices," *Journal of Agriculture and Food Chemistry*, 51 (2003), 1237–1241.

14. If you don't use salt with iodine, your multivitamin may do the trick. Dr. Andrew Weil suggests eating omega-3-rich fish (salmon, sardines, or mackerel), sea vegetables (like the sea shakes discussed in chapter 10), or choosing produce grown in iodine-rich soil—typically in coastal states. Less than one-half teaspoon of salt with iodine can provide the recommended daily intake of 150 micrograms of iodine. See A. Weil, "Iodine," *Dr. Weil's Vitamin Advisor* (Weil Lifestyle, 2007), http://www.drweil.com/ drw/u/id/ART02872, accessed Feb. 12, 2008.

CHAPTER 10

1. U.S. Department of Agriculture, "Dietary Guidelines for Americans" (2005), http://www.mypyramid. gov/guidelines/, accessed Feb. 9, 2008.

2. 1 serving = 1 slice bread, 1 cup dry cereal, 1/2 cup cooked cereal or pasta. "Three servings" is half the recommended five to ten daily servings of grains, depending on calorie needs.

3. Number of per capita miles is based on *Highway Statistics* 2003, U.S. Department of Transportation, http://www.fhwa.dot.gov/policy/ohim/sh03/htm/ps1.htm. Fuel economy data was gathered from U.S. EPA http://www.fueleconomy.gov and used 2008 fuel economy ratings. The 2008 ratings include updated estimates, which account for more realistic driving conditions. Note that the embodied energy of the vehicle, or the energy to manufacture and service the vehicle has not been included in this analysis.

4. The CO_2e emissions for the three types of automobiles assume the autos were driven 9,800 miles per year. The CO_2e emissions associated with three types of diets shown (High, Average, and Low) all assume a 3,700 calorie diet, but vary in the percentage of Calories from animal products (High Diet—38 percent; Average Diet—28 percent, and Low Diet—18 percent) and the type of meat eaten (High—red meat; Average—mixture of red meat/poultry; Low—poultry only). See text for further details of these calculations.

5. Although the average American needs about 2,100 Calories per day, food waste and overeating explain the relatively large per person production of food in the United States. See Eshel and Martin (2006).

6. The number of animal Calories consumed is based on per capita food supply data from the Food and Agricultural Organization, with chicken comprising 19 percent, eggs 5 percent, milk 41 percent, beef 32 percent, and salmon 3 percent. Vegetable-based Calories were divided between potatoes (30

percent), corn (30 percent) and soybeans (12 percent). While they don't represent the true variety of foods consumed, they serve as an estimate for the energy and carbon emissions. See Food and Agricultural Organization of the United Nations, *FAO Statistical Yearbook,* (2006), http://faostat.fao.org, accessed May 1, 2008.

7. The amount of beef Calories was varied between the 540 Calories/day (high), 180 Calories/day (average) and 0 Calories/day (low; all red meat replaced by poultry).

8. Most health professionals today suggest a reduction of animal products may be good for your health. Many studies have shown that high consumption of red meat may be a risk factor in major diseases such as obesity, some cancers, hypertension or heart disease. For example, A. Cross, et al. "A Prospective Study of Red and Processed Meat Intake in Relation to Cancer Risk," *Public Library of Science Journal PLoS Medicine,* 4 (Dec. 2007), e325.

9. "Whole Grains Gain Health Claim," *Food Product Design* (Sept. 1999), 24.

10. L. M. Crawford, "Speech before Whole Grains and Health: A Global Summit," (Food and Drug Administration, 2005), http://www.fda.gov/oc/speeches/2005/wholegrains0520.html, accessed Feb. 9, 2008.

CHAPTER 11

1. H. McGee, *On Food and Cooking: The Science and Lore of the Kitchen,* rev. ed. (New York: Scribner, 2004).

2. J. Wakefield, "UVM Launches Cheese Artisan Institute with $500,000 from Sen. Jeffords, John Merck Fund, Private Donor" (University of Vermont, 2004), http://www.uvm.edu/employees/?Page=News&storyID=5113, accessed Feb. 11, 2008.

3. B. Cox, "USDA Establishes Grass (Forage) Fed Marketing Claim Standard," *AMS News Release* (Agricultural Marketing Service, USDA, 2007), http://www.ams.usda.gov/news/178-07.htm, accessed Feb. 11, 2008.

4. J. Robinson, "Health Benefits of Grass-Fed Products," *Eatwild.com* (2007), http://www.eatwild.com/healthbenefits.htm; accessed Feb. 11, 2008.

5. Sustainable Table, "The Issues: Pasture Raised," (2007), http://www.sustainabletable.org/issues/pasture/, accessed Feb. 11, 2008.

6. A. Collins and R. Fairchild, "Sustainable Food Consumption at a Sub-National Level: An Ecological Footprint, Nutritional and Economic Analysis," *Journal of Environmental Policy and Planning,* 9 (Mar. 2007), 5–30.

7. R. Conniff, "Counting Carbons," *Discover* (Aug. 2005), 54–61.

8. National Honey Board, "Honey Is Not All the Same," *Honey Locator* (National Honey Board, 2008), www.honeylocator.com, accessed Feb. 11, 2008.

9. Earth Talk, "What Is Causing the Dramatic Decline in Honeybee Populations in the U.S. and Elsewhere in Recent Years?" *Health News Digest* (2007), http://healthnewsdigest.com/news/Environment_380/What_is_Causing_the_Dramatic_Decline_in_Honeybee_Populations_in_the_U_S_and_Elsewhere_in_Recent_Years.shtml, accessed Feb. 11, 2008.

10. Ibid.

11. D. Cruickshank, "Bee-sotted by the Goings on in the Bee Port, Otherwise Known as Hive," *San Francisco Chronicle Magazine* (July 1, 2007), 8.

12. V. Eyring, et al., "Multimodel Projections of Stratospheric Ozone in the 21st Century," *Journal of Geophysical Research-Atmospheres,* 112 (Aug. 2007), D16303 (article number).

13. For a good review of the current status of the ozone layer, see the most recent version of the World Meteorological Organization/United Nations Environment Programme's Ozone Assessment (2006). The "Twenty Questions and Answers" section provides a relatively quick update and details can be found in the report. Connections between global warming and ozone depletion are addressed particularly in chapter 5: Climate Ozone Connections, http://www.wmo.ch/pages/prog/arep/gaw/ozone_2006/ozone_asst_report.html. For a shorter review of ozone changes in the coming decades, see A. Tabazadeh and E. C. Cordero, "New Directions: Stratospheric Ozone Recovery in a Changing Atmosphere," *Atmospheric Environment,* 38 (2004), 647–49.

14. Collins and Fairchild (2007).

Resources

AMAZING CARBON

Australia
+61 2 6772 5605
www.amazingcarbon.com

**BLUEBIRD GRAIN FARMS
(SELLS THE GRAIN EMMER)**

Winthop, WA
509-996-3526
www.bluebirdgrainfarms.com

CARBON FARMERS OF AMERICA

Swanton, VT
802-524-0707
www.carbonfarmersofamerica.com

**THE CENTER FOR URBAN EDUCATION
ABOUT SUSTAINABLE AGRICULTURE
(CUESA)**

San Francisco, CA
415-291-3276
www.cuesa.org

**CENTRAL VERMONT PUBLIC SERVICE
CORPORATION/CVPS COW POWER**

Rutland, VT
802-747-5681
www.cvps.com/cowpower

**COMMON GROUND ORGANIC GARDEN
SUPPLY AND EDUCATION CENTER**

Palo Alto, CA
650-493-6072
www.commongroundinpaloalto.org

**COMMUNITY ALLIANCE WITH
FAMILY FARMERS (CAFF)**

Davis, CA
530-756-8518
www.caff.org

COSKATA

Warrenville, IL
630-657-5800
www.coskata.com

CROWN S RANCH, LLC

Winthop, WA
509-996-3849
www.crown-s-ranch.com

DUCK CREEK FARM

Salt Spring Island, BC, Canada
duckcreek@saltspring.com

ECOSYNERGY, INC.

Burlingame, CA
650-373-2929
www.ecosynergyinc.com/

**FOXGLOVE FARM, CENTER FOR ART,
ECOLOGY, & AGRICULTURE**

Salt Spring Island, BC, Canada
250-537-1449
www.fieldsofplenty.com

**HOLISTIC MANAGEMENT®
INTERNATIONAL**

Albuquerque, NM
505-842-5252
www.holisticmanagement.org

KAISER PERMANENTE

Farmers' Market Resource Guide
www.permanente.net/homepage/kaiser/
 pdf/46370.pdf
Dr. Maring's Blog
www.kp.org/farmersmarketrecipes (blog)

KITESHIP

Martinez, CA
925-550-6738
www.kiteship.com

MARSHALL'S FARM NATURAL HONEY

American Canyon, CA
707-556-8088 or 800-624-4637
www.marshallsfarmhoney.com

METHOW VALLEY CREAMERY

Twisp, WA
509-997-5471

**POINT REYES FARMSTEAD
CHEESE COMPANY**

Point Reyes Station, CA
800-591-6878
www.pointreyescheese.com

PRATHER RANCH MEAT CO.

San Francisco, CA
530-336-6667
www.pratherranch.com

RODALE INSTITUTE

Kutztown, PA
610-683-1400
www.rodaleinstitute.org

SELTZER SISTERS

Redwood City, CA
800-928-3755
www.seltzersisters.com

**SMITHSONIAN MIGRATORY
BIRD CENTER**

Washington, DC
202-633-4209
www.si.edu/smbc

STOPWASTE.ORG

Oakland, CA
510-891-6500
www.stopwaste.org

STRAUS FAMILY CREAMERY

Marshall, CA
415-663-5464
www.strausfamilycreamery.com

**UC SUSTAINABLE AGRICULTURE
RESEARCH AND EDUCATION
PROGRAM (SAREP)**

Davis, CA
530-752-7556
www.sarep.ucdavis.edu

WHITE OAK PASTURES, INC.

Bluffton, GA
229-641-2081
www.whiteoakpastures.com

**WILLIAMS ENGINEERING ASSOCIATES,
CAL POLY SAN LUIS OBISPO**

Woodland, CA
805-459-2985
wmsengr@the grid.net

WORLD CENTRIC

Palo Alto, CA
650-283-3797
www.worldcentric.org

Index

A

Ableman, Michael, 82
Acterra, 225
aerobic organisms, 31
agricultural waste, 131–32
agriculture: produces nitrous oxide, 19 shifting areas of, 36 as source of greenhouse-gas emissions, 81, 100
Aihara, Cornellia, 200–201
almonds, 69, 206
American Grassfed Association, 200
anaerobic organisms, 31, 106, 132
Annan, Kofi, 44
antioxidants, 161
apple versus iPod, 124–25
appliance carbon emissions, 7
Australian drought, 52
Auto/Food Comparison, 178
Autumn Tempeh Salad, 94

B

Backyard Bloody Mary Bar, 63
Backyard Broiled Figs with Goat Cheese, 90
Backyard Persimmon Martini, 64
Baked Millet and Quinoa with Onion and Corn, 192
baking grains, 181
barley, pearl, 179
Basic Stir-Fry: 3 Ways, 137
BBQ'ed Tofu with Lime, 89
Beans: Nitrogen-Fixing Pot o', 28–29; Jalapeño Rum, 29
beef: grain-fed, 98; pasture-raised versus grain-fed, 101, 199–202, 204–5; dry-aged, 201
bees, 212–14
beeswax, 212
Beets: in Black Soy Bean and Roasted Corn Salad, 91; Roasted, 170
Benziger Family Winery, 41–42
Best Choice Seafood with Peach-Ginger-Mint Relish, 48
Best Marinade Ever, 168
Bible, 77

biocompostables, 135
biodiversity habitats, 23–24
bird-friendly growing conditions: 22–24
Bisphenol A, 55
Black Soy Bean, Roasted Corn, and Beet Salad, 91
blanching, 160
Bloody Mary Bar, Backyard, 63
Blue Spruce Farm, 108
Boiled Buckwheat with Hard-Boiled Egg, 191
boiling grains, 181, 182
Bolsen, Wes, 131–32
Bosch, Carl, 18
bottled water: amounts used, 5, 51, 53; taste and safety of, 53, 54–57; energy analysis of, 61
Braggs Amino Acids, 184
Braised Tempeh, 115
braising grains, 182–83
Brazilian coffee, 23
bread: affects of carbon-dioxide levels on, 44; Rice Miso, 49
Bridport, Vermont, 108
brix number, 83, 86
Brown, Sally, 130, 131
buckwheat, 191

C

Café 150, 123–25
cancer, 180
Candied Shallots, Roasted, 175
Candy-Coated Brie, 19, 28
caramelization of vegetables, 155
carbohydrates, 179
carbon absorption, 16, 78, 80
carbon cycle, 21
carbon dioxide: as greenhouse gas, 10; and the carbon cycle, 21; atmospheric concentrations and cycles of, 26; response of plants to different levels of, 33–35; from plastic water bottles, 60; and transportation, 72–73; emissions of (CO_2e), 81; intensity of, 156–57, 178
carbon emissions: of appliances, 7; figuring, 127–29; per food Calorie, 156–57; comparisons of, 178

Carbon Farmers of America, 224
carbon footprint labels, 165
carbonic acid, 42;
carbon offsets, 224–25
carbon sequestration, 80, 82, 102
Carrot Sails, 138
Carrots, Roasted, 169
Cascio, Jamais, 158
cattle: as emitters of methane, 81, 98, 100; grain-fed
    vs. pasture feed, 101
Central Vermont Public Service Cow Power
    program, 108
Certified Humane-Raised and Handled, 205
Certified Organic, 205
charcoal briquettes, 158
cheese, 202–3, 206–7
cheese platters, 203, 206–7
cherries, example of, 72–73
Chicago Climate Exchange, 131
Chili: Dark Chocolate, 30; Paste, 112; Veggie
    Almond, 172–73
chill hours, 36
China greenhouse-gas emissions, 147
chlorofluorocarbons (CFCs), 215
Choate, Chris, 130–31
chocolate, artisan, 24
chocolate nibs, 24
cholesterol, 180
Clancy, Kate, 103–4
clear cutting, 22–23
climate, 4
climate change: meaning of, 6; fingerprints of, 9,
    21; in the past, 35; impacts of, 52
climate-model storylines, 39–40
Coale, David, 210
cocoa, 22–24
coffee, 22–24
Collard Greens with Black Olives and Piment
    d'Espelette, 174
Colombia coffee, 23
colony collapse disorder, 213
Common Ground Organic Garden Supply and
    Education Center, 210
Community Alliance of Family Farms (CAFF), 122
community-supported agriculture (CSA) boxes,
    120–23
composting, 133–35
Condiment Plate, 183–85

containerships, 118–20
cooking connection, 11
cool cuisine: composition of, 8; stages of, 12–13
Cool It, 225
Cooltini, 62
coral, 42
corn chips' carbon emissions, 127
corn syrup, 6
Coskata, Inc., 131–32
cover crops, 20, 80
cows: finishing, 99, 101; sacred, 103. See also beef,
    cattle
Cribb, Julian, 38
crop rotation study, 78–80, 82
crops: fertilizer used for, 19, planting diversity of,
    20, 22
Crostini, Grass-Fed Beef, 112–13
Crown S Ranch, 97, 101
Culinary Institute of America, viii
Culp, Dave, 118–20
cyclones, 52

D

Dallek, Aaron, 127
Dark Chocolate Chili, 30
Darwin, Charles, 25
deforestation, 10, 22, 81
Dickman, John, 123–25
digesters: methane, 108–10; dry, 130–31
Dijon Green Beans with Roasted Candied Shallots,
    175
droughts, 52
dry farming, 41
dry-aged beef, 201, 202
dulse shake, 185
Dunn, Dave, 108

E

earthworms, 24–25
EcoSynergy, 127–29, 224
Eden Foods, 91
Eden shake, 185
Eggplant with Greens and Pasture-Raised Ground
    Pork, 112–13
eggs, farm-fresh, 207–10
Eggs Full Monty, 44
Ellison, Larry, 119

embodied energy, 127

Emma Maersk, 118

energetics of food and cooking, 3, 179, 210

energy generation: as source of carbon dioxide, 81; from methane digesters, 108–10; from food waste, 129–30

environmental costs of food production, 7

Environmental Credit Corporation, 131

erosion, soil, 24–25

ethanol: corn-based, 22; from agricultural waste, 131–32

F

fair-trade products, 24

farmers markets, 120–23

Feenstra, Gail, 75

Feldman, Gene Carl, 42–43

fertilizer, oil-based, 18–20, 22

Fisher, Anthony, 38

flame tamer, 193

flavonols, 24

flaxseed, 185

floods, 52

food, energy efficiency of, 156

Food/Auto Comparison, 178

food devaluation, 6

food miles, 72–73

Food Service Partners, 122

food waste, 6, 129–30

Ford, Henry, 158

fossil fuels, 10, 21, 81

Fruit, Dried, in Roasted Nut Mix, 140

fruit, unripe, 140

Fruit Guys, The, 121

frying grains, 183

fuel costs, 8

Full Circle Food Cycle, 70

G

gasoline: recipe for one gallon of, 5

glaciers, 9

Global Change Research Information Office, 33

Global Change Reserve Act, 33

global warming, 6, 9

global-climate models, 37

global-warming diet, 5, 11

glomalin, 78

Gomashio: Popping Chocolate, 31; on Condiment Plate, 184; Basil, 195; Green Onion Basil, 196; Turkey Mole, 196

Google, 123–25

grain: availability of, 43–44; carbon dioxide affect on, 44; whole versus processed, 177–78; and health, 180; ways of cooking, 180–83; cooking chart, 181 seasonings for, 183–85; sauces for, 186–87; tips for cooking, 189

grapes: season of, 41–42, 69–70; thinning of, 76; harvesting of, 85–86

Grass-Fed Beef Crostini with Arugula, Green Peppercorns, and Dry Jack, 111

Grass-Fed definition, 205

Grass-Fed, Grain-Finished definition, 205

grazing, planned, 102

Great Pacific Garbage Patch, 54

Green Beans, Dijon, 175

Green Onion Basil Gomashio, 196

Green Tea Stir-Fry with Seasonal Vegetables and Chicken, Beef, or Baked Tofu, 196–97

greenhouse effect, 17

greenhouse gases: production of, 10; necessity of, 17; emissions of, 81, 100, 147

Grilled Persimmon Salad with Maple–Spiced Walnuts Spinach, and Frisèe, 92–93

Grilled Vegetables with the Best Marinade Ever, 168

grilling vegetables, 156, 158–59

guano, seabird, 18

H

Haber, Fritz, 18

Haber-Bosch process, 18

habits, 57

Harris, Will, 106

hato mugi, 191

hazelnuts, 206

heart disease, 180

heat waves, 52

herbs, 187–88

Hindus, 103

holistic land management, 101–102

honey, 211

honeycomb, 211–12

Honey Syrup, 64

Horwath, William, 78–80, 82, 129

Howard, Philip, 71–72
humus, 78

I

ice, fresh, 63
Incanto, 58–59
income, correlates with weight, 6
industrial food system, 4
insects, 9
Intergovernmental Panel on Climate Change (IPCC): future storylines from, 39–40
International Food Policy Research Institute (IFPRI), 38
International Stir-Fry Sauce—Orange-Maple-Chipotle, 150
iPod versus apple, 124–25
islands, 0

J

Jalapeño Rum Beans, 29
Japanese Hot Pot with Carrots and Kudzu, 46
Jones, Christine, 78
Jordan, Dean, 119
junk food, 4

K

Kaiser Permanente, 120–23
Kingsford, E. G., 158
Kingsolver, Barbara, 71
Kiteship, 118–20
knives, sharpening, 164
Kabocha, 94
Koran, 77
Kremen, Claire, 212–13, 214
kudzu: increase of, 34–35; with Japanese Hot Pot and Carrots, 46
Kyoto Protocol, 40

L

land management, 101–102
landfills, 129
Larson, Don, 210
Law of Signatures, macrobiotic, 86
Lettuce Cups with Grass-Fed Meat (or Braised Tempeh) and Peanut Sauce, 114

livestock: fertilizer used for, 19; as source of greenhouse-gas emissions, 81, 98, 100
Local Honey Sparkler, 64
locally grown foods, 71–77
Long-Term Research into Agricultural Systems (LTRAS) project, 79–80

M

macrobiotics, 179, 200–201
Maillard Effect, 155, 200
Maillard, Louis Camille, 200
Main Dish Salad, 138–39
Maple-Spiced Walnuts, 92
Marinade for Chicken or Tofu, 196
Marinade, The Best Ever, 168
marine life, 0, 42–43
Maring, Preston, 120–23
Marshall, Spencer and Helene, 214
Marshall's Farm Natural Honey, 213
Martini, Backyard Persimmon, 64
Mauna Loa Observatory, 26
McCarthy, Steve, 201–202
medical costs, 7
methane: as greenhouse-gas emission, 81, 98, 100; uses of, 107–8; from landfills, 129
methane digesters, 108–110
Methow Valley Creamery, 108–9
migration, bird and insect, 52
milk, organic, 108–9
Mittelstaedt, Chris, 121
monocropping, 20, 22–24
Monterey Bay Aquarium Sustainable Seafood Guide, 45, 48
Montgomery, David, 16, 20
Moore, Charles, 54
mosquitoes, 52
Most Local Foods Plate, 75
Muhammara, 171
mycorrhizal fungi, 78

N

Naturally Raised, definition of, 205
New Zealand lamb, 73
nitrogen-fixing, 18–19
nitrogen sustainability studies, 79–80
Nitrogen-Fixing Pot o' Beans, 28–29
nitrous oxide, 19

Norcal, 129–30
nori shake, 185
nuts, 206

O

oatmeal, 179
obesity, 6, 7
ocean studies, 42–43
oil: as part of industrial food system, 4, 5, 71; and
    plastic bags, 6
omega-3 fatty acids, 104
omega-6 fatty acids, 104
omelet, green egg, 210
Operation Bad Bacteria, 56–57
Oracle Corporation, 121
Orange Creamsicle, 65
Orange-Maple-Chipotle International Stir-Fry
    Sauce, 150
Organic Industry Structure, 71, 74
organically grown food, 77–82, 83
ozone depletion, 215

P

Pacific starfish, 52
packaging waste, 6
Pastore, Mark, 58
Pasture-Raised definition, 205
Peach-Ginger-Mint Relish, 48
Peanut Sauce, 114
peanuts, 206
pecans, 206
pests, 36
phytochemicals, 160–61
phytoplankton, 42–43
pistachios, 206
plants: C3 and C4 types of, 33; respond to changes
    in atmospheric carbon dioxide, 34
plastic: bags, 6, 57–58; water bottles, 51, 53
plowing, 18
Pollan, Michael, 103
Pomegranate Molasses Sparkler, 65
Pomeroy, Steve, 36
Popping Chocolate Gomashio, 31
popping grains, 182
Pork, with Eggplant and Greens, 112–13
Portola Valley, California, 69
Portola Valley Ranch, 70

Potatoes, Spanish Backyard, 217
Prather Ranch Meat Company, 201
Pressure-Cooked Brown Rice and Hato Mugi, 191
pressure-cooking grains, 181, 182
puffin birds, 52
pullet eggs, 209

R

Red Pepper Walnut Dip, Roasted, 171
Relish, Peach-Ginger-Mint, 48
Renz, Kathryn, 60
rice, brown, 191
Rice, Robert A., 23
Rice Miso Bread, 49
Rico, Ralph, 122
Risotto: Winter Emmer, with Roasted Root
    Vegetables and Rosemary, 192; Spring Barley,
    with Asparagus, Dill, and Fresh Artichoke, 194
Roasted and Fresh Vegetable Dip with Roasted Red
    Pepper Walnut Dip (Muhammara), 170–71
Roasted Carrots, 169
Roasted Corn, with Black Soy Bean and Beet Salad,
    91
Roasted Nut and Dried Fruit Mix, 140
Roasted Red Pepper Walnut Dip (Muhammara), 171
Roasted Root Vegetables, 193
Roasted Vegetables, 169
roasting vegetables, 156
Robinson, Jo, 104
Ruth Leserman's Caramel Brie, 28

S

Salatin, Joel, 145
salt, 162–64
salt bowls, 163
Salt Spring Island, B.C., 76
salt taste test, 163
satisfaction, 146, 148
sauces, 186–87
sautéing vegetables, 155
Savory, Allan, 101–102
Schmitt, Paul, 132
Scrambled Tofu, 220
sea levels, rising, 52
seasonal foods, 83–85
Seasonal Fruit Salad with Candied Ginger, 47
Seltzer Sisters, 59–60

Sesame Date Bars, 141
sesame oil, toasted, 184
shade-grown plants, 22–24
Sierra Nevada snowpack, 38
Silicon Valley Chickens, 216
Slow-Cooked Grass-Fed Beef Stew, 218
Smithsonian Migratory Bird Center (SMBC), 22–24
snorkling, story of, 15–16
soaking grains, 182
soil, 16, 18
soil carbon, 78, 80
solar cooking, 210
solar energy, 22
solar ovens, 210
soy sauce, 184
Spanish Backyard Potatoes, 217
spices, imported, 187–88
Spinach with Pear, Pecan, Red Onion, and Artisanal
    Blue Cheese, 95
Spring Barley Risotto with Asparagus, Dill, and
    Fresh Artichoke, 194
Spring Mix with Goat Cheese, Toasted California
    Almonds, and Fresh Strawberry Balsamic
    Vinaigrette, 90
steeping grains, 181, 182
Stew, Slow-Cooked Grass-Fed Beef, 218
Stir-Fry Sauce, 196–97
stir-fry carbon emissions, 128
stock, 187
StopWaste.Org, 129–30
Straus, Albert, 100
Straus Family Creamery, 108, 129
Strawberry Balsamic Vinaigrette, 90
Sukovaty, Louis, 97–99, 102–3, 105
Sunflower, Flax, Umeboshi, Basil Gomashio, 195
Sustainable Agriculture Farm System (SAFS)
    project, 79–80
Swecker, William, 200

T

Tahini Carrot Daikon Canapé with Black Olive, 151
Taste tests: parties for, 56; tap water versus bottled,
    61; pasture-raised versus grain-fed beef,
    201–202, 204; farm-fresh eggs versus factory-
    farm eggs, 208–9; honey, 214
temperatures, global, 35
terpenes, 200
tilling, 18

toasting grains, 183
Tofu: BBQ'ed, with Lime, 89; Scrambled, 220
Torah, 77
transportation and food miles, 72–73
true costs of food, 7
Truly Green Egg Omelet, 210, 221
Turkey Mole Gomashio, 196

U

Umami Broccoli, 48
umeboshi vinegar, 184
Union of Concerned Scientists, 36, 103
United Kingdom Department for Environment, Food
    and Rural Affairs, 72
United States farm bill, 7

V

VanderYacht, Elise and Ron, 108–9, 201
Vega Macrobiotic Study Center, viii
Vegetable Grilling Guide, 159
Vegetables, Roasted, 169
vegetables: how to eat more, 153–54; caramelizing,
    155; sautéing, 155; roasting, 156; grilling, 158–59
Veggie Almond Chili, 172–73
Vietnam coffee, 23
Vineyards, 38, 41. See also grapes

W

WalMart, 71
walnuts, 206
waste: manure, 108–10; food, 129–30; agricultural,
    131–32
water, bottled, 55–57, 60
water, sparkling, 58–60
water, tap, 55–57, 60
water taste test, 55
water bottles, 51, 53–57
water shortages, 36, 38, 41
weather, 4
weeds, 34
wheat, 43
White Oak Pastures, 108
Wilcox, John, 76
Williams, Douglas, 107–8
Wind-Powered Zucchini Boats with Cheddar,
    137–38

Winter Emmer Risotto with Roasted Root
    Vegetables and Rosemary, 192
World Centric, 135

Z

Ziska, Lewis, 34–35, 44
Zucchini Boats, 137–38

Y

yeast, nutritional, 185

Metric Conversion Chart

Liquid and Dry Measures

U.S.	Canadian	Australian
¼ teaspoon	1 mL	1 ml
½ teaspoon	2 mL	2 ml
1 teaspoon	5 mL	5 ml
1 tablespoon	15 mL	20 ml
¼ cup	50 mL	60 ml
⅓ cup	75 mL	80 ml
½ cup	125 mL	125 ml
⅔ cup	150 mL	170 ml
¾ cup	175 mL	190 ml
1 cup	250 mL	250 ml
1 quart	1 liter	1 litre

Temperature Conversion Chart

Fahrenheit	Celsius
250	120
275	140
300	150
325	160
350	180
375	190
400	200
425	220
450	230
475	240
500	260